MAILING ADDRESS
Ira S. Katz, PhD
Clinical Psychologist
831 Vida St.
Soledad, CA 93960

D1791854

Cognitive Therapy with Schizophrenic Patients:
The Evolution of a New Treatment Approach

Cognitive Therapy with Schizophrenic Patients: The Evolution of a New Treatment Approach

Edited by
Marco C.G. Merlo
Carlo Perris †
Hans D. Brenner

Hogrefe & Huber Publishers
Seattle · Toronto · Bern · Göttingen

Library of Congress Cataloging-in-Publication Data

is available via the Library of Congress Marc Database under the
LC Control Number 2001094326

National Library of Canada Cataloguing in Publication Data

Main entry under title:

Cognitive theraphy with schizophrenic patients : the evolution of a new treatment approach

Includes bibliographical references and index.

ISBN 0-88937-253-5

1. Schizophrenia—Treatment. 2. Cognitive therapy. I. Merlo, Marco C. G. II. Perris, Carlo III. Brenner, H. D.

RC514.C63 2001   616.89'820651   C2001-902506-8

Copyright © 2002 by Hogrefe & Huber Publishers

Hogrefe & Huber Publishers

USA:	P.O. Box 2487, Kirkland, WA, 98083-2487
	Phone (425) 820-1500, Fax (425) 823-8324
CANADA:	12 Bruce Park Avenue, Toronto, Ontario M4P 2S3
	Phone (416) 482-6339
SWITZERLAND:	Länggass-Strasse 76, CH-3000 Bern 9
	Phone (031) 300-4500, Fax (031) 300-4590
GERMANY:	Rohnsweg 25, D-37085 Göttingen
	Phone (0551) 496090, Fax (0551) 4960988

No part of this book may be reproduced, stored in a retrieval system, or transmitted, in any form or by any means, electronic, mechanical, photocopying, micro-filming, recording or otherwise, without the written permission from the publisher.

Printed and bound in Germany
ISBN 0-88937-253-5

Contents

Foreword IX

Preface XIII

Contributors XV

A. Theoretical Aspects

1. M.C.G. Merlo and W. Gekle 3
   Psychosocial Treatment of Schizophrenic Disorders: Structuring
   Information Processing and Information Exchange

2. B. Hodel and H.D. Brenner 18
   Therapies for Information Processing in Schizophrenia:
   Conceptual Basis, Present State, Future Directions

B. Practical Aspects

1. C. Perris 31
   A Comprehensive, Integrated Treatment Program for Patients
   Suffering From Schizophrenic Syndromes Based on Cognitive
   Psychotherapy

2. P.W. Corrigan 47
   Cognitive Rehabilitation of Schizophrenia

3. D.G. Kingdon and D. Turkington 59
   Using Cognitive Behavioral Therapy of Schizophrenia in a District
   Psychiatric Service

4. M.C.G. Merlo and H. Hofer 68
   Systemic Considerations for the Inpatient Treatment of First-Episode,
   Acutely Psychotic Patients

5. G.C. Zapparoli, M.C. Gislon and G. De Luca 75
   Delusional, Cognitive and Emotional Aspects of Communication
   with the Psychotic Patient

6. G. Liotti and M.A. Reda 84
   Why is Individual Psychotherapy Contraindicated in Schizophrenia? –
   Theoretical Reflections from a Constructivist Point of View

C. Empirical Evaluation

1. P. Zorn and V. Roder 95
   Social Skills Training Programmes for Schizophrenic Patients:
   What Works and How Can it be Improved?

2. W. Spaulding, D. Penn and C. Garbin 107
   Cognitive Changes in the Course of Psychiatric Rehabilitation

3. B. Hodel and H.D. Brenner 125
   A Training Program for Coping with Maladaptive Emotions:
   Further Development to the Integrated Psychological Therapy for
   Schizophrenic Patients

4. S. Kraemer 136
   Cognitive Behavior Therapy and its Differential Effects in the
   Treatment of Chronic Schizophrenic Patients

Appendix

H. Hofer
A. Important Concepts in Cognitive Therapy 167

B. Rating Instruments 175

C. Neuropsychological/Experimental Psychological Tests 178

References 181
Author Index 211
Subject Index 217

Foreword

The evolution of cognitive-based therapies for the treatment of schizophrenia marks a defining period in the history of psychiatric treatment, one highlighted by critical advances in the knowledge of neurocognitive functioning and treatment technologies. When one looks back upon the evolutionary development of the scientific understanding and treatment practices in psychiatric illness, it is somewhat remarkable to note the rapidity with which these advances have taken place. Essentially, nearly all of our current knowledge about schizophrenia has developed out of investigations conducted within the past 100 years. Before that point, an understanding of mental illness and the use of clinically viable treatment technologies was virtually nonexistent.

In earlier eras, disturbances in behavior were thought to be attributed to supernatural forces such as evil spirits, witches, demons, gods, or sorcerers. The response to such poorly understood phenomena often took the form of primitive and barbaric practices that included public humiliation, physical torture, exorcisms, and impri-sonment. Little change took place in the treatment of mental illness until the late 18th and early 19th centuries when the humanitarian movement triggered by the work of Chiaruggi, Pinel, Tuke, and Dix resulted in a more compassionate response to treating the mentally ill.

The understanding of mental illness as a disturbance similar in many ways to other medical disorders was later made possible through the work of Kraepelin and Bleuler who conceptualized schizophrenia as a medical disorder defined by its etiology, symptomatology, course, and outcome. Succeeding efforts attempted to seek physical origins for the cause of schizophrenia which led to the identification of genetic, neurodevelopmental, and environmental influences as key factors in the etiology of schizophrenia.

More recently, during the past 40 years, the field has been overwhelmed with investigations identifying neurocognitive disturbances associated with schizophrenia. These investigations led to the discovery that schizophrenia is associated with multiple deficits in information processing that include, but are not limited to, deficits in attention, memory, language, motor functioning, and executive or frontal systems functioning. One of the more prominent recent discoveries is that certain cognitive deficits are present primarily during psychotic episodes while other cognitive deficits are present both during and between episodes, the latter identified as so-called "vulnerability indicators".

These findings have led to changes in the conceptualization of treatment needs. Emerging treatment programs now emphasize the teaching of social skills, family management, coping strategies and interventions for improving information processing deficits to help protect patients from exacerbation of symptoms and consequent relapse. It is now recognized that patients are not only limited by their psychotic symptoms, but by their cognitive deficits as well. Indeed, some evidence exists to suggest that certain neurocognitive deficits may be related to psychosocial activities and to the acquisition of social skills; moreover these deficits may be more related to certain areas of functional outcome than psychotic symptoms. In toto, the scientific advances made in the conceptual understanding of schizophrenia in terms of both its clinical characteristics and cognitive deficits have grown exponentially in the past 100 years, and these advances can be linked directly to the advances achieved in formulating innovative treatments.

The heterogeneous symptoms, cognitive disabilities, and social and occupational deficits that are indigenous to the disorder point towards the need to continue to refine existing treatments and to continue to develop new ones. *Cognitive Therapy with Schizophrenic Patients: The Evolution of a New Treatment Approach* describes the latest state-of-the-art developments in the treatment of schizophrenia, highlighting the advances in knowledge about the role of cognitive deficits on behavior and including the latest innovative approaches in the treatment of psychiatric symptoms. With respect to the latter, the cognitive therapies have become increasingly popular forms of treatment, targeting the interactive relationship among thoughts, feelings, and behavior. These therapies have by-and-large replaced psychoanalytic treatments made popular during the early part of the 20th century.

Offshoots of the landmark contributions of Aaron T. Beck, the newer derivations of cognitive therapies and integrated treatment approaches presented in this book attempt to alleviate certain target symptoms of the disorder (e.g., delusions, deficits in social problem solving, emotional dysregulation) through selected cognitive-behavioral techniques. *Cognitive Therapy with Schizophrenic Patients: The Evolution of a New Treatment Approach* is well-suited for the scientist-practitioner, providing the theoretical and empirical basis for the development of innovative treatments along with detailed descriptions of the programs and treatment techniques. A chief contribution of this book is the emphasis on the integration of neurocognitive functioning with psychiatric rehabilitation.

There is a danger, however, in "lumping" all cognitive approaches into the same category. For example, the "cognitive" methods described in this book that aim to directly alter delusional and hallucinatory experiences have much more in common with the cognitively-based methods of "top-down" social skills training - where interpersonal problem-solving is a mainstay than they have with a "bottom up" strategy of modifying molecular functions of information processing. Experimental psychopathologists and clinical psychologists have much less in common than this book might suggest. The latter are adapting methods of cognitive therapy found to be useful in depressive and anxiety disorders to schizophrenia while the former are identifying "malleable" vulnerability factors that may be critical in the etiology of schizophrenia - then attempting to "normalize" these functions using innovative behavioral interventions followed by generalization of laboratory-based improvements into clinical improvement in real life settings.

If psychiatric rehabilitation is to continue to advance, much more effort must be expended by its proponents to integrate pharmacotherapy with cognitive-behavior therapy. For example, the new generation of atypical antipsychotic drugs may yield improvements in neurocognitive functioning that can serve as a platform or "plateau" for higher level assaults on disability and handicap. Another arena for cognitive rehabilitation is functional magnetic brain imaging which will allow for much more precise pinpointing of the neural pathways which need to be altered through cognitive remediation. A beginning has already been made in this arena with the charting of auditory hallucinations by two groups - one in New York and one in Los Angeles.

Robert P Liberman

Preface

We are very honored to dedicate this book to our co-editor, Prof. Carlo Perris, who passed away before we were able to finish the editing. It was very important for him that this work be published. All professionals who work in the field of psychosocial treatment of schizophrenic disorders are very much indebted to him for he has brought forward the whole field and established high standards. He also inspired and enriched many of us personally. We are sure that his influence will go on.

Prof. Perris has great merit in the significant changes in conceptual approaches undergone in the psychotherapy of schizophrenic disorders. With the advent of cognitive therapy and cognitive sciences, we can observe a paradigm shift in that therapists of different formations search for integrating dialogue. The improvement of real life situations has increasingly become the focus of psychotherapeutical interventions. There is no other human illness with as much relevance to a person's social situations as schizophrenia. Even the aims of psychopharmacological interventions are no longer limited to reducing signs and symptoms, but to optimize the cognitive and motor functions for a better social reintegration. Successful reintegration for which we today have well founded evidence that good cognitive and motor functioning are essential prerequisites. From psychotherapy there is also an acceptance of the importance of basic cognitive functions (e.g., memory, executive functions, attention) for successful therapeutic work. Thus we can see an increase in the common base for a better integration of psychotherapy and psychopharmacology.

This book integrates the clinical experience and research of different groups which have provided valuable contribution to the evolution of this new approach. It is divided into a theoretical introduction, descriptions of practical applications, and research results. In the first part *Merlo and Gekle* describe a model of information processing and information exchange. On the basis of theoretical considerations, demands for therapeutic interventions which focus on integrating patients back into their natural environment and fostering their autonomy in everyday life are elaborated. This chapter is followed by the contribution of *Hodel* and *Brenner* giving an overview of the theoretical basis of cognitive deficits in schizophrenic patients. They conceptualize schizophrenia as a systemic disorder and show the implications for therapy, as specified in the Integrated Psychological Therapy Program (IPT) for schizophrenic patients.

The second part of the book is introduced by *Perris* who presents the Integrated Treatment Program – a treatment method which has been used in special centers for young schizophrenic patients. The importance of an individualized therapeutic program is discussed. Corrigan deals with the question of why a combination of interpersonal skill training and cognitive remediation is forward-looking. The role of cognitive impairment with regard to limited information processing capacity is explained. An overview of laboratory-based approaches and available treatment programs is given. *Kingdon* and *Turkington* provide a detailed description of specific cognitive techniques used for schizophrenic patients, and conclude with information on their application and experiences in a clinical setting. *Merlo* and *Hofer* focus on the inpatient treatment of first-episode schizophrenic patients in the acute phase. The work on a specialized ward and the factors which influence multidisciplinary teamwork are discussed from a social system theory perspective. *Zapparoli, Gilson* and *De Luca* deal with specific aspects of psychotic communication that have to be considered in therapy. A case report of a chronic patient is presented to illustrate the utility of a combination of psychodynamic therapy and cognitive therapy. Based on their empirical work, Liotti and Reda discuss why individual psychotherapy may be contraindicated in schizophrenic patients. They also present a general review of autism and cognitive disabilities in schizophrenic patients. In the third part (C) of this book, empirical assessments of cognitive therapy are presented. *Zorn* and *Roder* have further developed the Integrated Psychological Therapy (IPT) for schizophrenic patients and present their program on residential, vocational and recreational rehabilitation. *Spaulding, Penn* and *Garbin* describe their research program for chronic patients and theirs results with a computer-based test battery, to analyze the relationship between cognitive functioning and social-behavioral functioning. *Hodel* and *Brenner* describe the relationship between cognitive impairment and emotional deregulation, and the development of a specific technique to target emotional coping skills. First results of this further developement of IPT are discussed. *Kraemer* addresses the question of how cognitive strategies might be used to help chronic patients to cope with stressful situations more effectively and presents. And presents the results of her studies. The book concludes with three Appendixes compiled by *Hofer*. Appendix A gives definitions of concepts commonly used in psychosocial therapy with schizophrenic patients. Appendix B contains short descriptions of rating instruments referred to in this book, and Appendix C describes the neuropsychological/experimental procedures mentioned herein.

The editors would like to thank all those who contributed for their engagement and cooperation. We would also like to thank the patients and their families, whose experiences are the basis for our growing knowledge about these illnesses which create such enormous suffering. For all the interesting advice and discussions, we also thank our collaborators who are too many to name. We also acknowledge Dr. G.-J. Hogrefe and Mr. Dimbleby, who helped publish this book. Last but not least, we are very grateful for the support and patience of our families in this time consuming endeavor.

Summer, 2001
Marco C.G. Merlo
Hans D. Brenner

Contributors

HANS D. BRENNER, Prof. Dr. med. et phil., Professor of Psychiatry, Universitäre Psychiatrische Dienste (UPD) Bern, CH-3072 Bern, Switzerland

PATRICK W. CORRIGAN, PsyD, Associate Professor, University of Chicago, Center for Psychiatric Rehabilitation, 60477 Tinely Park IL, USA

CALVIN GARBIN, PhD, Psychologist, University of Nebraska, Lincoln, Nebraska, USA

WALTER GEKLE, Dr. med., Consultant, Universitäre Psychiatrische Dienste (UPD) Bern, CH-3072 Bern, Switzerland

MARIA C. GISLON, PhD, Psychologist, Centro di Psicologia Clinica della Provincia di Milan, Milan, Italy

BETTINA HODEL, Dr. phil., Psychologist, Universitäre Psychiatrische Dienste (UPD) Bern, CH-3072 Bern, Switzerland

HELENE HOFER, Dr. phil., Psychologist, Universitäre Psychiatrische Dienste (UPD) Bern, CH-3072 Bern, Switzerland

DAVID G. KINGDON, MD MRCPsych, Professor of Mental Health Care Delivery, Unversity of Southampton, Southampton, United Kingdom

SIBYLLE KRAEMER, Dr. phil., Psychologist, Psychiatric University Hospital of the Technical University of Munich, Munich, Germany

GIOVANNI LIOTTI, MD, Psychiatrist, Director of Training of the Italian Association for Cognitive Therapy (SITCC), Rome, Italy

GIUSEPPE DE LUCA, PhD, Psychologist, Centro di Psicologia Clinica della Provincia di Milan (Como), Italy

MARCO C.G. MERLO, Dr. med., Consultant, Hôpitaux Universitaires de Genève, Départment de Psychiatrie, CH-1225 Chêne-Bourg, Switzerland

DAVID PENN, PhD, Assistant Professor, Departement of Psychology, University of Nebraska, Lincoln, Nebraska, USA

CARLO PERRIS, MD, Professor of Psychiatry, University of Umeå, S-90185 Umeå, Sweden

MARIO A. REDA, MD, Professor of Psychiatry, Università degli Studi di Siena, Institut di Psicologia Generale e Clinica, I-53100 Siena, Italy

VOLKER RODER, Dr. phil., Psychologist, Universitäre Psychiatrische Dienste (UPD) Bern, CH-3072 Bern, Switzerland

WILL SPAULDING, PhD, Professor of Psychology, University of Nebraska, Lincoln, Nebraska, USA

DOUGLAS TURKINGTON, MRCPsych, Senior Lecturer, Unversity of Newcastle, Newcastle on Tyne, United Kingdom

GIOVANNI C. ZAPPAROLI, MD, Professor of Psychiatry, Centro di psicologia clinica, Milan, Italy.

PETER ZORN, Psychologist, Universitäre Psychiatrische Dienste (UPD) Bern, CH-3072 Bern, Switzerland.

A. Theoretical Aspects

Chapter A.1

Psychosocial Treatment of Schizophrenic Disorders: Structuring Information Processing and Information Exchange

Marco C.G. Merlo and Walter Gekle

1.1 Introduction

In this chapter, the authors try to bring together biological and neuropsychological knowledge with more recent approaches to schizophrenic disorders, which are influenced by information theory. The consequences and advantages of a thorough analysis of interpersonal dynamics and information exchange, together with intrapersonal information processing for the biological and psychosocial treatment of schizophrenic patients, are discussed. We should establish which verbal information should be given to a schizophrenic patient, which member of the therapeutic team should do this and how and when that should be done. We also need to establish which of his/her actions and activities should be encouraged. These questions are addressed here by applying the infomedical model in order to find ways to structure psychosocial interventions with schizophrenic patients in an optimum fashion.

While there is overall consensus about the efficacy of neuroleptic medication in the treatment of schizophrenic disorders (Davis, 1975), there is an equally valid realization of the importance of non-pharmacological treatment interventions. A recent meta-analytic review of the role of psychosocial treatments of schizophrenic disorders demonstrated the additive and supplementary effects to somatic treatment as well as the durability of their effects (Mojtabai *et al*, 1998). The combination of pharmacological and psychosocial treatments are best integrated in the bio-psycho-social model (Engel, 1977). Different authors have applied this approach to the understanding of schizophrenic disorders (M. Bleuler, 1978; Ciompi, 1988; Lempp, 1992; Perris, 1981; Seltzer *et al*, 1989). In the following, we will extend this fundamental concept with an **infomedical paradigm** proposed by Foss & Rothenberg (1988). These authors have analyzed illness processes from an information theoretical point of view. The infomedical model links together information from multiple levels of organization (mind, culture, body). We will follow this approach in order to integrate the complexity of different and often diverting phenomena resulting from a psychotic breakdown. Two major domains will be differentiated: the intrapsychic information processing and external, interpersonal information exchange.

In these terms, psychosocial treatment is believed to help the patient by means of verbal communication focusing on optimizing information processing and information exchange (for the value of psychotherapy when used in conjunction with medication from a patient's stance see Anonymous, 1986). This is not psychotherapy in a narrow sense. The concern lies in structuring the information exchange in a way that a common understanding among those who take part in treatment is possible.

Along with a comprehensive model of information processing, the relationship between different intrapsychic levels of dysfunction in schizophrenic patients will be discussed. Disturbances of information exchange are also regularly found in these patients (e.g. restriction of interpersonal relations to almost exclusively professionals). Apart from cognitive impairment and psychopathological symptoms and signs, an understanding of social problems is of major importance for treating this disorder. Information processing and information exchange are linked through the way information is implemented. In other words, successful information processing and information exchange are perceivable in an individual's verbal communication and willed action. Therefore, regular evaluation of patients' activities has also to be considered by psychosocial treatment.

In the different domains of dysfunction, a typical pattern in schizophrenic disorders consists of changes between **extreme positions**, e.g. lack of interest or excessive interest, overactivity or apathy, intensive emotions or anhedonia. Therapeutic interventions should counteract these extremes, and at the same time, avoid either over- or understimulating situations.

1.2 Disturbances in Information Processing

1.2.1 Cognitive impairment

In order to compare and integrate the techniques of different psychosocial approaches, we propose a model of **information processing** and information exchange that helps to distinguish different levels of psychosocial intervention. This model is based on the concept of memory-driven and state-dependent brain information processing (Koukkou & Manske, 1986; Koukkou et al, 1991). Figure 1 displays a model of how information is intrapsychically processed. Perceptual and attentional processes are responsible for the input of information which comes from both inside and outside the body. In consciousness, one becomes aware of thoughts, emotions and actions, as well as of distinguishing between those elements belonging to oneself or to another person. Usually the term 'cognitive functions' is used in a broad sense, which also encompasses unconscious information processing. These functions are divided into basic functions and functions related to cognitive schemata; the latter constitute semantic memory. In working memory, incoming information is continuously controlled for discrepancies between internal meaning structure (i.e. semantic memory) and external information (Goldman-Rakic, 1991). Input can be distorted by altered *basic cognitive functions* (perception, attention) or by a low capacity of the working memory (Corrigan, chapter B.2, this book). On a higher level, distortions in thinking can occur, e.g. in concept formation, abstraction, taking perspective and in relating to the self.

The importance of basic cognitive impairment in behavior therapy with schizophrenic patients has been emphasized by Brenner (1987) who proposed a persuasiveness model to explain the effect of such impairment on the interface between biological substrate and social functioning. Recently, Frith has introduced the concept of '**theory of mind**'. This shows that many signs and symptoms of schizophrenic disorders can be understood as an impairment of the capacity of a normal person to represent beliefs and intentions (Frith, 1992). During the acute psychotic breakdown and during the postacute or stabilizing phase, schizophrenic patients suffer from difficulties in describing the contents of their consciousness. Even after remission and in full awareness of their experiences during the psychotic episode, they show marked problems in talking about what happened to them (Hurlburt, 1990). Frith (1992) interprets these findings as a confirmation of a lack of

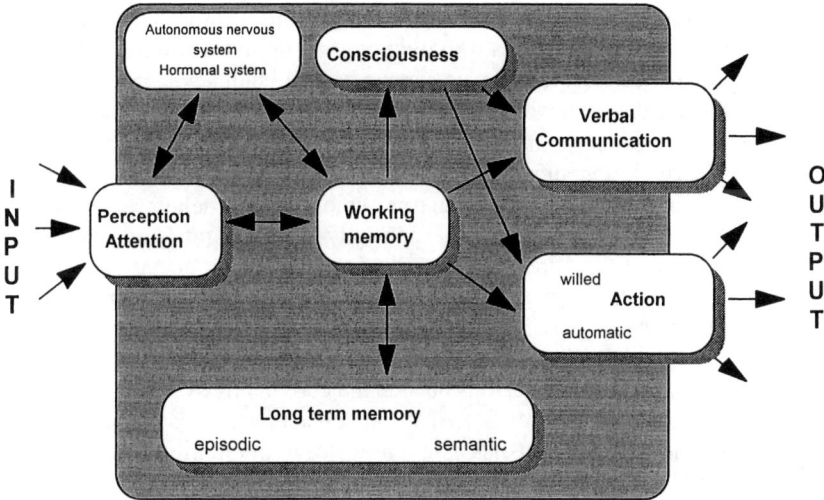

Figure 1. Information processing: Input from inside and outside of the body is processed in the working memory and compared to earlier experiences and one's personal value system. Verbal communication and willed action are accessible to consciousness.

a 'theory of mind' or - in other words - an awareness of one's own mental state. For acting adequately in social situations every individual (older than five) has to be aware of other people's mental states, i.e. can distinguish between his own knowledge, intentions, emotions, beliefs and those of others. This ability to reflect on one's own or others' thoughts is also called metathinking.

1.2.2   Distortions in cognitive schemata

According to social cognitive theories, cognitive schemata interpret and organize incoming information (Hewstone & Macrae, 1990). Cognitive schemata are conceptualized as dynamic and long lasting structures of relevant information, which make up the meaning-structure of the psyche. This organization of internal information can be roughly divided into two domains: one is that of goals and means and the other, of concepts of the self and others. This differentiation divides meaning-structures into those that consist of elements of the world of things and those of the world of relations.

Means are the instruments by which a person interacts with other persons and by which he hopes to succeed in accomplishing his goals. They are tools for organizing communication and action. For social situations, social skills are important tools, which have been intensively studied in schizophrenic patients (Wallace, 1986). There is much evidence that the majority of schizophrenic patients are impaired on this level. In addition, both schizophrenic patients and also many of their relatives show disturbances in their ability to appraise social situations. They have difficulties in distinguishing between what can or cannot be considered 'normal' and 'adjusted' social behavior (Harrow & Quinlan, 1985; Harrow et al, 1989). In other words, schizophrenic patients have a distorted internal map of what is accepted social behavior. The patient's cognitive schemata for interpretation of social interactions may not be transferable to persons who did not grow up in the same family unit (for example, one patient explained that his parents had told him never to show emotions to other people because that would be dangerous).

Schemata of the self and others develop during social interaction and are acquired very early during an individual's life. They are, in most cases, coined by the family system, its communication patterns, emotionality, beliefs, socioeconomic circumstances as well as other factors. Especially in very rigid family systems that have built up a sort of a "firewall" towards the surrounding social systems, these schemata might not be applicable to social situations outside the family. At the same time, schizophrenic patients often lack or have little contact with a peer group. They have few social interactions and therefore have limited possibilities of expanding their experience to persons outside the core family system. Both distorted internal maps of social contact or lack of social contact make breakdown more likely to occur when the individual at risk is going to leave the family of origin. On the other hand, within the family there can be distorted communication as shown by studies of *expressed emotion* (EE) (Kavanagh, 1992; Bebbington & Kuipers, 1994; Butzlaff & Hooley, 1998) and communication deviance (CD) Nugter et al, 1997). On the basis of these communication dysfunctions, dysfunctional cognitive-emotional or emotion-logical structures (Ciompi, 1991) of the self and others are imprinted in the psyche. An important aspect of these distortions is the difficulty of differentiating between the wishes and beliefs that belong to the patient's self and those that come from another persons. It has not yet been shown whether this lack of differentiation is a neuropsychological disorder as postulated by Frith (see above) or if it is caused by distortions of cognitive schemata (see also 1.2.4), which originally may have their roots in a dysfunctional communication style within the family.

1.2.3 Emotional disturbances

The emotions are strongly connected to cognitive functions, and are also of great importance for the intrapsychic processing of information. Janzarik (1959, 1988), in his concept of structural dynamics and Ciompi (1988, 1991), with his affect-logical concept have emphasized this relationship between *cognition* and emotion. Both authors have applied their respective theories to the understanding of psychotic decompensation and the cause of illness. They contend that emotional overstimulation causes an overload of information, resulting in a derailment of cognitive functioning.

Schizophrenic patients describe their psychotic anxiety as the most terrible and frightening experience a human being can go through (Podvoll, 1990). On the other hand, some are also exposed to the other end of emotional extremes, i.e. anhedonia and apathy, which go together with understimulation, social withdrawal and chronicity. Both extreme states of feelings can evolve in the same patient and can be understood as a dysregulation of adaptive internal processes. They also involve a dysregulation of the autonomic nervous system and the hormonal system; data from several neuropsychohormonal studies show how intensive these dysregulations are (Lieberman & Koreen, 1993).

In interpersonal situations, schizophrenic patients not only sometimes express inappropriate affect, but they even have difficulties in perceiving their own and others' emotions (Hodel & Brenner, chapter C.3, this book). This causes great insecurity in interpersonal contacts and may explain why many patients often avoid social situations: though this social withdrawal does not mean that they lack the desire for friendship or partnership per se.

1.2.4 Difficulties in performing willed actions

Since Kraepelin's time (1902), both clinicians and researchers have described the insufficiency of willed actions in schizophrenic patients. Various theories have been proposed to better understand the difficulties schizophrenic patients have to transpose their intentions into willed action. Some authors have interpreted these phenomena as lack of intentionality. Other authors have explained this incapacity in terms of hypofrontality of the brain (Weinberger *et al*, 1986). In connection with the 'theory of mind', Frith (1992) has also interpreted this dysfunction as a disturbance of the prefrontal cortex, i.e. a neuropsychological disorder. It is important to differentiate between abulia (i.e. reduced impulse to perform willed action) caused by brain dysfunction (sometimes even by excessively high dosages of neuroleptic medication) and a lack of perspective as a result of inadequate goals and insufficient exchange of information.

Another concept for explaining insufficient willed action can be drawn from Mead's (1934) social-behavioral theory of the self, which differentiates between 'I' and 'me'. The latter is the part of the self that has developed from the interaction with others. It coincides with those schemata which are experienced as belonging to one's self. Whereas the 'I' provides the feeling of freedom and initiative, the 'me' connects us to the social world; at the same time, the 'I' gives us a certain amount of freedom to carry out willed actions. Both parts of the self are necessary prerequisites for human behavior. It is the human dilemma that behavior is never only autonomous or heteronymous action (Blankenburg, 1991) but a process of 'related individuation' (Stierlin, 1978). Kraus has applied Mead's theory to the understanding of functional psychoses (1987). According to this, schizophrenic patients have both a reduced 'me', because of distorted schemata, and a lack of 'I-activity' in that they show little autonomy or initiative.

1.3   Disturbances in Information Exchange

When treating schizophrenic patients, therapists should not only consider information processing as a dysfunction of the individual, but also consider disturbances of **information exchange** in the social system of this patient. Keeping the focus on information, structural deficits in this social domain become evident and therapeutic interventions can be combined with individually based approaches. Information exchange is comprised of the relationships within the family system as well as with significant others that are part of a natural environment or of persons with professional roles. The importance of the therapeutic relationship between individual therapist and patient is undisputed. The quality of the relationship between primary carer (family and significant others) and patient in its relevance for long-term outcome is well established (Kuipers, 1998). Nevertheless, some therapists and other caregivers still have difficulties in widening the focus from an individually centered approach to a systemic one. The latter means that the social system of the patient is also considered (e.g. family burden, peer group, general practitioners and teachers).

The social problems of schizophrenic patients are at least twofold. On the one hand, patients have difficulties with everyday life, employment, and recreation; on the other, their social network often lacks acquaintances, companions or friends. This is why family ties are much more important and more susceptible to crises than in a person of the same age who has sufficient extra-familial relationships. Thus, it is important to assess the relational resources of the patient and to analyze with him/her where changes are necessary and possible. Visualizing the present social network with a sociogram may sometimes be of value for the patient and significant others as well as for the therapist.

Often the social system of the patient is not only restricted to a small number of personal resources, but there is also a reduction in the quantity and quality of information exchange. The content of the verbal interactions of patients with family members and professionals is often limited to matters concerning the illness. Often patients and families receive contradictory, confusing and negative information about schizophrenic disorders. This makes information exchange more redundant and reduces input for new experiences. The restriction to contents concerning only pathology causes a loss of quality of life and of resources: he/she becomes entrapped in a vicious circle of negative information as a modern form of 'institutionalism'. This is a possible danger of educational programs focusing only on psychopathology, deficit-syndromes and the cognitive and emotional shortcomings of schizophrenic people. In the analysis of this domain it is important to consider not only the verbal information but also the indirect information resulting of real life experiences (e.g., what is the activity of the patient during the day? How are the living facilities?). Before trying to implement a therapy, a thorough evaluation of the information on the concepts of the illness and the resources already available in the patients' social systems, should be undertaken.

1.4 Domains and Strategies of Therapeutic Interventions

1.4.1 Deciding the level of approach for psychosocial interventions

The therapeutic aim of ameliorating the disturbances of intrapsychic information processing is to help the patient reintegrate their selves into a natural social environment and to foster their autonomy in everyday life. By clearly structuring information exchange within the patient's actual system (formed by the patient, their families, significant others and professionals) a positive influence (at least not a confusing one) might be exerted on the patient's disturbed information processing. Different approaches are needed for this complex task. Whereas cognitive remediation strategies are directed towards an improvement of the performance of *basic cognitive functions* (such as attention), psychotherapy, in a narrower sense, may increase social competence by acting on cognitive schemata.

Descriptions of specific techniques for *cognitive remediation* and cognitive psychotherapy can be found in other chapters of this book. In this chapter, some general considerations on how to structure psychosocial interventions will be discussed.

1.4.2 Situational therapy versus structural therapy

During the acute phase of illness, verbal communication with the schizophrenic patient should focus on the here-and-now. The term 'situational therapy' is used in this sense and describes the efforts of the therapist to help the patient to process information about the present situation. It is assumed that the structure of a patient's personality has evolved out of experiences during his life, and it is strongly connected with schemata of the self and others. Therefore, this is of high importance to the patient and, if endangered by psychosis or questioned by others, elicits strong emotional reactions. The extreme insecurity found during acute psychotic states and also during the first part of the post-acute phase necessitates a comforting approach on the therapist's part and not a challenging or provoking one. Thus, structural therapy during acute phase or in patients without a good social integration would be overstimulating.

Structural interventions are used in cognitive and psychodynamic therapies. The former works on cognitive schemata; the latter connects present experiences with emotionally important events of the past in order to overcome maladaptive behavior. This 'insight-oriented' therapy (Gunderson *et al*, 1993) seems more appropriate in a later phase of therapy and more effective for treating negative symptoms of schizophrenic disorders. As it is a maieutic approach (see 1.4.5), it also furthers improvements in Ego functioning. Although the use of psychodynamically oriented therapies remains controversial, Mojtabai and colleagues (1998) showed, in their meta-analytic review of psychosocial treatments of schizophrenic disorders, that psychodynamic therapies are equally effective, but that patient characteristics and common elements of therapy are more important as determinants of outcome.

1.4.3 The consensual sphere as a requirement for communicative structure

The consensual sphere is the basis for any communicative act, i.e. two persons who want to exchange information have to agree on a minimum of rules in order to achieve this exchange. In Mead's theory, both participants in a communicative act have to have internalized socially accepted attitudes, i.e. to have developed a 'me'. For instance, both have to accept that they must share the same language, time and space for communicating. Neologisms and word salad are extreme examples of a distortion of fundamental communicative rules. Other dysfunctional ways of perceiving and thinking may also impede the formation of a consensual sphere. This sphere is not only defined by cognitive contents but also by the state of feelings and emotions. The latter define the context of a communicative act, e.g. a pleasant emotion gives a different connotation to a word or a sentence than an angry emotion. Therefore, patients with inappropriate affect have difficulties in developing a consensual sphere with any partner in communication. It is not useful to go to a metalevel (i.e. to interpret the inadequate communication of the patient) in this early phase. Instead, the therapist should be aware of the feedback he receives from the patient, and consider his subjective experience of the present situation. By this, it is possible to reduce stressful emotions during the encounter and to establish an emotionally neutral or even positive emotional framework of what is to become the beginning of the consensual sphere.

Delusions and hallucinations are common symptoms of schizophrenic disorders, which strongly impede the effort to establish a consensual sphere with the patient. Nevertheless, recently there have been several attempts to deal with these disturbances. Psychoanalytically oriented authors (Seltzer et al, 1989) as well as cognitive-behavioral authors (Perris, 1989; Chadwick & Birchwood, 1994; Kingdon & Turkington, 1994) agree on approaching these positive symptoms by avoiding escalation with the patient about what is true of their experiences. They emphasize the priority of a good therapeutic alliance (see also below). If this first step is completed successfully, it may be possible to work through the attitudes and assumptions that are connected with the hallucinations or delusions with the patient (see also Kingdon & Turkington, chapter B.3.)

1.4.4   The therapeutic alliance

A good therapeutic alliance between patient and therapist is of fundamental importance for any successful therapy. In the treatment of schizophrenic patients, this is a major problem because of the great amount of suspiciousness they often show. Sometimes the patient does not even accept the minimal consensus that he/she needs some help. The therapist is often in a dilemma because the patient does not accept treatment, and at the same time, a delay of treatment might have deleterious consequences. Recent concepts of early intervention (McGorry & Jackson, 1999) aim at developing new strategies for the initial contact with the patient. A good alliance formed within the first six months of treatment is related to better compliance with prescribed medication and to a better outcome after two years (Frank & Gunderson, 1990). A therapeutic alliance requires the therapist to be committed to the patient's subjective experiences and to accept the need to get involved in a 'treatment partnership' (Seltzer et al, 1989; Böker, 1992). Perris (1989; chapter B.1., this book) compares it with a scientific expedition and calls it 'collaborative empiricism'. He also deduces from Bowlby's (1982) attachment theory the concept of a *secure base* to describe this relationship, which encourages the patient to explore new possibilities.

Feedback about the quality of the therapeutic alliance should be drawn only to a minor extent from what the patient talks about, but more from the actions he has been able to perform. This point should be discussed openly with the patient. The therapist should refrain from gathering information behind the patient's back.

1.4.5 Instructive versus maieutic interventions

Schizophrenic patients experience psychotic symptoms as intrusions into their personal space. This phenomenon can be explained as a lack of differentiation between one's own thoughts and feelings and those of others. Advice from a staff member may be misinterpreted by the patient as an intrusion. On the other hand, patients have disturbances in carrying out willed actions (see below), and when planning therapeutic interventions, the therapist has to consider these disturbances. An instructive intervention is necessary to transfer information, e.g. about relapse prevention, but has the disadvantage that the therapist does not know how much of this information the patient accepts. The maieutic approach (Perris, 1989; chapter B.1., this book) has the advantage of letting the patient express the solutions he has in mind. This approach is also used in psychodynamic and systemic family therapy. Its disadvantage is to be found in the requirement of a stable psychological state and of a minimum of introspective capacity in the patient.

The maieutic approach combined with feedback from the patient's activities is the best way to overcome difficulties in performing willed actions, because it conveys to the patient the feeling that he has found the solution, thus enhancing self-esteem and self-confidence. If the capacity of the 'I' is too weak to propose a new solution, it is helpful to propose two or three possibilities to the patient and let him choose one of them. As in the domain of performance, it is important not to over- or understimulate the patient in this domain of willed actions either.

1.4.6 Time frame

An important criterion for organizing psychosocial interventions is the time frame. Strauss and colleagues (1985) have shown in a longitudinal study that the pattern of the course of illness are variable; phases with more active coping alter with more retired states. They also identified different individual-environmental interactions over the time course. Later, Strauss and Carpenter (1991) proposed an Interactive Developmental Model in order to describe the interactions between the individual and the environment. Recently, Cortese and colleagues (1999) differentiated with this approach three patterns (positive incline, fluctuating and stable course). In long-term treatment, these patterns of course should be considered as well as the phases of the disorder.

In both individual and family therapy, there is much evidence that intervals between the sessions should not be too short. Usually, schizophrenic patients only accept small changes during the post-acute phase. The 'change' of psychotic decompensation has been so frightening that many patients prefer to stay at a minimal level in order to avoid relapse. A pattern of extremes can also be found in this domain, as other patients tend to change too much in too short a time. Some want to take a full-time job immediately after recovering from psychosis, while others seem to lack any feeling for time and may be willing to stay for months or even years in the institution. The timing of therapy sessions and of changes in benefits and life situation (e.g. new job, new residential solution) is of major importance for resocialization. As a guideline, patients and their families should learn to accept that only one change at a time is possible.

1.4.7 Choice of content

As soon as a minimal therapeutic relationship has been formed, it is important to concentrate, with the patient, on the subjective experiences of psychosis and to try to find an explanatory model for decompensation. Kingdon & Turkington (chapter B.3., this book) emphasize a 'normalizing' rationale, and use normal psychological phenomena for understanding it. Similar approaches have also been proposed by Seltzer *et al* (1989) and Süllwold & Herrlich (1990). A common ingredient is distancing, i.e. to help the patient to learn how to differentiate between psychotic dysregulation and his/her personality. This distinction is fundamental for developing an active attitude towards the illness and for performing self-determined actions. Autonomy and self-esteem also grow parallel to the success the patient has in coping with new critical and stressful situations where early signs of psychosis may signal an impending relapse. In this way, psychotic symptoms become warning signs to the self when stress begins to exceed a certain level. The transmission of the vulnerability-stress-coping model is often a good starting-point for elaborating the individual stressful situation and possible coping behavior.

Using the term 'crisis' is part of the intention of normalizing the psychotic experience. The concept of crisis provides a possibility of working through those attitudes that patients should change in order to avoid situations with too much stress in the future. This positive connotation however, is not meant to negate the potential harm resulting from psychosis and the enhanced risk of a relapse in the subsequent three to five years. The vulnerability-stress-coping model and the concept of crisis should also be accepted by family members or significant others. Above all, during the therapeutic exchange, the therapist should bear in mind the normalizing aspect and avoid devaluing terms (Kingdon & Turkington, chapter B.3., this book). Recently, Birchwood emphasized that the early phase of psychosis is a critical period and stressed the importance of focusing on the prevention and management of depression, hopelessness and suicidal thinking during this phase (Birchwood & Iqbal, 1998; Birchwood, 1999). The evaluation of the psychotic experience as loss, humiliation and entrapment should be worked through with the patient as soon as possible. The topics of shame and self-stigmatization are of high priority.

Together with the vulnerability-stress-coping model, a pattern of verbal communication with the patient should be the way the patient learns to recognize situations of over- or understimulation. Both extremes influence the course of illness negatively (Wing & Brown, 1970). Often, patients have overly high or overly low expectations concerning their own performance, hence the risk of becoming over- or understimulated.

A theme, which is often well accepted in family therapy sessions, is that of self-esteem, which is often very much weakened by the experience of psychosis (Birchwood, 1999). Strong feelings of shame and guilt in the patient and other family members often accompany loss of self-esteem. Therefore, a 'no fault' atmosphere, in which self-esteem can be restored, is of crucial importance for overcoming psychosis. Willed actions (see below) play an important part in strengthening self-esteem, especially when these actions make sense to oneself and are accepted by the significant others.

Often, patients do not accept help from professionals, and contend that they do not need it. As in the emotional sphere, this is another aspect of a pattern of extremes: either they need nobody and do everything by themselves or they are completely passive and let others take care of even the most elementary activities. Behind such behavior there is often a dysfunctional concept of the self. The patient has to accept the fundamental human position that the self is constituted by interaction with others and that there is no 'pure self' beyond autism. Some patients misuse meditative techniques in order to find this imaginary 'pure self', but instead, they experience a relapse with the disintegration of their identity. Blankenburg (1991) described this human dilemma as a dialectic process between autonomy and heteronomy. Using Mead's social psychological concept, the schizophrenic patient has difficulty in integrating the 'me' with his 'I' (Kraus, 1987). However, by experiencing a positive relationship with the professional and establishing a consensual sphere, the patient may gradually learn to accept this interactionally

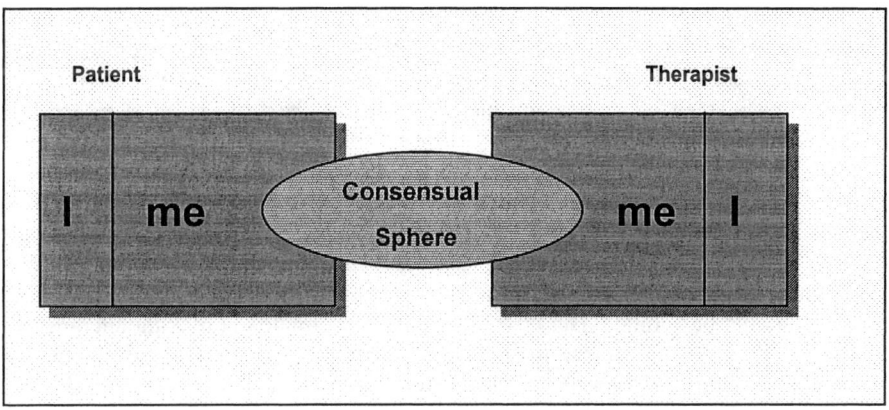

Figure 2. Consensual sphere: In order to establish a consensual sphere between patient and therapist it is necessary that both parts have internalized a 'me' structure.

constituted part of his self. Positive interpersonal experiences should reinforce the 'me' through contacts in peer groups. Many misinterpretations among family members can be overcome in family therapy sessions, and those parts of the 'me', which developed out of the family context, can be reintegrated. Consensual spheres between the patient, on one hand, and his family (as well as professionals or members of peer groups) on the other, become the basis for the development of self-consciousness, self-esteem, and self-confidence (Scharfetter, 1990).

1.4.8   Learning to cope with strong emotions

Many schizophrenic patients have difficulties in social situations possibly because they are overwhelmed by strong emotions or have been overwhelmed by them in similar situations in the past. Interpersonal interactions which escalate to strong criticism voiced by significant others (as measured by expressed emotion; Kavanagh, 1992; Bebbington & Kuipers, 1994; Butzlaff & Hooley, 1998) also elicit emotional overstimulation. On the other hand, overinvolvement of significant others can produce a state of anhedonia and loss of emotional investment on the side of the patient.

As described by Hodel & Brenner (chapter C.3., this book), some patients need training to recognize both their own emotions and those of others before coping strategies can be taught. 'Personal Therapy' (Hogarty et al, 1995) also focuses on coping with strong emotions. Zapparoli et al (chapter B.5., this book) propose an approach which attempts to understand the delusional, the emotional and the cognitive levels of emotional experience. Emotional-physiological reactions have been studied by Liotti and Reda (chapter B.6., this book). They found that close interpersonal relationship coincides with emotional uneasiness in schizophrenic patients. They interpret these findings as a reason for avoiding individual settings and preferring community, group and family settings. The latter settings have the advantage that emotional reactions can be the subject of direct therapeutic interventions.

Psychoanalysts (e.g., Racamier, 1982) have contended that schizophrenic patients may be very afraid of showing their own interests and wishes. At the same time, they are afraid of not being themselves, of losing their mind or of falling asleep. They feel influenced by others or by physical forces. They are afraid of being themselves and at the same time, of not being themselves. Kierkegaard has called this dilemma 'the illness that brings one to death' (1989). In terms of Mead's concept, the impulses of the 'I' and those of the 'me' are not integrated. In therapeutic situations, it is crucial that patients do not feel manipulated by the therapist in their sphere of the 'me'. Rules of interpersonal interactions should always convey that the 'I' as human essence is more important than abstract ideals or ideologies. For instance, it is necessary to inform patients that they need medication or that cannabis should be avoided. But it would not be appropriate to break the therapeutic alliance if they do not adhere to these arrangements. The therapeutic alliance is always more important than a slavish adherence to "law and order " in psychiatry, and therapists have to be able to walk on this thin line. It is important that patients experience interactions with therapists and others positively in order to assimilate the underlying social rules as a more or less complex cognitive scheme into their 'me'.

1.4.9 Helping to transpose information into willed action

Significant incapacities of schizophrenic patients include a distorted way of relating to other people, as well as an impaired ability to transpose inner concepts, wishes and needs into action. They have difficulties in willed actions, although they are sometimes able to express their wishes verbally. This incapacity in willed action has different aspects. One is that the patient does not want to do anything in the present situation, but tries to convince the therapist that, for instance, after discharge he will be able to get work. The therapist should encourage the patient to show willed actions in the shared situation, and therapeutic approaches that emphasize the 'here-and-now' position focus on this aspect.

Another aspect of the disturbances in willed action is patients' small degree of autonomy, or in terms of Mead's theory, their insufficient 'I'. This is strongly connected with a lack of perspective in their lives: they often have unrealistic and over-idealized goals, which are sometimes so high that they continue to experience disappointments. Often, these high expectations come from parents who cannot accept that their child will not perform as well as they would like them to. If the patient suffers learning disabilities caused by basic cognitive dysfunctions, it is important to help the parents to recognize and accept the neuropsychological limitations.

To be active and able to experience self-confirmation, a person has to be convinced that the things he is about to do have something to do with himself, i.e. to feel that 'I do it'. Some patients show such apathy that therapists or significant others become convinced that they have no wishes of their own and they start to take even small decisions for the patient. Then, both sides resign more and more, causing a vicious circle. Therapists and significant others therefore have to refrain from taking over too much responsibility, especially in the post-acute or stabilizing phase. They should focus on fostering the patients' own responsibility and adequate autonomy.

1.4.10 Restructuring the social network

It has been repeatedly shown that schizophrenic patients lack a supportive extra-familial social network, but systemic therapy aims at broadening the patient's natural system to a peer group. The problem of chronic patients is that almost all the people who interact with them are related to the illness. It is very difficult, if not impossible, to find the way back to normality from a position socially or geographically outside normality. Therefore, a major goal is to promote new relational systems outside the context of illness. A similar approach comes from sociotherapeutic strategies which promote vocational, residential and recreational activities for the patient in community-based environments whenever possible. As discussed above, the patient's self-esteem and motivation are strongly influenced by concrete positive experiences.

Before initiating long-term psychosocial treatment with schizophrenic patients, it is necessary to evaluate the interpersonal structure surrounding the patient. This structure consists of those persons who interact with the patient. If these people hear about the illness, they form their own concepts of it and may influence the patient. Therefore, the therapist should consider these opinions and try to work out a 'functional' illness model to be shared by all significant persons (also see above).

There is consensus among therapists that an acute schizophrenic patient is best treated by an interdisciplinary team. Milieutherapeutic approaches provide the main basis for psychosocial interventions in the acute phase of illness. Recently, the concept of expressed emotion (high EE: criticism, hostility or overinvolvement) has also been applied to staff members (Bebbington & Kuipers, 1994; Kuipers, 1998). These authors concluded that the reviewed studies showed the usefulness of this construct as an indicator of potential problems in staff-patient interaction. For instance, there was poorer outcome in schizophrenic patients who had been treated in a hostel characterized by high-EE staff, compared to a hostel with low-EE staff (Ball *et al*, 1992). Snyder *et al* (1994) found an association of critical attitudes in staff with poorer quality of life for residents. High-EE attitudes may evolve when staff members at a premature point in therapy are convinced that the patient has the free will to act in a certain way; on the other hand, some staff members are overly concerned with getting the patient 'to do something' without considering his inner state and motivation (Seltzer *et al*, 1989). The process of recovery requires a healthy environment that is characterized by a positive, warm relationship with the patient (Kuipers, 1998).

From the beginning of treatment in the acute phase, it is important to get into contact with the patient's relatives. Two different approaches have been applied to families with a psychotic member: the psychoeducational approach and systemic therapy. Goldstein (1994) has summarized the strategic goals and tactics of psychoeducational family therapy. Its critical issues are: integration of the psychotic experience; acceptance of vulnerability to future episodes; dependence on psychotropic medication for symptom control; the significance of life events for relapse; and distinguishing personality from disorder. Common features of psychoeducational programs with families include: early engagement of the family in a 'no fault' atmosphere; education about schizophrenic disorders; communication training; problem-solving training; and crisis intervention. These approaches are highly structured and are based on the vulnerability-stress-coping model; they emphasize the training of social skills to cope better with stressful life events and to learn how to communicate more clearly about the illness.

Constructivism has gained importance in cognitive therapy (Neimeyer & Mahoney, 1996) and systemic family therapy, and focuses on the construction of a social reality. Systemic therapy considers the consensual sphere between the patient and significant others as 'constructed reality'. Based on a maieutic approach, the therapist aims at enhancing self-structuring processes and fostering resources. One main tool is circular questioning (Selvini-Palazzoli *et al*, 1980; Tomm, 1985), which has been referred to as 'the Socratic method'. This way of questioning is an exercise in appreciating a different perspective, i.e. taking another person's perspective into account (Merlo *et al*, 1991). Other strategies of systemic therapy are: reintegrating the 'mad' person into the family's communication system; improving communication skills; questioning the exclusiveness of patient's role as the unwell family member; the passivity attached to this role; and working on relapse prevention (Retzer, 1994).

As shown by the analysis of the social network, the patient's relations to a peer group outside the family of origin, plays a major role during adolescence and fosters adequate autonomy and related individuation. One of the biggest advantages of treating First Episode Patients in a specialized service designed to meet their needs is found here. Sometimes the first extra-familiar peer relations occur among these young patients, and these relations might form a model after discharge (Merlo & Hofer, chapter C.4, this book).

1.5   Conclusions

The following statements sum up the major points that have been proposed as a common basis for psychosocial intervention in the treatment of schizophrenic patients.
1. In the intrapsychic domain of information processing, there is a need for reorganizing cognition, emotions and actions:

a) cognitive therapy should be tailored to the specific needs of the individual patient;
b) instructive intervention should be coordinated with interventions which help the patient to develop autonomy using a maieutic approach;
c) coping with strong emotions should be a major focus and 'decatastrophization' should be applied in order to reduce anxiety;
d) at the beginning, psychosocial therapy should focus on the present situation (situational versus structural therapy);
e) the way a schizophrenic patient relates to another person ('theory of mind'/self-other representation) deserves special interest;
f) achievable goals in life should be worked out (intentionality);
g) the patient should be encouraged not to succumb to routine activities, and learn to cope with new situations by structuring time (flexibility/adaptability);
h) the importance of fostering willed actions should be considered in order to facilitate new, positive experiences and to strengthen self-esteem.

2. In the domain of information exchange, the following aspects are important:
a) helping the patient to develop consensual spheres which he can share with other people;
b) analyzing the familial and extrafamilial social network on the interpersonal level, and involving both systems in the therapeutic process.

As this summary shows, the main focus of psychosocial therapy is on the resocialization of the patient, i.e. providing him with the capacity to reconnect with his own intrapersonal world as well as with the interpersonal world in an autonomous way. Repeatedly, we have experienced that structuring external information exchange helps reconstructing the patients' internal information processing. These thoughts provoke the question: Does the psychotherapy of schizophrenic disorders have to be much more phase specific and phase adapted than it is now? It might be possible that, in the future, the same multidisciplinary team follows the patient through the acute psychotic phase in which the treatment is highly medically and biologically oriented. Nevertheless, it is in this phase where the most traumatizing experiences occur and where, at the same time, the foundations of what is to become the crystallization point of the consensual sphere or therapeutic relationship, are laid down. With increasing stabilization, the patient might choose or been allocated to one team-member who is to follow the patient and might develop into the patient's individual therapist within the team. Therapy could now, according to the patient's state, evolve from an originally psychoeducative approach to cognitively oriented techniques and from there to even psychodynamically influenced strategies. Sometimes, patient and therapist might have to step back, if they proceeded too fast. Some patients might not be willing to go down this road; some therapists might not be experienced enough to walk the thin line between drawing from different schools and mere eclecticism. However, we have to overcome the insufficient position that the most inexperienced therapists often treat the most severely ill patients. We have always to bear in mind that a good therapeutic relationship remains the secure basis of all therapeutic interventions, and that it needs experience to build up this relationship with schizophrenic patients.

Chapter A.2

Therapies for Information Processing in Schizophrenia: Conceptual Basis, Present State, Future Directions

Bettina Hodel and Hans D. Brenner

2.1 Conceptual basis for the Integrated Psychological Therapy Program

Our current understanding of the nature of schizophrenia as a systemic disorder reflects an impressive body of research which suggests that neurobiological, psychological and social factors influence both the onset of illness and its course (cf. Böker & Brenner, 1992). Inherited and/or acquired structural changes in the brain underlie individual cognitive and perceptual abnormalities, i.e. information processing deficits which interact with environmental factors in transforming biological deviations from the norm into full-blown psychotic symptoms. The vulnerability-stress model of schizophrenia defines structural brain changes as an expression of biological vulnerability, and individual dysfunctions in information processing as an expression of cognitive vulnerability (cf. Brenner *et al*, 1992).

Cognitive vulnerability and biological vulnerability, however, interact with one another, reinforcing or weakening each other's effect. The information processing systems of the central nervous system develop along with the genetically-determined neuronal differentiation of the neo-cortex, i.e. especially with the post-natal development of the axons and the formation of synapses. For their maturation, however, they require continuous sensory experiences so that neuronal activity is a decisive structuring factor. If neuronal activity is modulated by external information, the latter factor also influences the development of the neural network and related structural characteristics of the organization of the brain. This explains why adverse psychosocial factors can result in enduring attentional, perceptual and cognitive impairment, depending on the functional state of the brain. In other words, such *impairment* can be potentiated or diminished by internal or external factors (cf. Koukkou *et al*, 1991).

Recent research findings in the field of neurobiology have paved the way for the development of systemic neuropathophysiological models of illness which vary to some extent, depending on the importance assigned to the findings on structural brain abnormalities in which deficits in information processing are pivotal (cf.

Brenner et al, 1992; Hemsley, 1994; Nuechterlein, 1994). This makes a compelling case for the viability of cognitive remediation, designed specifically to treat the information processing deficits in schizophrenic patients based on a model of vicious circles. This model describes the disruptive effects of impaired information processing on other levels of functioning (Brenner et al, 1992). It is based on the hypothesis of pervasiveness, which assumes that disorders in information processing not only reinforce each other, but also have pervasive detrimental effects on behavioral planning and on social competence. As shown in Figure 1, a first circle involves elementary and complex cognitive impairments, which reinforce and potentiate each other; a second circle covers the deterioration of social competence due to the first circle.

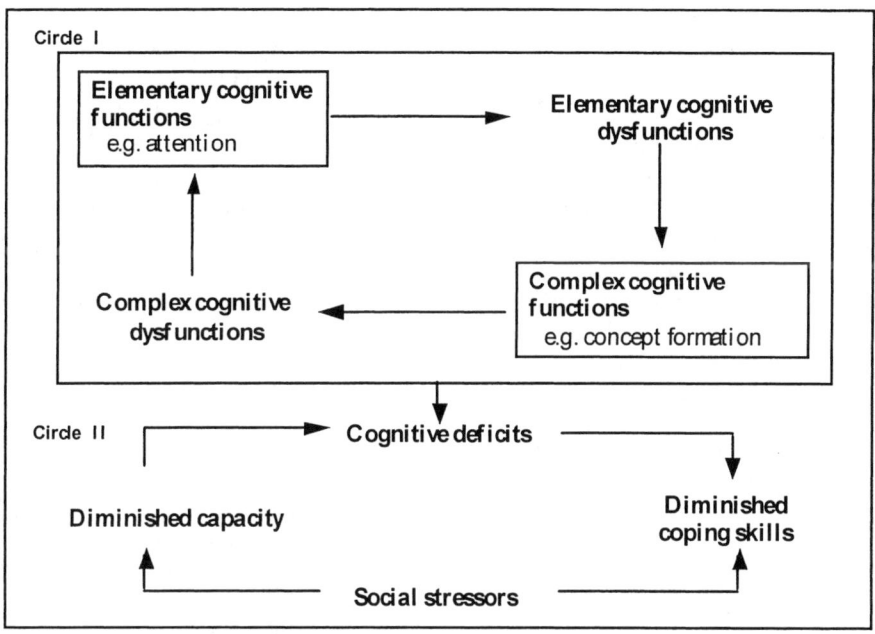

Figure 1. Schematic representation of the vicious circle between cognitive and social dysfunction.

The therapeutic corollary of this model is that *cognitive remediation* programs for schizophrenic patients must address both of these vicious circles: isolated improvements in cognitive performance may not be durable if compromised by social deficits. Conversely, behaviorally-oriented interventions also seem to be insufficient, since poor social functioning can re-emerge in connection with the first feedback loop. In addition, it is most likely that cognitive improvements remain stable over time only when tangible changes in behavior have been achieved, and behavioral interventions are efficacious only if cognitive mastery is acquired in treatment.

From such a perspective, current therapy and training procedures aimed at reducing the information processing deficits associated with schizophrenia can be divided into direct, indirect, or combined types. Direct procedures involve quasi-experimental and highly prescriptive intervention steps, aimed at remediating elementary cognitive impairments. Indirect procedures are primarily behaviorally-oriented interventions which explicitly address the cognitive impairments exhibited by schizophrenic patients. Combined procedures consist of both direct and indirect treatment strategies.

Direct intervention procedures target attentional, mnemonic, and conceptual skills so as to diminish impairments at various levels of functioning by rehearsing cognitive tasks. This could be described as a 'stimulation-approach' as defined by Green (1993). Early attempts at attentional skills training can be traced back, to e.g. Wagner (1968), who trained schizophrenic patients to match task and test stimuli. Wishner & Wahl (1974) and Benedict & Harris (1989) both developed a method of letter recognition training under auditory distraction conditions. Rosenbaum *et al* (1957) and Meiselman (1973) pioneered training procedures with reaction time tests, using instructions, reinforcement or punishment to improve performance.

Hammond & Summer (1972) and Larsen & Fromholt (1976) seem to have been the first to train mnemonic functions by means of serial rehearsal of syllables and words. Despite evidence of therapeutic efficacy, this line of training has not been pursued, presumably due either to concurrent advances in pharmacotherapy or to the underlying assumption that cognitive impairments are merely epiphenomena which are nuclear and are irremediable (Spring & Ravadin, 1992).

New developments along this line of cognitive treatment include computerized training programs devised to directly treat elementary attentional and perceptual functions. Lamberti *et al* (1988), using a training procedure involving similar learning tasks to those employed by Wagner (1968) and by Wishner & Wahl (1974), reported positive changes in attentional function. Gestrich & Hermanutz (1991) succeeded in reducing schizophrenic patients' reaction time in learning tasks which involved computerized auditory and visual stimuli. Gansert & Olbrich (1992) and Olbrich (1993) reported positive preliminary results with a training module which includes a combination of attentional, mnemonic, and conceptual skills (verbal and nonverbal). Current cognitive remediation also supports the potential of directly treating schizophrenic patients' conceptual functions (Green, 1993) by means of training procedures primarily based on the Wisconsin Card Sorting Test (WCST: Heaton, 1981). For instance, Goldberg *et al* (1987) asked patients to sort WCST cards according to certain criteria. Bellack *et al* (1990) reported improved test performance by omitting instructions and by providing positive reinforcement for correct solutions. Summerfelt *et al* (1991), Green *et al* (1992), Hellmann *et al* (1992) and Delahunty *et al* (1993) obtained the greatest gains in the WCST by using a combination of these procedures.

The indirect approach to treating cognitive impairment in schizophrenic patients incorporated cognitive restructuring and principles of learning into strategies devised to modify deficient behavior and to improve social skills and behavioral control was called 'behavior modification'. Corresponding strategies used to reduce schizophrenic patients' behavioral deficits by altering their language, attention, and thinking behavior were shaped by the innovative procedures devised by Meichenbaum & Cameron (1973). They involved training in task-relevant self-instruction to enhance focusing and attentional control by means of concentration exercises. Diaz & Colon (1985) reported a method of controlling schizophrenic patients' behavior; they were thought to recognize socially inadequate ways of behaving by comparing these to desirable ones, using a self-verbalization technique. Highly structured and systematic social skills training programs which are directed at equipping patients to survive outside the confines of a psychiatric hospital and employ the principle of overlearning are yet another method of indirectly affecting cognitive change (Bellack & Hersen, 1978; Bellack & Morrison, 1982; McFall, 1982; Wallace, 1982; Liberman et al, 1985; Liberman et al, 1986). Despite the relative effectiveness of these training procedures, practical experience suggests that persistent cognitive impairment has a disruptive effect on improvement on the behavioral level that may occur, thereby leading to a new decompensation.

One category of new developments in behavioral modification which explicitly takes into account the cognitive impairment associated with schizophrenia is based on the concept of social problem-solving skills as defined by Liberman (Liberman, 1988; Liberman & Wallace, 1990; Liberman et al, 1993). Training modules in such areas as job finding and leisure time have been designed to equip mentally ill patients with the social and problem-solving skills needed to prepare them for community living. The therapeutic procedures which are used incorporate techniques applied in earlier social skills training programs, as well as videotapes and other visuals (Eckman et al, 1992; Vaccaro et al, 1992; Wallace et al, 1992). Secondly, new developments in this direction have also been guided by the concepts of social perception and *social cognition* (Bellack, 1989). In social skills training programs for schizophrenic patients, special emphasis is therefore placed on sensitizing participants to the emotional cues involved in social situations and to their meanings (Bellack, 1997).

Combined intervention procedures used to treat cognitive impairment in schizophrenia are based on both the 'stimulation' and the 'behavior modification' approaches. In particular, they rely on substitution transfer processes (Green, 1993), i.e. specific training tasks generate compensatory processes on the same level of information processing and on other levels of functioning. One of the first of such interventions was devised by Adams et al (1981), who offered ideation training in attentional tasks and in self-instruction to a patient with severe paranoid, and discussed his delusions with him so that he could understand them in a situation-relevant manner. Evidence collected in two other recently conducted single-case studies suggests that social skills training is more effective if it is preceded by attentional training (Wong & Woolsey, 1989; Massell et al, 1991). The cognitive treatment methods developed by Perris (Perris et al, 1988; Perris, 1997) may also be regarded as a combined intervention approach. Based on similar theoretical underpinnings to those in the model of vicious circles, Perris et al (1988) have called for the treatment of both cognitive and social dysfunction in schizophrenic patients proceeding from cognitive aspects to a focus on social behavior. Guided by the principles of cognitive behavior therapy (Beck, 1979), i.e. 'Socratic dialogue', and a kind of 'collaborative empiricism', the patient and his therapist work together towards modifying maladaptive cognitions by devising alternative ways of appraising and interpreting social cues and by recognizing internalized negative and distorted viewpoints. Nevertheless, Perris (1997) has suggested that other therapeutic techniques, e.g. self-instruction, as well as social skills and problem-solving training procedures should also be incorporated as a part of this approach.

Table 1. Schematic overview of the Integrated Psychological Therapy Program for Schizophrenic Patients (IPT).

Subprogram	Focus of Intervention	Intervention Techniques
Cognitive Differentiation	Attentional skills	Card-sorting exercises Verbal concept exercises
Social Perception	Analysis of social information	Description of depicted social situations Interpretation of social situations depicted Discussion of individual interpretations Elaboration of a consensus
Verbal Communication	Conversation skills	Verbatim repetition exercises Analogous repetition exercises Exercises with interrogatives Conversation about one topic Free conversation
Social Skills	Competence in social skills	Cognitive prestructuring for skills acquirement Role play
Interpersonal Problem Solving	Application of (interpersonal) problem solving strategies	Identification and analysis of a given problem Cognitive prestructuring Transfer of the focused solution to real-life situations

The combined intervention procedure which probably has received the most recognition in European countries is the *Integrated Psychological Therapy Program for Schizophrenic Patients* (IPT) (Brenner *et al*, 1987a, 1990, 1994; Roder *et al*, 1988, 1992). Table 1 shows the formats of intervention used in IPT. This is based on the inverse corollary of the model of two vicious circles (cf. Figure 1), targeting cognitive impairments and their effects on social behavior. A series of controlled studies on IPT has demonstrated significant treatment effects on both cognitive and social levels of functioning. However, the assumption that cognitive functions have a pervasive effect on social behavior was not confirmed. Nor was generalization of trainings effects found to take place on a more elementary level of cognitive functioning.

2.2 Evaluation of the Integrated Psychological Therapy Program

For a more detailed analysis of IPT, a study was undertaken with 21 chronic schizophrenic patients diagnosed according to DSM III-R (Hodel, 1993a). These patients had a mean age of 31.0 years (sd = 10.2), a mean total length of illness of 9.7 years (sd = 5.2), and a mean total length of hospitalization of 30.2 months (sd = 21.2). The purpose of the study was to find out whether improved cognitive functions have pervasive effects on subsequent social interventions (bottom-up effects, Brenner et al, 1992), or conversely, whether improved social functioning has pervasive effects on subsequent cognitive intervention (top-down effects, Brenner et al, 1992).

Patients were randomly assigned to one of two groups. The IPT program was administered in a mirror design (Friedrich & Henning, 1988) to ensure a high degree of internal consistency without the use of control groups. One group of ten patients began the study in the normal IPT order [Cognitive Differentiation, Social Perception (cognitive interventions), Social Skills, Interpersonal Problem Solving (social interventions)], thus following a bottom-up approach. The group then engaged in IPT in the reverse order [Social Skills, Interpersonal Problem-Solving (social interventions), Cognitive Differentiation, Social Perception (cognitive interventions)]. The other group of 11 patients started out on the behavioral sub-programs before moving on to the cognitive ones, in line with a top-down approach. They then worked through the program a second time in the normal order. Both groups attended a total of 24 therapy sessions of 45-60 minutes each over a period of 12 weeks. The groups were led by the same therapist and co-therapist.

Another research associate, who was not involved in therapy, tested each group prior to and after all therapy sessions. The following measures were used to assess performance level: (a) cognitive functioning: Syllable Memorizing, Word Recognition, Crossing out Numbers [subtests of the Repeated Psychological Measures, (RPM; Fahrenberg et al, 1977)]; (b) subjective cognitive impairments: Frankfurt Complaint Questionnaire (FCQ; Süllwold & Huber, 1986), Self-Image Scale (SIS; Hodel, 1988); (c) social adjustment: Nurses' Observation Scale for Inpatient Evaluation (NOSIE; CIPS, 1981); (d) psychopathological symptoms: Brief Psychiatric Rating Scale (BPRS; CIPS, 1981).

The Mann-Whitney-U test showed no significant differences between the groups in the prior measurements. Wilcoxon tests were used for analyzing changes within the groups by comparing the pre-post results (see Table 2): The group representing the top-down approach demonstrated significant improvements in both measures of subjectively experienced cognitive impairment (FCQ, SIS) and a slight improvement in Syllable Memorizing. On the other hand, the group following the bottom-up approach did not evidence treatment gains in any of the cognitive measures used, whereas they showed comparable results in NOSIE and BPRS. Additionally, the post-measurements were analyzed by means of Mann-Whitney-U tests. Between the groups, significant differences were found in the measures of subjective cognitive impairment (Frankfurt Complaint Questionnaire, FCQ: $p = 0.03$, $z = -2.586$; Self-Image Scale, SIS: $p = 0.04$, $z = -2.160$).

The results of this study indicate that improvements in cognitive functions alone probably do not have a beneficial effect on subsequent social IPT interventions so that the bottom-up approach cannot be confirmed. Nor do they corroborate the top-down approach, as there was no group differentiation in the NOSIE and BPRS. Instead, factors which have neither been recognized nor controlled for to date are probably linked to the mechanisms of effectiveness. The following assumptions may be formulated about IPT effects: (a) cognitive intervention might improve cognitive functions which are not relevant to social functioning; (b) social intervention at the

Table 2. Comparison of two different intervention sequences of Integrated Psychological Therapy for Schizophrenic Patients (IPT) (pre-post comparison by Wilcoxon Tests).

Group with 'cognitive-social'-'social-cognitive' intervention sequence (N=10)

Measures		Mean		SD		z	p
		pre	post	pre	post		
Syllable M.		3.3	4.3	2.9	1.5	-1.784	n.s.
FCQ		23.9	18.3	14.7	15.1	-1.681	n.s.
SIS		10.7	8.8	4.3	6.0	-1.826	n.s.
NOSIE	social adaption	42.1	38.3	9.8	8.1	-2.701	0.006
BPRS	depression	14.8	10.0	8.0	9.2	-2.801	0.005
BPRS	anergia	9.7	5.1	11.2	3.5	-2.650	0.008
BPRS	hostility	7.1	4.8	4.3	4.5	-2.073	0.038

Group with 'social-cognitive'-'cognitive-social' intervention sequence (N=11)

Measures		Mean		SD		z	p
		pre	post	pre	post		
Syllable M.		3.9	5.1	2.1	2.3	-1.886	0.053
FCQ		26.7	6.9	25.1	19.2	-2.521	0.012
SIS		8.5	11.7	9.3	4.7	-2.170	0.030
NOSIE	retardation	12.5	9.5	12.3	10.1	-2.487	0.012
BPRS	depression	11.8	7.6	5.6	2	-2.547	0.011
BPRS	anergia	8.7	5.3	7.8	4.5	-2.488	0.013
BPRS	thought disorders	7.5	4.9	4.3	3.5	-2.366	0.018

beginning of therapy could - in contrast to cognitive intervention - reduce heightened arousal in schizophrenic patients; (c) social intervention used at the beginning of therapy seems to motivate patients, due to its relevance to real-life problems, whereas cognitive intervention focuses on cognitive functions, which does not appear to be so pertinent to daily life.

Thus, on the one hand, the therapeutic procedures employed in the cognitive sub-programs do not specifically meet the needs of schizophrenic patients, and on the other hand, the integration of cognitive and social tasks requires a greater consideration of metafunctions in information processing.

2.3 Discussion

The doubts expressed in the current literature concerning the value of cognitive therapy and the reservations and objections voiced about various cognitive remediation procedures reflect a corresponding lack of consistent research evidence (Green, 1993; Bellack, 1992; Bellack & Mueser, 1993; Liberman & Green, 1992). Cognitive therapy has mainly been criticized on five counts: (a) lack of specificity of knowledge on the locus and nature of cognitive impairments (i.e. insufficient distinction between cognitive and motivational problems); (b) our understanding of the malleability of cognitive impairment is limited; (c) lack of conclusive knowledge on the efficacy of interventions; (d) lack of information on the generalizability of cognitive improvements acquired in therapy to more complex levels of functioning, and their relevance to symptomatology or to social behavior and social competence (i.e. social skills or interpersonal and problem solving skills); (e) improvement in cognitive functioning is secondary to symptoms specific to schizophrenia, and cognitive therapy is of minor importance, compared to pharmacological treatment. Responses to these critical questions regarding the clinical relevance and effectiveness of cognitive approaches can be summarized as follows:

(a) Localization and nature of disorders: various research groups have developed test batteries to assess both elementary and more complex information processing deficits, particularly those specifically associated with schizophrenia, e.g. COGLAB by Spaulding *et al* (1989b, 1997). Studies on COGLAB suggest that the information processing deficits which schizophrenic patients show can basically be divided into two categories: primary and secondary deficits (Spaulding *et al*, 1997). Primary impairment is caused by neurophysiological factors, and can therefore be localized accordingly. These are long-standing deficits which can be observed both in family members and in children at high risk, and are therefore believed to be vulnerability-linked (Green, 1993). On the other hand, secondary impairment is a general cognitive type, such as 'limited capacity' (Nuechterlein & Dawson, 1984b), or is due to side-effects of medication (Green, 1993). In relation to the nature of the disorders, the dynamic testing approach involving repeated testing (Wiedl, 1997) has opened up new vistas in differentiating such moderating variables as the patients' motivation or their learning capacity from improvements in functioning (Green *et al*, 1997).

(b) Malleability of cognitive impairments: the availability of task-relevant instructions improves performance in the Wisconsin Card Sorting Test (Green *et al*, 1992). Also, training procedures using items derived from the Span of Apprehension Test reveal that even vulnerability-linked cognitive functions are modifiable in part (Kern *et al*, 1995).

(c) Lack of conclusive data on efficacy: One of the most effective strategies for reducing cognitive impairment in schizophrenic patients involves a combination of 'task-relevant learning and reinforcement' (Green *et al*, 1992, Green *et al*, 1997; Kern *et al*, 1995).

(d) Generalizability and relevance of cognitive improvement: There is conclusive evidence that the beneficial effects of cognitive remediation can be generalized to measures of social performance. Bowen *et al* (1994) showed that cognitive vigilance (indexed by means of the Continuous Performance Test) correlates with improvements in social functioning. Kern *et al* (1992) and Corrigan *et al* (1992a, 1994) found that verbal memory in particular is related to the ability to learn new social skills.

(e) Pharmacological strategies of treatment: Medication strategies are not devised according to whether primary or secondary cognitive impairment is causative of the symptoms to be treated, which in turn explains the variability of the effect of medication on cognitive functions, or why the pharmacological approach normalizes some functions (e.g. certain attentional disorders) yet fails to have an effect on others (e.g. memory or learning processes). Furthermore, it explains the emergence of additional secondary impairments in the course of medication treatment (Green, 1993; Brenner *et al*, 1991).

Future directions in cognitive remediation for schizophrenic patients can be mapped out based on the current state of knowledge of the form of modality reviewed in this paper. They can be formulated in terms of the following hypotheses:

(a) Further progress in the understanding of the neurophysiological bases of dysfunctional information processing typical of schizophrenia might pave the way for cognitive therapies which effectively target more specific functions of the prefrontal dorsolateral cortex and the medial temporal lobe, and thereby represent the quasi-experimental approach.

(b) At the same time, future intervention should evolve along the lines of a combined therapy approach, founded on empirically-based relationships between deficient cognitive functioning and behavioral functions. Spaulding *et al* (1997) for example, demonstrated correlations between attentional dysfunction and problems in psychosocial adjustment and between cognitive impairment, lethargy, and withdrawal.

(c) Cognitive training procedures with a group format are particularly effective in treating interindividual, vulnerability-related primary disorders, whereas individual therapy is more effective and appropriate with secondary impairment.

(d) The emotional aspects involved in relevant social interaction merit greater consideration in rehabilitation (Bellack, 1997). The IPT program has been expanded to include sections on home care, work skills and leisure skills (Roder, 1993), and interventions intended to optimize emotional management in social interaction (Hodel & Brenner, 1996; Hodel et al, 1998). Current evidence suggests that including emotional management as an integral part of the therapy program enhances its effect incurred on information processing functions (Hodel & Brenner, 1996; Hodel et al, 1998).

(e) Short-term reduction or compensation of cognitive impairment might be sufficient to exert a beneficial effect during phases of intensive psychosocial treatment. Yet regardless of this mechanism, the treatment of schizophrenia is a long-term endeavor, whether it involves cognitive therapy or other forms

(f) of psychosocial treatment, which requires regular booster sessions.

Thus there is hope that Liberman's prediction (Liberman & Corrigan, 1993) of the advent of a 'new generation' of more robust and more effective training procedures will come true, by continuing along the lines recently elaborated in cognitive remediation for schizophrenic patients.

2.4 Summary

Schizophrenia may now be understood as a systemic disorder in which changes in brain structure underlie individual cognitive abnormalities which, for their part, interact with environmental factors at the onset of the illness and during its course. The rationale for cognitive therapy for schizophrenic patients may be deduced from this. Existing approaches may be grouped into direct, indirect, and combined procedures. The latter are based on the assumption of the pervasive effects of elementary and complex cognitive impairments at the level of overt behavior. However, a mirror-design study which was conducted on 21 patients with schizophrenia diagnosed according to DSM-III-R criteria to compare the differential effects of two intervention sequences failed to confirm this assumption. These findings and other considerations have cast doubt on the purpose of cognitive therapy, in particular with respect to the locus, nature and malleability of cognitive impairments, as well as the generalizability of cognitive improvement. Possible future directions in cognitive therapy for schizophrenic patients have been outlined here.

B. Practical Aspects

Chapter B.1

A Comprehensive, Integrated Treatment Program for Patients Suffering from Schizophrenic Syndromes Based on Cognitive Psychotherapy

Carlo Perris

The aim of this chapter is to describe a comprehensive and individualized cognitive psychotherapy approach to young patients suffering from a schizophrenic disorder. The basic propositions which will be dealt with in the following comprise: (a) a short presentation of the rationale behind the use of cognitive psychotherapy with schizophrenic patients; (b) an overview of the treatment program; and (c) a few remarks on the feasibility of the proposed approach based on the results obtained so far. A more thorough discussion of these three issues has been made available in previous publications where more detailed reference to the relevant literature is also given (Perris 1988a, b, 1989).

1.1 Treatment

Aspects concerning the rationale of our treatment program will be dealt with under two main headings: the first concerning a general conception of 'schizophrenia', and the second dealing with a few basic notions on cognitive psychotherapy.

1.1.1 A general view of schizophrenic disorders

It is a truism that the approach which is taken to the treatment of patients suffering from a mental disorder in general and 'schizophrenia' in particular, depends not only on the immediate therapeutic goals but also upon the attitude of the psychiatrist to the nature of mental disturbances, their origins, and their expected outcome. For example, if it is thought, as it occasionally was in the early 1970's, that 'schizophrenia' is not at all a real mental disorder, but nearly a 'life-style', then no efforts will be made to find suitable treatments. On the other hand, if disorders labeled as schizophrenic are more or less implicitly assumed to have a genetically-determined, irrevocably progressive deteriorating course with a malignant outcome, then such a belief will inevitably affect or influence the setting of goals for treatment. Thus, since the main focus of this article is on the use of cognitive psychotherapy with schizophrenic patients, I must begin with a few introductory remarks to give an indication of the rationale behind the treatment which we propose.

It is generally acknowledged that both Kraepelin (1902) and E. Bleuler (1950) regarded their concept of dementia praecox and schizophrenic psychoses as a preliminary attempt to summarize clinical experience without any pretense of describing a single disease with a consistent etiology. However, although E. Bleuler (1950) had been quite explicit about the possible heterogeneity of schizophrenia by entitling his seminal treatise 'The Group of Schizophrenias', a tendency to regard schizophrenia as an unitary disease (albeit with phenomenologically different subgroups) has been dominating for a long time.

More recently, however, there has been some agreement that schizophrenic disorders are a heterogeneous group of morbid conditions still in need of being identified more closely. On the other hand, although research workers as well as clinicians seem to accept this view, this insight seems to be easily forgotten by biologically-, psychoanalytically- or socially-oriented authors alike, as soon as they discuss treatment or possible causative factors. A further common practice concerning the latter is that all too often either biological, intrapsychic or social factors are assigned decisive importance, depending on the ideological preferences of the particular author. The main problem is that anyone who reads carefully the various theories presented in the literature cannot but admit that there is something convincing in all of them, and that 'schizophrenia' can indeed be conceived as a biological disorder, as a result of maladaptive intrapsychic processes, or as a failure in a struggle against pathogenic social forces. However, the trouble seems to be that each author has perceived only one aspect of the truth, and has therefore described 'schizophrenia' on the basis of only one of its many-sided aspects, all too often without considering that explanatory models about health are but a subset of rationalizations that individuals and groups make about the world in general. My personal stance is that assumptions exclusively based on depth psychologies, biochemical hypotheses or social explanations are but reductionistic. Hence, the concept of the genes, life experience and current environmental milieu all interact to determine behavior and must be incorporated into any theory which explains psychiatric disorders.

Among the conceptions with which I sympathize are those which regard the occurrence of psychopathological manifestations in general, and of schizophrenic syndromes in particular. Within a theoretical framework they should focus on individual vulnerability, which takes into account the continuous dynamic interaction between potentially pathogenic factors belonging to different domains (cultural, biological, psychological, social) and the developing individual (e.g. Gottesman & Shields, 1971; M. Bleuler, 1979; Zubin & Spring, 1977; Marsella, 1988; Öhman & Magnusson, 1987). In particular, the model which we propose to conceptualize the development of schizophrenic syndromes is quite close to those described by Nuechterlein and Dawson (1984) and Ciompi (1988). Those models focus on the comprehension and processing of information (i.e. cognitive processes) as one major characteristic of individual vulnerability (cf. Brenner *et al*, 1983; Brenner, 1987).

Unfortunately, at this juncture I cannot go into details concerning this interactional theoretical framework (which I assume is valid for other psychopathological disorders as well; Perris, 1991, 1997) and the reader has to be referred to the previous publications mentioned above (Perris, 1988a, b, 1989). However, I would like to emphasize a few points which are at the core of the framework. First of all, the model is not reductionistic. A continuously ongoing transaction is assumed to occur between the individual on the one hand, and the factors belonging to the different domains on the other hand, which influence its (normal or deviant) development. Thus, the factors that ultimately become pathogenic, are assumed to be the results of such interactions and not the effects of any single factor, even though the phenotypical manifestations can be very similar. In particular, neither genetic factors, nor particular social influences, nor intrapsychic processes occurring very early in life are, per se, regarded as necessary and sufficient determinants of psychopathological manifestations occurring later in life. Secondly, in our model a 'time dimension' is implicit. This implies that 'vulnerability' is not regarded as a static, unchanging condition, but rather as one which changes continuously throughout a person's lifetime. In this context, both factors which might enhance individual vulnerability (e.g. a perinatal trauma or communication deviance within the family), and factors which may act as protective for a particular individual (e.g. availability of a supportive network) can be taken into account. Possible changes in the level of vulnerability over time become particularly important when considering the long-term course of a schizophrenic disorder and its marked interindividual differences (Ciompi, 1980, 1985). Further, the concept of interaction together with recognition of individual vulnerability allows the significance of *life events* to be brought into proper perspective. In this context, it is well known that similar life events do not affect all people to the same extent. At the same time, as it can be easily assumed that many stressful situations do not occur by chance but result from the interplay between a certain individual and his environment at a certain point in time. Erlenmeyer-Kimling (1979) has pointedly emphasized that "life events are obviously handled or mishandled in different ways by different people". The importance of a time dimension has to be stressed once more with regard to life events. It implies, in fact, that the impact of events on an individual is likely to be different according to their context and timing. In particular, chronological time (i.e. the developmental, maturational phase), social time (i.e. timetables in the change of social roles), and historical time (i.e. times of marked socio-economic changes) when life events occur merit consideration. Finally, the concept of interaction is of specially great importance with regard to treatment and cannot be reduced to the possible results of simultaneous administration of different medications. There is a great amount of evidence indicating the occurrence of both positive and negative interactions between the administration of psychotropic medications and psychotherapeutic or psychosocial interventions (Karasu, 1982; Leff & Vaughn, 1981; Falloon & Liberman, 1983; Hogarty, 1977). Gottesman and Shields (1971) stressed that adherence to an interactional model not only fills the chasm between geneticism and environmentalism, but may also help in clarifying "how psychotherapy or phenothiazines or a good mother may each contribute to symptom amelioration without necessarily casting light on etiological questions" (p.521).

Since a focus on individual vulnerability is not reductionistic, treatment approaches guided by this conception will not be reductionistic either. Thus, there is no sense, in my opinion, either in searching for an exclusive biological method of treatment which will be able to cure 'all' patients suffering from a schizophrenic syndrome, or in prolonging psychodynamic treatment for decades before acknowledging the limits of analyzability. According to our framework, instead, only a highly individualized treatment approach that tries to maximize the effects of each treatment component might produce results which are satisfactory in the long run. For this reason, the treatment program applied in our centers is integrated or 'holistic' in the sense that it comprises individual psychotherapy, psychosocial interventions, and the use of psychotropic medication tailored to the needs of each patient. It is important to stress that our treatment program is not just 'eclectic', but 'integrated' as well as that each intervention is related to the other in order to maximize each single effect.

1.1.2   Basic elements on which cognitive psychotherapy is founded

The most basic tenet of cognitive psychotherapy is that the contents of a person's thoughts affect his feelings, and lead to a definite behavioral response. Hence, therapeutic interventions are primarily focused on the patient's dysfunctional cognitions and on their modification. However, to avoid some common misunderstandings, it is important to give two specifications of this principle. Firstly, the term 'thought' does not exclusively refer to thinking of which one is subjectively aware, but also includes determinants of thinking and action resulting from influences which have been perceived without being noticed, and are thus 'unconscious' (Bowers, 1984). In other words, cognitive psychotherapy does not reject the notion of unconscious processes, but regards them from the vantage point of neuropsychology rather than identifying the notion of unconscious influence in psychoanalytic terms (Liotti, 1986). Secondly, the connections between thoughts, *emotions* and behavior are not regarded as exclusively one-directional. Instead, they are conceived as being controlled by feed-back mechanisms, hence are understood as an interactional circuit or loop. Greenberg & Safran (1987) have emphasized that it is a mistake to assume a one-directional relationship between *cognition* and emotion, and have maintained that they are fused together completely interdependently.

Within the broad term 'cognitions' three distinct elements are taken into account in cognitive psychotherapy: **'cognitive products'** (Hollon & Kriss, 1984), that is, thoughts, images, daydreams, ruminations, etc. Cognitive products are the output of information processing, largely accessible to the individual. Of particular importance in this group of events is the concept of 'automatic thoughts' described by Beck (1976) in his theory of emotional disorders. The second element refers to **'cognitive processes'**. Among those taken into account for therapeutic interventions, particular attention is paid to errors in recognition and in the processing of information or 'cognitive distortions'. Also of special relevance are processes related to variations in attention capacity and variations in the distribution of attention (e.g. self-absorption), and processes related to the encoding, retention and recall of information. Examples of cognitive distortions, most frequently occurring in psychiatric patients (even though they are not necessarily pathological per se) comprise 'selective abstraction', 'arbitrary inference', 'dichotomous or polarized thinking', 'mindreading' and 'personalization'. Both delusional and hallucinatory experiences can be conceptualized as cognitive distortions. Finally, the concept of **cognitive**

structure or **schema** constitutes the third and most important element. Cognitive structures are conceived as organizational entities which contain all of an individual's knowledge at any given moment about himself and the world (Hollon & Kriss, 1984). Mandler (1984) pointed out that *schemata* are also processing mechanisms, that is, they are active in selecting evidence, in screening the data provided by the environment, and in providing appropriate hypotheses. Piaget (1954), whose concept of schema is often referred to by cognitive psychotherapists, clearly stated that emotion and cognition are two indissoluble aspects of behavior. He maintained that emotional life and cognitive life are inseparable because all interaction with the environment involves both structuring and evaluation. More recently, several theoreticians have restated Piaget's opinion and stressed the emotional component of schemata (Décarie, 1978; Ciompi, 1988; Lundh, 1983; Mandler, 1984). Of particular importance for cognitive psychotherapy are those cognitive structures which encompass one's *self-concept* and knowledge of one's own relationship with the environment (including past and present experiences, and future predictions). To stress the importance of the interpersonal context, Safran and Segal (1990) have suggested the term 'interpersonal schema'.

1.1.2.1 A few remarks on the development of cognitive structures

A process of paramount importance is the one concerning the development of cognitive structures. According to current modern views in developmental psychology, it is assumed that the individual enters the world with genetically-determined and highly-differentiated capabilities for perception and reaction. Those capabilities might be regarded as rudimentary cognitive structures which are later developed and revised by the individual in his coming to terms with the environment by the well-known processes of assimilation and accommodation. As a result of those processes, our schemata continuously structure our experience and are structured by them. According to the first of the two mechanisms mentioned, a stimulus may be altered or assimilated such that it becomes consistent with the pre-existing schema. Conversely, the schema itself may be modified, according to the second type of process, to accommodate discrepant information.

Even though most cognitive structures go through a continuous process of restructuration and transformation, it is assumed, however, that the most fundamental ones, i.e. those relating to the self-concept (or self-schema), are relatively lasting and resist interference once they have been established. The fact that we are capable of selection from a continuous flood of information lends support to this stability. Selections means in this case that we choose to recognize and process information which is congruent with our self-schema, and conversely, to neglect or reject information which is contradictory by making various cognitive distortions (Markus, 1977). In this respect, the cognitive distortions previously mentioned are to be regarded as a self-confirmatory bias.

One consequence of such prevalently assimilative processes is that the self-schema becomes difficult to alter since a great deal of information consistent with its basic theme has continuously been accumulated.

1.1.2.2 The general cognitive paradigm of psychopathological disorders

The general cognitive paradigm of the occurrence of psychopathological disorders is illustrated in Figure 1. It assumes, on the one hand, that a dysfunctional self-schema has developed. On the other hand, it is assumed that such a dysfunctional schema is easily activated by internal or external stimuli which may be erroneously perceived or faultily processed. These stimuli get translated into automatic dysfunctional products at the same time as negative emotions (and concomitant somatic sensations) are experienced. As indicated in the figure, a complex of systematic feed-back relationships is also assumed to occur.

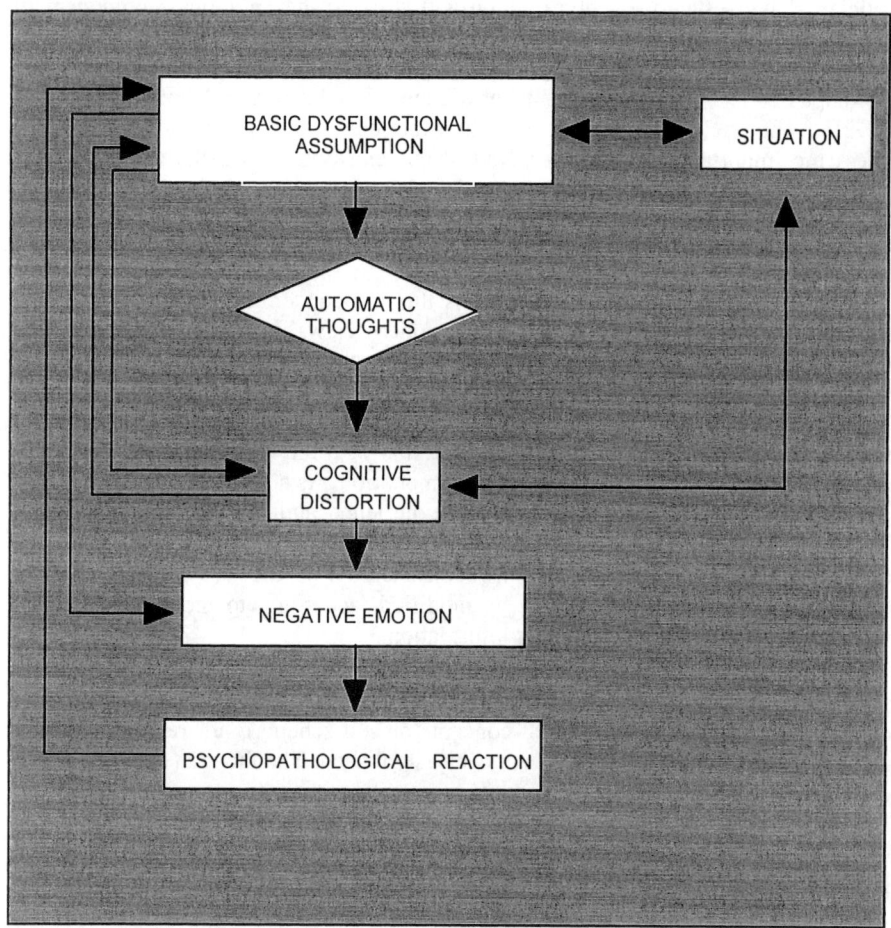

Figure 1. Complex of systematic feed-back relationships.

According to the model depicted in Figure 1, it is the existence of rigid dysfunctional assumptions or 'personal rules of living' (Wessler & Hankin-Wessler, 1986), subsumed under the concept of 'dysfunctional schema', that allow a cognitive conceptualization of an individual's vulnerability to psychopathological disorders.

In line with the theoretical point of view discussed in a previous section, dysfunctional schemata are assumed to develop during past periods as a result of various noxious influences (biological, psychological, social ones, etc.). They are, later, easily activated when the individual experiences stimuli which are analogous to those which occurred when the assumption developed. Once activated, these dysfunctional assumptions are generalized to an ever larger number of situations, henceforth leading to more and more negative cognitive products.

1.1.2.3 Assumptions on which cognitive psychotherapy with schizophrenic patients is based

The assumptions on which the appropriateness of cognitive psychotherapy for schizophrenic patients stands, derive from the interactional vulnerability-stress-model that I have previously mentioned and might be summarized as follows (Perris, 1989):

(a) The individual who will develop a schizophrenic disorder has, for various reasons related to his particular predicament, developed a fundamentally dysfunctional self-schema comprising both a dysfunctional *self-concept* (i.e. an abstracted record of his past experience with personal data) and dysfunctional basic assumptions concerning his relationship with his environment. Both the self-schema (encompassing the individual's emotional capabilities and motivational dispositions) and the dysfunctional basic assumptions related to it are assumed to be largely unconscious.

(b) The dysfunctional self-schema and the dysfunctional basic assumptions thus incorporated, are continuously sustained and reinforced by a variety of cognitive distortions in the comprehension and processing of information. These distortions might relate to the actual perception of a certain situation or to a subsequent evaluation of the event.

(c) Schema-related, automatic dysfunctional thoughts (or images) occur, involuntarily and repetitively, each time the dysfunctional self-schema is activated by both external and internal stimuli which are perceived by the individual as a threat to his personal domain. Even dysfunctional automatic thoughts are assumed to occur out of focal awareness and, thus, to be largely unconscious.

It should be evident that the assumptions presented above allow for taking into consideration the pathogenic impact of both biological and psychosocial factors and any possible interaction between them. I have, once again, to refer the reader to another publication (Perris, 1989) for a more detailed presentation of some of those interactions. I would like to stress at this juncture that a conception, based on an interactional view of vulnerability and focusing on attentional processes and on the processing of information, has heuristic value in studies of high-risk populations. But it also allows putting the findings which suggest that cognitive distortions also occur in healthy relatives of schizophrenic patients in an plausible perspective (Süllwold, 1986b).

1.1.2.4 The goals of therapy

The goals of therapy can be conceptualized within a **molecular** or within a **metacognitive** frame of reference (Carmin & Dowd, 1988). Those conceptualizations are not mutually exclusive but should rather be understood as being complementary. The main difference between them concerns the intention of the therapeutic approach. Within a metacognitive frame of reference, the prime goal of therapy is to help the patient to become aware of his dysfunctional assumptions, and to learn to recognize both the automatic negative thoughts that they promote and the cognitive distortions which he makes to sustain his dysfunctional self-concept. Interventions specially focused on the monitoring of automatic thoughts or aimed at restructuring dysfunctional self-instructions, and interventions focused on challenging and correcting cognitive distortions are the most frequently used therapeutic strategies within a molecular framework. Since cognitive distortions in the perception and processing of information comprise the mechanism by which the most basic dysfunctional convictions are continually confirmed, their correction eventually implies that the confirmatory feedback is severed and even the most basic schemata become less active. An emphasis on long-term goals, which characterizes the metacognitive approach, also comprises a guided recollection of how dysfunctional cognitive structures might have developed, and a (as thorough as possible) restructuring of an individual's self-schema. This process, comparable with the psychoanalytic concept of 'working through', means that cognitive psychotherapy must be regarded within this framework as an insight-oriented, restructuring psychotherapy and not merely as a supportive or symptom-oriented one. It should be emphasized, however, that the activity and directiveness proper of cognitive therapy allow for achieving important therapeutic results in a much shorter time than it is the case when using a psychoanalytically oriented therapeutic approach.

1.2   The Integrated Treatment Program

In the following, only a general overview of the treatment program will be given, whereas a more detailed description of the various treatment components is available elsewhere (Perris, 1989, 1993). However, two introductory remarks of a more general character are warranted: one concerning the use of psychotherapy with schizophrenic patients, and the other concerning a conceptualization of the *disability* of the schizophrenic patient.

1.2.1   The use of psychotherapy with schizophrenic patients

So far, psychoanalytically oriented psychotherapy has represented the most common psychotherapeutic approach to the treatment of selected schizophrenic patients. Elsewhere (Perris, 1988a, 1989) I have had the opportunity to analyze in detail the findings in the literature on which an unbiased evaluation of the use of this type of psychotherapy might be based. Some of those findings will be summarized in the following.

- Psychodynamic psychotherapy can lead, in isolated cases, and in the hands of dedicated therapists, to exceptionally good results. However, the total number of cases which have been treated during the last fifty years can still be counted in three figures. One possible reason for the relatively small number of patients which have been reported is that there are still very few therapists who are engaged in the treatment of schizophrenic patients.

Another important reason is that economic constraints have markedly limited the number of patients who have had access to this type of treatment. Changes in diagnostic attitudes, poor knowledge about the spontaneous course of the disorder in single patients, lack of adequate control over possible confounding factors, uncertainties concerning the factors operating in the selection of patients, and lack of well defined criteria for judging outcome, make it almost impossible to draw conclusions which can be generalized to the whole population of patients suffering from schizophrenic syndromes. On the other hand, it would be unjustified to maintain that psychotherapy has no effect whatever, if it is considered that psychodynamic treatment implies, independently of any other intention, the establishment of a confiding and supporting relationship over several years.

- No special theoretical psychodynamic approach (i.e. Freudian, Jungian, Sullivanian, based on object-relations theory etc.) seems to provide better or more permanent results than any other, and no particular method has been able to claim superiority. The adequacy of current theories for the intended purpose has, on the other hand, been questioned (Gunderson, 1979). None of the current psychoanalytic interpretations, for example, is able to accommodate available knowledge concerning heredity or the action of psychotropic medications.
- The establishment of a special patient-therapist relationship, variously conceptualized in terms of 'relatedness', 'corrective emotional experience' or 'basic trust' etc. is unequivocally regarded to be an essential requirement for any effective psychotherapy with schizophrenic patients. As mentioned above, it can easily be assumed that such a relationship extending over a period of several years might have been one important determinant of improvement in many patients.
- On the other hand, the duration of treatment is in many cases disproportionately long in relation to the alleged results achieved. When therapy continues for several years or even decades, and the same time the criteria of outcome are poorly defined, it becomes particularly difficult to identify the remedial components of the treatment.
- Those few scientifically acceptable studies which are available indicate that reality-oriented supportive psychotherapy can produce better results than exploratory, insight-oriented psychotherapy.
- Training in psychodynamic psychotherapy has become increasingly lengthy without producing significant changes in the results obtained during different periods. Such lengthy training sets serious limits as concerns the number of professionals who can be involved in this type of treatment.

In my conclusions to the present chapter, I will comment in what respect cognitive psychotherapy represents a more appropriate alternative.

1.2.2   The disability of the schizophrenic patient

Wing (1974) emphasized that the total *disability* of the schizophrenic patient should be considered under three main headings. The first includes 'primary' *impairments* that are directly related to the disorder. Wing names the schizophrenic thought disorder as an example. The second group comprises all those 'secondary' *handicaps* which result whenever primary impairments are present, e.g. loss of self-confidence or maladaptive personal habits. Negative effects of institutionalism and late negative consequences of heavy medication should be considered in this group as well. In addition, Wing points out that many patients, irrespective of diagnosis, suffer from further social handicaps in the form of lack of social skills and professional expertise which depends both on the precarious conditions (not necessarily in economic terms) in which many patients have grown up, and the fact that many have never been given a chance to solve these problems. A very common example is found in young patients (especially males) who have been inhibited in attaining independence from their parents. Whereas those last mentioned handicaps represent an important contribution to overall vulnerability as defined in an earlier section, one should not be tempted, however, to generalize the importance of deficient social skills to all schizophrenic patients. A not negligible proportion among them have in fact developed greatly, both socially and professionally, before the onset of the disorder which destroys a lot of what they had accomplished. On the other hand, a focus on social skills should not be neglected whenever a comprehensive, long-term treatment of patients with a schizophrenic syndrome is implemented (Roder *et al*, 1988; Perris, 1988a, 1989). Lack of attention to this third type of handicaps is one important factor which limits the thoroughness of any psychodynamic approach.

1.2.3 The implementation of small, community-based cognitive therapy centers for young patients: General characteristics

For a few years, two small treatment centers for the treatment of young patients primarily suffering from a schizophrenic syndrome have been implemented within the network of psychiatric services developed by the Department of Psychiatry of the Umea University at Umea (Sweden) (Perris, 1986, 1987). A third one has become operative since 1988. Since that time, similar small units in which the same treatment approach as in Umeå is applied, have been developed in several other places throughout Sweden. All of these centers are located in ordinary houses in the community. They can accommodate six to eight patients of both sexes who live in a family-like atmosphere, taking care of to the daily chores, the shopping and the preparation of the meals. In all of the centers the staff comprises in all of the centers six full-time mental nurses, one full-time occupational therapist and one part-time physiotherapist, all of whom have been trained in cognitive psychotherapy. One senior doctor (the present author) has the medical responsibility for the centers. He also acts as the supervisor of the therapeutic program in general and supervises the individual therapy sessions once a week. At each center two therapists, chosen among the nurses who are responsible for the individual therapy sessions, are assigned to each patient.

Priority is given to patients ranging between 18-35 who meet DSM-III-R criteria for schizophrenic disorder, independent of whether they are still presenting psychotic symptoms or whether they are in a phase of remission. However, patients suffering from an Axis II personality disorder are, occasionally, also accepted. Excluded are patients with verified brain damage, patients with a history of prolonged alcohol- or drug abuse, and patients with recurrent psychotic syndromes of a manic-depressive or schizoaffective type. Since participation in the treatment program is voluntary, the patient must be prepared to stay at the Center for the period of treatment that is stipulated in the initial contract (see below), and to accept the general conditions of the program.

The duration of treatment is individualized and flexible. It is based on the results achieved at the end of an initial period of five months which represents the minimum period for each patient. So far, no patient has remained at the Center for more than three consecutive five-month periods. However, a few patients may participate in individual therapy on an out-patient basis when they have been discharged from the Center and have settled in the community. Occasional visits of mostly a social nature are encouraged. Booster sessions at six months and at one year after discharge are consistently scheduled for every patient, independently of the duration of the initial treatment. At those sessions, follow-up assessments are carried out; among those, a video recording is made to be able to document the state of the patient.

1.2.3.1 Goals of treatment and the issue of contemporaneous medication

Although we speak of treatment, it should be obvious that simply controlling of psychopathological symptoms is not the primary goal of our treatment program. In fact, such control can be easily achieved in a larger proportion of patients by the appropriate use of psychotropic medications. To put it in simple terms, our major aim is to promote the patient's self-esteem and feeling of competence, hence, to foster the patient's ability to live as comfortably and as independently as possible in an everyday social context. Only with a few highly motivated patients is a more ambitious aim attempted, i.e. working through their personal narrative, within a cognitive therapy framework, including the experience of previous traumatic experiences which might have contributed to the development of a dysfunctional self-schema.

The above formulation of our goals implies that we do not see any contradiction in the contemporaneous use of psychotropic medications. Most of the patients who are referred to our centers are already on medications and beginning treatment at any of our centers does not imply that medication is stopped. Our general conception, sustained by experimental evidence in the literature, is that the same neurohumoral processes on which antipsychotic medications act are also involved in the processes regulating attention and in those responsible for the processing of information. Furthermore, research results by Hymowitz and Spohn (1980) suggest that medication treatment contributes to enhancing the schizophrenic patient's capacity to utilize verbally-oriented psychotherapy. Hence, we regard pharmacotherapy and cognitive therapy as complementary treatments rather than as mutually exclusive. Furthermore, we have found that dosages of medication can be successively reduced the more progress is made in therapy and that the patient himself is able to learn to actively participate in deciding on whether and which dosages have to be continued. Moreover, cognitive psychotherapeutic principles can be profitably used to help the patient to correct uninformed or prejudicial assumptions concerning medication and to evaluate the pros and cons of the continued use of medications when it is deemed necessary.

1.2.3.2 Components of the treatment program

The treatment program adopted in our centers is articulated at various levels as follows:
- a milieu therapeutic level, including training in interpersonal relations;
- a group level comprising weekly sessions with various contents;
- an individual level comprising weekly individual psychotherapy sessions.

In addition, patients are encouraged to become involved in various activities in the community during their stay at the center. Finally, psychosocial interventions with family members are also planned. Despite the fact that this chapter is not long enough to be able to describe the treatment program at length, I expect that even a short description can give a general idea about its conception.

1.2.3.3 The milieu therapeutic level

Life at the Centers is organized in a family-like fashion (enhanced by the presence of pets), the guiding principle being Bowlby's concept of a **secure base** (Bowlby, 1973). Bowlby emphasized that human beings of all ages are able to use their talents to their best advantage when they are confident there is one or more trusted persons who will come to their aid should difficulties arise. These trusted persons can be conceived as a secure base from which the patient operates. Even though other concepts could be used to characterize the atmosphere at the Centers, we prefer Bowlby's terminology, because there is also an implicit component of action in addition to a conception of basic trust which is in line with the more general 'active' characteristic of cognitive psychotherapy.

One main characteristic of the therapist-patient relationship in cognitive psychotherapy has been defined by Beck (1976) as 'collaborative empiricism'. This implies that therapist and patient are expected to actively work on the analysis of the patient's cognitive/emotional dysfunctions, putting forward hypotheses, and testing them in order to reject or accept them if necessary. To be able to do this, the patient has to feel that he can trust his therapist and at the same time that he has the opportunity of exploring new solutions to his problems. Hence, the significance of the concept of secure base.

The milieu therapeutic approach takes advantage of the daily interactions between therapists and patients and those which occur among the patients themselves. At the same time, participation in all daily routines at the Center represents direct training in ordinary social family life. One major difference between a simpler behavioral training program and the training program at our centers is that whereas the former is exclusively based on training new behaviors expected to be more adaptive, the cognitive approach used in the latter also implies that dysfunctional cognitions which have previously hampered the development and/or the use of appropriate abilities are identified and corrected.

Since our centers have attracted the attention of mental health professionals from other parts of Sweden and from abroad, they frequently receive visitors who wish to learn more about our program. By having to interact with the visitors, guide them around and tell them about the treatment program, the patients have further opportunities to practice social interactions with strangers. At the same time, those interactions help the patients to overcome prejudices about their own illness.

Other milieu therapeutic processes are conceptualized in terms of 'structure', 'support', 'validation' and 'involvement' as originally described by Gunderson (1978) which are always promoted with attention paid to the needs of each single patient. Details about how those processes are used with inpatients have been given elsewhere (Perris, 1988c).

1.2.3.4 Group activities

Group activities are scheduled weekly and comprise both special sessions with the physiotherapist, the occupational therapist and two therapeutic groups. The physiotherapist is also responsible for individual training (e.g. body knowledge and posture, and setting limits) tailored according to the particular needs of each patient. The occupational therapist is responsible for a group session on creative painting.

The two more formal group therapeutic sessions are devoted to interpersonal skills training and to training in the recognition, differentiation, and expression of *emotions*. In both training programs a cognitive approach is followed in the sense that cognitions related to the required performance are consistently elicited and possible dysfunctional cognitions are the target of intervention. A special training manual has been developed to give a consistent structure to social skills training.

1.2.3.5 Individual therapy

The frequency of individual sessions varies according to the needs of each patient and to the phase of treatment. However, two weekly sessions is the general rule. Attention is paid to keeping the therapeutic sessions separate from ordinary interactions between therapists and patients during the day. Other general rules are to address the healthy aspects of the patient's personality in order to discourage regression (in line with what several psychodynamical therapists also do).

A first consequence of an emphasis on the healthy aspects of the patient is a shift in focus from the symptoms which may be present to actual problems which the patient might experience as difficult or insurmountable. We prefer to begin with problems which the patient experiences in the 'here-and-now' and which can be managed with a certain likelihood of success, considering the patient's present resources. Solving problems which at first glance seem to be of negligible importance in the whole pattern of the patient's total disability, often represent a first step toward enhancing the patient's self-esteem and highly contribute to reinforcing both his motivation for treatment and the therapeutic alliance. In addition, the therapist gets an opportunity to identify more closely the most common cognitive distortions made by the patient and the most basic dysfunctional schemata which rule the patient's assumptions.

The main focus of the therapeutic sessions, however, is on challenging the cognitive distortions presented by the patient. Those frequently comprise not only instances of those distortions mentioned in a previous section, but also cognitive errors (e.g. desymbolisation, lack of awareness of asymmetry in human relations, egocentric overinclusiveness) which occur more frequently in schizophrenic patients. In the course of the therapeutic sessions consistent use is made of the techniques and strategies characteristic of cognitive psychotherapy. A detailed description of them would be beyond the scope of the present article.

1.3 General Remarks on the Efficacy of the Treatment Program

Since our centers have been operating for a relatively short time, only some general remarks on the efficacy of our treatment can be made at this juncture. A more detailed analysis of the results of the ongoing evaluation program will have to wait for a future publication. However, some preliminary results of a 3-year follow-up will be mentioned in the following.

First of all, it should be stressed that if a reductionistic view of 'schizophrenia' as an unitary disease is rejected and emphasis is laid upon schizophrenic syndromes which can develop and unfold in a vulnerable individual as a result of the interplay of pathogenic factors in different domains, then also the view that a single type of treatment could be appropriate for the whole range of pathological manifestations which occur in schizophrenic patients has to be rejected. It is well-known that not all patients respond equally well to medication, psychotherapy or psychosocial interventions. Further, we are still unable to accurately predict the long-term course of illness in any single patient or which patient will benefit most from which therapeutic intervention. On the other hand, evidence has been accumulating which suggests that a combination of different treatment strategies can achieve the best results. Thus, if the question as to whether psychotherapy has its given place in the treatment of patients suffering from schizophrenic syndromes is not put in an 'either-or' fashion, then the answer should be unconditionally affirmative. Open to discussion, however, is which kind of psychotherapy is most feasible, especially at the present time, when the organization of psychiatric services is going through marked changes and traditional hospitals have become obsolete. So far, psychodynamically-oriented psychotherapy has been the most common approach. In a previous section, I have summarized some of the issues concerning the use of psychodynamically-oriented psychotherapy. In the following, some of the arguments which support the view that cognitive psychotherapy has to be considered as an important alternative, particularly for schizophrenic patients, will be summarized.

a) First of all, the emphasis is on 'structure' and on 'activity' which are the principle characteristics of cognitive therapy. Patients suffering from schizophrenic disorders go through chaotic experiences and tend to withdraw. Structure in the therapeutic approach promotes order, and activity counteracts passivity and withdrawal.

b) Secondly, the flexibility characteristic of cognitive psychotherapy allows for tailoring its use to the very needs of each patient. In particular, reductionism involving viewing the patients' problems mostly in terms of intrapsychic processes, is avoided. The therapist can move along different levels of intervention and still remain consistent with the guiding theoretical framework.

c) Thirdly, just because of its flexibility, cognitive psychotherapy can be used with a wider range of patients than dynamic psychotherapy. Hence, most factors which operate in the selection of patients for psychodynamic psychotherapy can be avoided.

d) Fourthly, the goals of therapy are made more explicit and the process to reach those goals is well defined. In addition, several measurement instruments are available which make it possible to provide tangible evidence of the assumed changes. Research by Roder *et al* (1988) clearly supports this statement.

e) Fifthly, frequent 'homework' assignments make it possible to ascertain that changes which have occurred in the course of therapy really generalize to situations outside the therapeutic sessions. The patient has an opportunity to test the insight gained during treatment in real situations. Feedback to the therapist enables him to identify and correct dysfunctional cognitions which could still be operating.

f) Sixthly, the combined use of psychotropic medications acting on relevant neurotransmitter systems and cognitive psychotherapy can easily be conceptualized as being complementary rather than mutually exclusive or contradictory to each other. In fact it has been shown that an appropriate use of psychotropic medications positively influences both attentional processes and the processing of information.

g) Finally, structural changes in the patient (i.e. restructuring basic dysfunctional schemata) can be achieved in a much shorter time. In our experience they are comparable to those which can be achieved after several years of psychodynamically-oriented psychotherapy.

In addition to the above mentioned reasons, other aspects concerning the advantages of cognitive psychotherapy can be added. One concerns the training of the therapists. All the personnel working at our services (about one hundred) receive basic training in cognitive psychotherapy (Perris, 1988c), whereas the personnel at the centers has received more intensive training. According to the experience gained in those occasions, it can be maintained that cognitive psychotherapy is relatively easy to teach to mental health professionals belonging to a variety of disciplines including psychiatric nurses. It is thus possible to recruit a larger number of therapists than if only doctors and psychologists participated in the training program.

1.4 Preliminary Results and Issues of Generalization

1.4.1 Preliminary results

With the exception of the very initial period of our activity when there was a very low drop-out rate, none of the patient have interrupted treatment without consent from his therapists. This might be due to the fact that the criteria for inclusion have been better defined. Besides a minimal readiness to participate in the therapeutic program, there must be no history of alcohol or substance abuse as the main reason for care, nor the presence of brain damage, or a low intellectual level (estimated IQ below 80) which would impair the patient's capacity to participate in treatment. Another possible reason for the low drop-out rate is that the details of treatment are always specifically adapted to the needs and resources of each single patient so that a threshold of optimal frustration is never crossed.

An ongoing comprehensive evaluation of the patients participating in the treatment is being conducted at the centers. Some preliminary results of a small series (n=21) of patients who have completed treatment and participated in at least a three-year follow-up phase, have been reported elsewhere (Perris & Skagerlind, 1994; Perris, 1993, 1994). None of those patients have remained at the Center for more than three consecutive periods of five months. There have been significant improvements in both symptomatology and social functioning in the whole group. Even more important is that improvements at the end of treatment have increased at follow-up. At the end of follow-up, nineteen of the patients are either able to live on their own or with a partner of their choice, and two still live with their parents. It is important to note that 52 % of the patients have paid employment (at least part-time) at the end of follow-up, and that another 19 % are engaged in some form of occupational training, which is not limited to former mental patients. Also, 7/21 are able to manage without any medication at all at the end of follow-up. The mean dosage of drugs for those receiving neuroleptics calculated in chlorpromazine equivalents is 114 mg (range 33-250). Another important finding is that no instance of suicide has occurred either during treatment or during follow-up, either in this small series or among the other patients treated at the centers.

1.4.2   Issues of generalization

On the occasion of public presentations, the program that we have developed has sometimes been objected to on the grounds that is feasible only with verbally competent and particularly motivated patients. This has not been our experience. A thorough assessment of the patient's resources, marked flexibility in the structure and sequence of interventions, and access to non-verbal strategies make the program both feasible with and acceptable to most patients, also those with manifest psychotic symptomatology.

Over the past ten years since we started the therapeutic approach described above, several similar units (at present about twenty) have been implemented in other regions throughout Sweden, and a few more are in the planning stage in other countries (Finland, France, Italy, Spain). On the whole, the structure of the program is the same as in Umea despite some minor differences. No major problems have occurred in the running of those units. Such a development strongly supports the generalizability of the approach that has been described in this chapter. In a few places, where economic or other constraints did not allow for utilizing particular houses as in Umea, the program has been implemented, with a few modifications, in day centers, coupled or not to protected living for the patients participating in the program, or in re-structured hospital wards. However, such changes in general layout or setting imposed by local circumstances, do not seem to affect the feasibility of treatment in any noticeable way. The approach described by Merlo and Gekle (chapter A.1., this book) supports this view about generalizability.

In conclusion, the treatment program described above seems to be easily acceptable to most patients, also severely disturbed ones. Openness towards the patients' relatives, and frequent scheduled and non-scheduled contacts with them highly contribute to improving negative feelings that relatives may have about psychiatric care, and to mitigating conflicts which may occur between relatives and patients.

Apparently, patients make pronounced therapeutic gains at the end of treatment and these gains increase during follow-up, suggesting that their originally dysfunctional internal working models of self and others have actually been restructured. However, further studies are necessary to verify the findings obtained so far.

Chapter B.2

Cognitive Rehabilitation of Schizophrenia

Patrick W. Corrigan

2.1 Introduction

Since schizophrenia was first described, cognitive *impairments* have been considered pathognomonic of the disorder and have been classically described in terms of positive symptoms like hallucinations, delusions and thought disorder (Bleuler E., 1950; Kraepelin, 1902). More recently, researchers have redefined cognitive impairments in terms of laboratory measures of discrete information processing (IP) functions with schizophrenic patients showing impairments in sustained attention (Nuechterlein, 1977), iconic memory (Saccuzzo, 1986), short term recall memory (Koh, 1978; Oltmanns & Neale, 1975), executive functioning (Weinberger *et al*, 1988, 1986; Zec & Weinberger, 1986) and response selection (Broen, 1968). Both pharmacological and rehabilitative treatments have been tested in terms of these impairments.

Most psychopharmacological interventions target the positive symptoms of schizophrenia. Hallucinations, delusions and conceptual disorganization of some schizophrenic patients have been shown to decrease significantly when appropriate doses of neuroleptic medication are given. However, the effects of these medications on other patients have been limited, with some patients experiencing residual symptoms (Asarnow & MacCrimmon, 1982) while other 'treatment resistant' patients are completely unresponsive (Csernansky *et al*, 1985). Moreover, evidence regarding the effects of neuroleptic medication on discrete IP deficits has been mixed (Spohn & Strauss, 1989). Some studies have found that medicated patients have better scores on attentional measures than unmedicated patients (Orzack *et al*, 1967; Spohn *et al*, 1977). Other studies found no effects on attentional or higher cognitive functions (Killian *et al*, 1984). Antiparkinsonian medication may actually diminish cognitive functioning as well (Baker *et al*, 1983; Tune *et al*, 1982).

Cognitive rehabilitation strategies have been developed to augment the effects of neuroleptic medication. Furthermore, cognitive strategies have been developed in the laboratory that target discrete attention, memory, and conceptual dysfunctions. However, clinical investigators realized over time the limitations of affecting cognitive impairments in vitro. As a result, skills training investigators developed rehabilitation programs that targeted the cognitive processes involved in social functioning. Empirical findings outlining strengths and weaknesses of each of these approaches will be reviewed in this chapter.

2.2 Explanatory Models of Cognitive Impairments and Cognitive Rehabilitation

Meehl and Cronbach (1955) counseled clinical researchers to couch intervention strategies in a theoretical network rich with description and prediction regarding the clinical population and behavioral phenomena of interest. By wedding cognitive remediation strategies to putative models of information processing in schizophrenia, a conceptual framework is provided for developing and subsequently testing interventions. Research into the schizophrenic patient's cognitive functioning has yielded several explanatory models which may provide fruitful heuristics for the design and evaluation of cognitive rehabilitation strategies. For example, early investigators sought to identify **one** pathological dysfunction in the series of processing stages from which all other IP deficits might result. Yates (1966) argued that the schizophrenic patient's **attention impairments** are primary such that any subsequent processing dysfunctions (e.g., limited recall memory, failure to change set) result from skewed information entering the system. Hence, targeting and ameliorating the patients' attentional deficits would secondarily improve all other impairments.

Conversely, Broen and Storms (1966; Storms & Broen, 1969) identified the opposite end of the information process - **response selection** - as deficient. During normal functioning, several responses are elicited in reaction to environmental stimuli. Responses that surpass a hypothetical response threshold are most likely to be performed with response strength, a function of previous experience and current arousal. Schizophrenic patients demonstrate collapsed response hierarchies such that, especially during hyper-aroused situations, multiple responses are above threshold and response selection is random. Interventions that decrease arousal (thereby increasing the response thresholds) or improve processing of cues (thereby decreasing the range of retrieving responses) will diminish cognitive impairments (Spaulding et al, 1986).

More recently, the cognitive impairments of schizophrenia have been explained within the framework of **limited information processing capacity** (Callaway & Naghdi, 1982; Knight & Russel, 1978; Nuechterlein & Asarnow, 1989; Nuechterlein & Dawson, 1984a; Nuechterlein, 1990). Normal cognition is limited by the amount of information that can be processed simultaneously (Kahneman, 1973; Hasher & Zacks, 1979); for example, most individuals find it difficult to closely attend to a radio show, read the newspaper and converse with a friend at the same time. The schizophrenic patient's cognitive capacity suffers even greater limits such that their cognitive abilities are easily overwhelmed by demands of many everyday informational tasks. This model has been used to explain the diverse range of cognitive impairments in schizophrenia, including attention, memory, executive functioning and response selection (Nuechterlein & Dawson, 1984a). Cognitive tasks at different processing stages that exceed the patient's limited capacity will be deficient. Diminishing the task demand or increasing available capacity will improve the schizophrenic individual's cognitive performance.

Given its success in explaining various information processing deficits, limited capacity appears to be a useful model for explaining the effects of cognitive remediation. Although limited capacity has high heuristic value, I do not mean to suggest that the cognitive literature is unequivocally supportive of this view. More accurately, limited capacity provides a useful conceptual framework within which to relate available data on the effects of cognitive remediation. In this role, limited capacity also exemplifies some of the limitations in current experimental psychopathological research - at times other explanations of cognitive remediation effects seem to have greater power or are simpler - and shows the need for further theoretical development in this area. In regards to cognitive remediation, weaknesses in the ability of limited capacity theory to thoroughly describe therapeutic effects will provide avenues for future research.

2.2.1 Factors that affect capacity level

Alternative hypotheses have been offered to explain the schizophrenic patient's limited capacity. On the one hand, schizophrenic patients are thought to have insufficient capacity in steady 'reserve', thereby unable to manage normal cognitive tasks. Conversely, the level of capacity is believed to be relatively equal between schizophrenic and normal groups, but less available for the patients. Further research needs to resolve the differences between reservoir and availability explanations. Nevertheless, three factors have been identified that might account for limited capacity in schizophrenia and explain cognitive therapy strategies.

(1) Inefficient Allocation Policy: The schizophrenic patient is not distributing capacity optimally. 'Allocation policy' refers to a hypothetical executive function which divides capacity among the various processing stages according to environmental contingencies such that the well-functioning individual will select those processing stages which yield the greatest reward (Kahneman, 1973). The schizophrenic patient is unable to integrate perceptual and cognitive processes (Magaro, 1980), thereby ignoring relevant internal and external cues necessary for capacity allocation to relevant stages. Cognitive rehabilitation strategies that improve allocation policy by making salient the internal goals and environmental cues that control the distribution of capacity will improve information processing.

(2) Effects of Arousal: Available capacity is limited by the schizophrenic patient's arousal levels. The relationship between arousal and capacity is described by a Yerkes-Dodson inverted U such that during periods of under-arousal or over-arousal the normal individual experiences diminished capacity (Gjerde, 1983). Research suggests that schizophrenic patients demonstrate steady state hyper-arousal (Broen, 1968; Gjerde, 1983; Venables, 1964; Zahn, 1975) or both hypo- and hyperaroused patterns (Dawson & Nuechterlein, 1984; Gruzelier, 1978). Cognitive rehabilitation strategies that optimize the level of patient's arousal will improve the processing of information.

(3) Impaired Automaticity: Hasher and Zacks (1979) have viewed information processing capacity demand as a continuum with automatic and effortful processing at the extremes. Automatic processes require relatively little capacity and can occur outside awareness for tasks like attending to or encoding well-learned information. Effortful processes, on the other hand, are conscious and require substantial capacity. Schizophrenic patients do not have as much available capacity as normals and therefore find effortful tasks more

difficult. Moreover, when a skill is first learned it tends to be effortful. Through intrinsic mnemonics and repeated practice, effortful processes become more automatic (Bandura, 1986; Fitts & Posner, 1967). Patients with schizophrenia do not show a normal transition from effortful to automatic processes (Magaro, 1984).

2.3 Discrete, Laboratory-Based Approaches to Information Processing Deficits

Many investigators who have studied IP deficits resulting from schizophrenia have transposed a variety of laboratory-based measurement strategies from cognitive psychology. Strategies have included reaction time, dichotic listening, card sorting, backward masking, span of apprehension and continuous performance. Rehabilitation interventions have been derived subsequently from these measurement strategies to ameliorate impairments by instructing patients to perform numerous times variations of the task. Unfortunately, it seems that investigators have been seduced by the precision and sophistication of these measures without showing any evidence that improvement of discrete, laboratory-based functions should be relevant to patients' cognitive functioning. Repeated practice of these tasks may eventually lead to improved cognitive functioning. From a limited capacity perspective, repeated practice makes an effortful process more automatic and hence requires less cognitive capacity. In this study, investigations are presented in terms of targeted IP deficit: attention, memory and conceptual flexibility.

2.3.1 Attentional deficits and readiness to respond

Operant contingencies have been used to focus attention and improve reaction time in several studies. From a limited capacity view, operant contingencies focus allocation, so that the schizophrenic patient assigns sufficient cognitive capacity to the processing of appropriate external stimuli. Without the incentive of reinforcing contingencies, patients are distracted by external and internal stimuli, capacity dedicated to the attention or reaction time test is diminished, and concentration or processing speed is lower than normal.

Along this line of thought, Wagner (1968) randomly assigned schizophrenic subjects to either an attention task (in which subjects were instructed to match a target stimulus with its replica embedded in a stimulus array) or an abstraction task (one of the three stimuli in the subsequent array shared a common physical or semantic attribute with the target stimulus). Correct performance was reinforced on fixed ratio schedules; mistakes resulted in a mild response cost. Results showed that subjects in the attention training group demonstrated improved scores on the attention task, while subjects in the abstract training group did not show significant improvement. No crossover effects were found; i.e. subjects in the attention training group did not improve abstract test scores. These findings suggest that monetary contingencies improve primary attentional function but have little impact on more abstract encoding functions.

Previous research had shown that reaction times of schizophrenic subjects are significantly slower than normal controls when stimuli are presented simultaneously over auditory and visual channels (Broen, 1968; Silverman, 1964; Venables, 1964). To improve reaction times in dual modality tasks, Meiselman (1973) compared the effects of feedback (contingent reinforcement) to repeated practice. During the prototypical single modality task, subjects are instructed to respond to the offset of a light or tone by lifting their finger from a telegraph key. During Meiselman's dual modality task, half the trials were tone off and half the trials were light off, in random sequence. After pre-tests, subjects in the feedback group were told a bell would ring after each response in which reaction time was ten milliseconds shorter than the mean reaction time demonstrated during the pre-test, and a buzzer would be heard for any responses slower than the mean. Subjects received five cents for each bell and lost five cents for each buzzer. Subjects in the repeated practice control group completed the pre-test reaction time trials again. Results showed that all ten subjects in the feedback plus reinforcement condition improved reaction time to dual modality stimuli; however, six subjects in the control condition were quicker as well. The decrement in reaction times of the feedback group was significantly greater than the one of the repeated practice group.

Reaction times of 32 schizophrenic patients in another study were manipulated using punishing contingencies (Rosenbaum *et al*, 1957). During baseline, subjects were to lift their finger from a telegraph key after hearing a buzzer. During the punishment condition, subjects received a mild electric shock that started with the onset of the buzzer and ended when the individual lifted his finger from the key. Subjects' reaction time decreased significantly from baseline during the shock condition. The studies by Rosenbaum *et al* (1957) show that negative reinforcement and punishment improve reaction time (and cognitive capacity).

A limited capacity model does not provide the most parsimonious explanation of the effects of reinforcement on attention. An alternate hypothesis might suggest that reinforcement directly focuses the disturbed patients' attention on the appropriate stimuli. This is a more behavioral perspective in which attention and reaction time are viewed as operant behaviors. Future research needs to test these competing hypotheses; findings that would support the limited capacity model should show that the increased capacity that results from reinforcing contingencies not only improves attention to target stimuli, but also enhances other functions like encoding, consolidation and subsequent retrieval of these stimuli.

Conclusions drawn from these studies are limited by the experimental methods employed. Investigators in each study failed to validate the diagnoses of subjects participating in the study. While it is unlikely that a homogenous diagnostic group exists for which the attentional functioning of all members responds similarly to operant strategies, accurate diagnostic description of subjects is necessary to apply a specific attentional intervention to appropriate patient groups. The ecological utility of attentional rehabilitation must also be examined. Although studies have shown that operant strategies improve attentional functioning significantly, the size of effects has not been reported. Does attentional functioning of schizophrenic patients approach normal levels after participation in these protocols? To answer this question, investigators should consider including a 'normal' control group to determine whether post-test scores of the patient sample approximate scores of the control group.

2.3.2 Memory deficits

Koh (1978) argued that although the schizophrenic patient's recognition memory is relatively intact, scores on recall tasks are significantly below normal. Greater cognitive capacity is required for recall than recognition tasks; hence, performance differences may be attributed to limited capacity deficits. Koh further explained these deficits by concluding that patients may lack basic organizational skills that facilitate the original acquisition and subsequent retrieval processes essential to recall memory, thereby making recollection more effortful. Similarly, other investigators have attributed memory deficits in schizophrenia to poor encoding of information into meaningful constructs (Calev et al, 1983). Hence, strategies that compensate for insufficient organization may improve information recollection.

Koh and his colleagues (1976, 1980, 1981) found that patients who rated words on a memory task (and thereby aided encoding) in terms of pleasantness were able to increase recall to almost 'normal' levels. Using a similar method, Larsen and Fromholt (1976) instructed schizophrenic subjects to sort a word list into idiosyncratically meaningful categories. After patients had sorted the list into the same categories in two consecutive sorting trials, subjects were asked to recall as many words as possible. Subjects in this group were able to recall words as well as normals. Improvements in recall memory have been shown in nonverbal domains as well. Patients who rated a series of faces on a pleasantness continuum were able to recall those faces as accurately as a normal control group (Koh et al, 1981).

Findings from studies in this area are particularly remarkable because of cognitive function improvement to near-normal levels in schizophrenic patients as the result of an IP intervention. Unlike attentional deficits, which have been ameliorated by manipulating the contingencies governing existing cognitive functions, short term recall was facilitated by an adjunctive IP strategy. Encoding and organization strategies significantly ameliorated memory deficits in this population.

At first glance, this finding appears consistent with the view that early processing deficits skew subsequent cognition. If information enters the system in a coded form that parallels reality reasonably faithfully, subsequent, more complex processes like information recall will occur at near normal levels. The encoding task facilitated attentional processes of the schizophrenic subjects. However, supporters of the limited capacity view might argue that encoding and organizing strategies provide a prosthesis with which patients are able to increase the automaticity of an otherwise highly demanding cognitive task. Moreover, the capacity required to subsequently recall well-encoded information is greatly diminished.

An independent measure that covaries with the amount of cognitive capacity that an individual employs while completing a task would be an important metric in sorting out theories that compete with limited capacity explanations. Beatty (1982) suggested that pupil size is a good measure of cognitive task demand in normals; e.g., as the number of digits in a short term recall task increase, pupils enlarge. Although this research has not been replicated on schizophrenic samples, it suggests that pupil size, or some other psychophysiological measure, may provide a metric for calibrating capacity demand. This would not be a straightforward replication, given the abnormal patterns of arousal evinced by schizophrenia. However, this measure may provide a more precise tool for determining processing load. In terms of resolving the competing hypotheses for improved recall, research supporting a limited capacity view should find that the psychophysiological measures of capacity covary with improved performance on memory tasks.

2.3.3 Conceptual flexibility

When processing information normally, individuals are able to identify commonalties across stimulus categories and also to recognize rules that govern relationships between these categories. Moreover, normal individuals are able to change rules as changes occur in the task. Conceptual flexibility has been measured using the Wisconsin Card Sorting Test (WCST; Heaton, 1981) in which subjects are asked to match stimulus cards to one of four key cards. When taking this test, subjects must determine the rule by which stimulus cards are matched to key cards (match by color, number or shape) and sort accordingly. Unbeknown to the subject, the rule is changed after ten consecutive correct matches. Perseverative errors result when individuals incorrectly match stimulus cards to key cards according to a no longer operative rule. Schizophrenic patients show significantly more perseverative errors than normals on this task, thereby suggesting an inflexible ability to change matching rules according to environmental information (Heaton, 1981; van der Does & van den Bosch, 1992).

The executive functions implied in this measure are especially relevant for a capacity model. Patients with deficient executives (who are conceptually inflexible) may not allocate cognitive capacity according to environmental stimuli. Hence, rehabilitation strategies that improve more complex cognitive functions will more than likely improve the schizophrenic patients' overall ability to manage processing capacity in light of changing environmental rules and information.

In an attempt to improve patients' ability to recognize and alternate between cognitive rules, Goldberg and his colleagues (1987) trained schizophrenic patients in the WCST. After making several perseverative errors during a pre-test, 44 schizophrenic subjects were provided both overall and card-by-card instructions about the test. Overall instructions included information about the nature of the categories and the occurrence of shifting sets. During card-by-card instructions, subjects were told the operative rule; "Right now you should be matching by color. You must ignore the number of things and the shape of things." For patients who received overall and card-by-card instructions, perseverative errors diminished significantly during training. However, subsequent testing showed that the number of perseverative errors for subjects **returned to baseline** when instructions were no longer provided. Goldberg and his colleagues concluded that the inability to change rules flexibly to changing environmental information cannot be ameliorated through cognitive remediation.

Two subsequent studies sought to combine operant conditioning methods with trial-by-trial instructions to improve patients' rule-bound behavior. Bellack and his colleagues (1990) tested two cohorts of DSM-III-R diagnosed schizophrenic patients. Responses of subjects in the first cohort failed to improve despite contingent or noncontingent reward (5 cents for correct response). Patients in the second cohort who received contingent reward and card-by-card instructions significantly increased performance during training **and** during a subsequent testing session. Bellack and his colleagues concluded that by providing monetary reinforcers, patients had incentive to attend to and learn the step-by-step instructions.

Green et al (1990) found mixed results when trying to train schizophrenic patients on the WCST using a similar reinforcement contingency. Ten schizophrenic patients received instructions and response contingent monetary reinforcement to motivate subsequent performance. All patients increased WCST performance during training. However, after removing instructions but continuing reinforcement, half the subjects returned to baseline while half the subjects maintained improved functioning. Green and colleagues concluded that perhaps a learner/nonlearner distinction can be made that reflects etiological subtypes. Learners might benefit from cognitive remediation while nonlearners may not.

Providing instructions and feedback in the latter two studies may have served as external organizers which decreased the capacity demand of the tasks. However, the findings by Goldberg and colleagues (1987) suggest that the usefulness of providing stepwise instruction or repeated practice alone for tasks that require cognitive flexibility is limited. Adding reinforcing contingencies provides salient stimuli that help patients allocate necessary capacity for learning the task. The distinction between learners and nonlearners is more difficult to reconcile with a limited capacity approach to this problem. Green et al's (1990) findings suggest a qualitative difference in the effects of cognitive remediation on schizophrenia. The limited capacity model suggests that cognitive differences between schizophrenic patients are solely quantitative; e.g., the more cognitively disordered, the less available capacity. Hence, categorical differences should not be found in the data. Perhaps the interventions by Green and colleagues were not sufficiently focused, such that patients with the greatest capacity did not benefit. Alternately, instead of showing a bimodal distribution, learners and nonlearners defined a linear distribution with the point dividing successful from unsuccessful acquisition arbitrarily drawn.

Other yet unidentified subject variables may interact with limited capacity to account for this finding. For example, countless studies have shown that the symptoms, social deficits and course of schizophrenia are frequently worse in male than female patients (Angermeyer et al, 1990; Childers & Harding, 1990). Similar interactions might be found in future studies that help account for the learner-nonlearner distinction.

2.3.4 Generalizability of laboratory-based approaches?

Few studies have tested whether improvement in specific cognitive skills generalizes to facilitation of other cognitive processes. If information is processed serially, improvement in early cognitive functions should facilitate later more complex functions as well. For the most part, research in this area has not tested this hypothesis.

The ecological validity of laboratory-based approaches is poorly demonstrated as well (Ellis, 1986; Weingaertner, 1971). Does enhanced functioning that results from laboratory-based strategies translate into improved 'real-world' cognition? Studies have not demonstrated relationships between targeting specific information processing deficits and amelioration of positive symptoms. For instance, does improvement on a digit distracter task relate to whether the patient hallucinates? Similarly, only one study was found that addressed the relationship between cognitive functioning and other psychiatric symptoms (Adams et al, 1981). However, the effects of laboratory-based cognitive interventions on social functioning have not, for the most part, been investigated.

2.4 Cognitive Rehabilitation Strategies and Interpersonal Competence

Many patients who complete social skills training programs significantly increase their repertoire of interpersonal skills (Fecteau & Duffy, 1986; Morrison & Bellack, 1984; Wallace et al, 1980; Wallace & Liberman, 1985) and secondarily diminish psychiatric symptoms (Bellack et al, 1984; Falloon et al, 1982; Hogarty et al, 1986, 1987; Liberman et al, 1984). Unfortunately, some patients with severe cognitive impairments do not readily respond to skills training approaches (Liberman et al, 1985; Martinez-Diaz et al, 1983; Massell et al, 1991). Adding cognitive rehabilitation techniques to traditional skills training programs may improve the patients' ability to both process social information and perform appropriate interpersonal skills. Cognitive rehabilitation training programs have been specifically developed and tested for the acquisition of interpersonal skills and work behaviors.

2.4.1 Improving social skills

Brenner and his colleagues (Brenner, 1987; Brenner et al, 1987a, 1989, 1997; Kraemer et al, 1987; Roder et al, 1988) developed a comprehensive rehabilitation program called *Integrated Psychological Therapy for Schizophrenic Patients* (IPT) to ameliorate both cognitive and social dysfunctions of schizophrenia.

IPT has been tested in three independent investigations (Brenner et al, 1992). In the first study, 44 schizophrenic patients were assigned to an IPT group, a standard rehabilitation treatment group or a no-treatment control group. After three months of treatment, subjects who completed IPT demonstrated significantly greater performance on attention tasks and diminished overall psychopathology compared to both control groups. These effects were still present eighteen months later. However, IPT had no effect on measures of more complex cognitive functions like visuo-motor integration. The longitudinal effects of IPT were tested in the second study. A modified time series design was used in which eighteen patients with schizophrenia participated in a six week IPT program. A wider battery of cognitive measures assessing attention, verbal concept formation and categorization ability were administered prior to treatment, after three and six weeks of treatment and at a three week follow-up. Measures of social adjustment were gathered as well. Results showed that concept formation improved after three weeks of treatment, while IPT had little effect on other cognitive or social functions.

The relative effects of the cognitive and social components of IPT were investigated in a third study which was conducted as a single case design. Attentional and social adjustment measures were administered to two subjects during a two-week baseline, after completion of the Cognitive Differentiation and Social Perception Modules and after completion of the Social Skills and Problem Solving Modules. Results showed that both patients demonstrated steady improvement in all measures after the first set of Modules and maintained this improvement after completion of the second set of Modules. However, the cognitive and social adjustment scores were still below 'normal' levels at the completion of IPT. The authors concluded that treatment effects occurred in the first weeks of treatment and soon plateaued at levels below normal functioning. These findings challenge the results of the other two studies which suggested that the combination of strategies that target social and cognitive functioning produced improved performance in the interpersonal domain.

On the whole, these findings have been hampered by methodological limitations. Sample size has been small, thereby diminishing the power of the evaluation. Random assignment has not been used in the between group study. Dependent measures assessing cognitive functioning have varied across studies, making comparisons difficult. Still, there were several features of IPT that recommend it for further study. Brenner's research and treatment program systematically attempt to combine cognitive and psychosocial rehabilitative approaches. As a result, the potential for examining effects within these domains, as well as the interaction of cognitive and social approaches, was outlined. Moreover, the group format provides an efficient use of staff resources. Several patients with severe cognitive impairments can be treated at once.

Using a narrower approach to improve learning social skills, Liberman and his colleagues (1986) described an attention-focusing procedure that augmented conversational skills training. This protocol involved repetition of attentional prompts over several trials within a conversation training module. A confederate began a trial by making a predetermined statement to the patient, e.g., "I went shopping last night." If no response or an inappropriate response was made, the trainer prompted, "Ask her a question." If the patient continues to respond incorrectly, the trainer provides a second prompt. One good question is 'What did you buy?' The combination of several trials and repeated prompts during an otherwise traditional social skills curriculum increased skill acquisition. Results of two additional studies using single subject design showed greater conversational skills after participating in the attention focusing program (Massell et al, 1991; Wong & Woolsey, 1989).

Use of attention focusing procedures seems to improve the schizophrenic patients' processing of social information. Rather than being overwhelmed by information, patients are able to focus on details relevant to the skills being taught. Once the information is encoded correctly, subsequent retrieval of the skills is easier.

2.4.2 Improving work-related skills

The attentional skills of nine subjects were shaped during participation in the Continuous Work Performance Test (CWPT) (Spaulding et al, 1986). The CWPT includes folding, cutting, stapling, unstapling and sorting paper. During completion of these tasks, patients were paired with trainers who helped them accomplish daily work goals by prompting attention, providing encouragement, offering performance feedback and reinforcing effort. Subjects who were able to work without distraction for five continuous sessions graduated from CWPT. By the end of the study, seven of nine subjects reached criterion and continued to progress in subsequent stages of vocational training. Five of the successful patients also showed improved global psychiatric status. Improved instrumental skills seemed to be related to decreased psychiatric dysfunction.

Attention to instrumental tasks has also been improved by using shaping procedures. In a recent study, seven chronic schizophrenic males participated in attention shaping procedures embedded within language and mathematics training classes (Menditto et al, 1989). During each class, subjects received shaping chips, verbal praise and access to a tray of consumables, each time a task was accomplished within a two to three minute interval. As subjects met shaping criteria, the amount of time in which subjects were to attend to task was lengthened. Subjects who were disruptive during training lost access to their tray of consumables were prompted that access to the tray would return when the inappropriate behavior ceased, and were ignored until more appropriate behaviors returned. After twelve months, six of the seven participants showed noticeable improvement in their ability to attend to task. Four of these six graduated from the shaping class and entered a more demanding academic program at the hospital.

These two studies on the interaction of cognitive strategies and improved work skills recapitulate other findings about the therapeutic effects of reinforcement and corrective feedback on the cognitive aspect of activities. Specifically, environmental contingencies help to mitigate patients' limited cognitive capacity by facilitating allocation of capacity to appropriate tasks resulting in improved functioning. However, as seen in the study by Menditto et al (1989), individually tailored contingencies can be an expensive undertaking, often requiring one-to-one assignment of staff members to patients.

2.5 Summary

Taken in its entirety, the research suggests that the effects of rehabilitation on the varied manifestations of cognitive impairment in schizophrenia are substantial and significant. Despite these victories however, the overall state of cognitive remediation research is one of multiple independent studies of unrelated interventions; in fact, the literature as a whole reflects several, separate rehabilitation movements with little common direction. For example, laboratory-based interventions have been shown to improve the schizophrenic patients' attentional, memory and higher order executive functions. However, the line of theoretical development across laboratory-based studies has been thin and unguided. Moreover, the attempt to establish the ecological validity of these interventions has been lacking. Few studies have attempted to determine how better information processing, as shown on laboratory-based tests, leads to diminish psychotic processing of information or improved social cognition.

Rehabilitation strategies that combine interpersonal skills training and cognitive methods probably offer the most generalizable interventions. The greatest success of cognitive remediation will be realized when the social cognitive skills of patients improve. Hence, patients who more accurately perceive the obvious cues of interpersonal situations as well as the subtle rules, roles and goals that govern them will be more successful. Another social cognitive skill is the ability to learn new social and coping skills. Hence, cognitive remediation strategies that improve interpersonal skill acquisition meet a key rehabilitative goal.

Generalization of treatment effects are being reconceptualized from the assumption that transfer of therapeutic effects is a natural consequence of treatment to the view that strategies need also to be actively incorporated into rehabilitation to facilitate generalization (Stokes & Osnes, 1989). Hence, clinicians utilize interventions like in vivo role play, independent homework and natural consequences to foster transfer of newly learned behaviors to other settings (Corrigan et al, 1992b). Similar strategies need to be developed that help generalize cognitive remediation effects as well.

The generalization of discrete effects to broader dysfunctions provides an even more challenging question for investigators. This kind of generalization may occur in three forms. Generalization may occur as transfer from target process to secondary process, for example, the effects of attentional rehabilitation may be observed to improve short term recall. Alternately, generalization may occur as transfer from target process to broader task. Rehabilitation of attentional deficits specific to psychosocial skills training leads to improved skills learning and subsequent interpersonal functioning. Finally, generalization may manifest itself as a nonspecific improvement of life satisfaction, e.g., diminution of troublesome delusions through collaborative restructuring yields increased patient statements about *quality of life*. Clinical investigators need to account for these varied forms of generalization in developing and testing cognitive interventions.

The limited capacity model that explains the cognitive impairments of schizophrenia was successfully used in this study to explain rehabilitation effects of some cognitive strategies. Components of the limited capacity model also suggested new directions for rehabilitation research that have not been actively pursued before. For example, the relationship between arousal and capacity suggested that cognitive remediation strategies should attempt to moderate patients' level of physiological arousal. This hypothesis implies that psychophysiological measures of arousal should have a more central role as covariates in this research. Moreover, relaxation strategies that reduce the anxiety of hyper-aroused patients and intervention strategies that stimulate hypo-aroused patients may have positive cognitive effects.

The quality of theoretical explanation seemed to be lacking when limited capacity was used to explicate the effects of cognitive remediation on more 'macro-cognitive' impairments. Comprehension of the various forms of cognitive impairment and rehabilitation in schizophrenia requires several different explanatory heuristics, with these independent models interrelated through a superordinate framework; the *vulnerability-stress-model* may provide this higher order framework (Cromwell & Spaulding, 1978; Zubin & Spring, 1977). Some investigators have made the stress diathesis their core concept for explaining more macro-phenomena associated with the disorder, including the patients' social dysfunctions and positive symptoms (Goldstein, 1987).

A vulnerability-stress model may also enhance cognitive models of rehabilitation over the course of the disorder. Current rehabilitation research has been limited by presenting a static picture of the patients' cognitive impairments. In reality, information processing dysfunctions vary with course of the disorder, e.g., during periods of acute exacerbation many cognitive functions are diminished. More than likely, as patients are intensely anxious and psychotic, available capacity diminishes causing dysfunctions in all information processes. However, even when symptoms remit, some cognitive impairments remain. As cognitive remediation strategies continue to develop, clinical investigators need to specify the strength of treatment effects on specific episode-linked versus vulnerability-linked deficits.

Chapter B.3

Using Cognitive Behavioral Therapy of Schizophrenia in a District Psychiatric Service

David G. Kingdon and Douglas Turkington

Over the past years, we have been developing and using cognitive behavioral techniques with patients with schizophrenia (Kingdon & Turkington, 1994) in a district psychiatric service. Their use has been compatible with working in a busy psychiatric environment although inevitable compromises have been necessary in relation to the amount of time which has been devoted to individual patients' therapy. We outline here the approach used.

3.1   Explanations of Schizophrenia

Providing an explanation of the symptoms of depression (Beck *et al*, 1979) or anxiety (Beck *et al*, 1985) to patients is fundamental to the application of cognitive therapies in these conditions. Similarly constructing explanations of schizophrenic symptoms seems necessary, if we are to develop the use of cognitive therapies with them.

Explanations presently used with patients and their relatives tend to concentrate on biological or complex psychological rationales of schizophrenia. The former particularly emphasize distinctions between schizophrenic symptoms and normal experience. Not only does this make understanding them more difficult than if they could be related to culturally familial experiences, but such divisions can also be quite artificial. Strauss (1969) examining Present State Examination data, collected as part of the World Health Organization International Pilot Study of Schizophrenia, concluded that "phenomena like delusions and hallucinations represent points on continua of function". The use of terms such as 'over-valued idea' and 'pseudo-hallucination' also suggests at least gradation of experience.

There is also a considerable body of research which describes the occurrence of symptoms and signs similar, if not always identical to those in normal subjects. Hallucinations and delusions can occur in organic confusional states which are recognized as producing psychopathological phenomena indistinguishable from those in schizophrenia. They can also occur in hostage situations and solitary confinement (Grassian, 1983) and in sleep (Oswald, 1974) and sensory deprivation experiments

(Leff, 1968). Indeed, Leff concluded in his study of the latter that "the perceptual experiences of normal people under conditions of sensory deprivation overlap considerably with those of mentally ill patients".

It is also possible to relate delusional beliefs to commonly occurring beliefs in society. Delusional beliefs such as those involving thought broadcasting and insertion have a culturally, even if not scientifically, acceptable equivalent in beliefs in telepathy. The Present State Examination recognizes this by inquiring, whether the subject thinks "anything like hypnotism or telepathy is going on?" (Wing, 1974) where there is indication of delusions connected with thinking processes. Similarly, delusions of control by external forces closely resemble beliefs in supernatural phenomena such as poltergeists, astrology, and in religious and magical forces, and again hypnotism. Although such beliefs are, of course, scientifically disputable if not disprovable, that they are held by many members of most societies is not (Eysenck, 1986).

Fleeting ideas of reference, paranoia and grandiosity have been described as very common (Gottesman & Shields, 1982), possibly even universal, in the normal population. They were said to occur spontaneously and are usually dismissed rapidly. However, at times of stress, the 'effort after meaning' might lead to more ready acceptance of such beliefs. This would particularly be the case where an individual was isolated or felt unable to discuss intimate matters with parents from whom he is separating and with whom relationships may have deteriorated, or with a partner, because close relationships outside the family had not yet developed. Such beliefs would also be more accepted where communication could occur within such a close relationship at times the partner or parents' beliefs or way of communicating with them might be so abnormal as to confuse further rather than enlighten.

In developing rationales for schizophrenic experience, those which relate such culturally acceptable beliefs to psychotic phenomena have in our experience assisted in destigmatizing them to the patient and his family and laying them open to rational argument by the use of cognitive behavior therapy (Beck *et al*, 1985).

3.1.1 Vulnerability and stress

The symptoms patients developed were explained to them in terms of the effects of stress on a vulnerable individual. Life events and circumstances have been described as significantly increased prior to the onset of acute schizophrenic episodes. Such events were elicited and explored with patients. Although there remains much controversy about the specific place of such events in the etiology of schizophrenia, there seems less doubt that they can act as precipitating factors (Lukoff *et al*, 1984). Stressful events are recognized as increasing suggestibility (Ludwig, 1966) and therefore increasing the likelihood that vulnerable individuals would be less critical in accepting beliefs they would in normal circumstances reject.

This vulnerability would be described to patients and relatives as consisting of genetic and neuropsychological components, the latter manifested by perceptual and attentional deficits (Brenner, 1989). In a proportion, this may be related to birth injury or other damage leading to ventricular enlargement but only becoming prominent after a period of maturation has occurred (Murray *et al*, 1988). The basic concept of a vulnerability-stress diathesis has therefore been explained in terms such as that: "Stress seems to affect people in different ways, depending on the individual make-up which includes any family susceptibility, personality and possibly brain structure. The same sort of stressful events may make some people depressed or anxious, others may not be affected at all, whereas in your circumstances, you have begun to hear voices and/or got a bit mixed up about the significance of the feelings that you are getting or events that are occurring around you". The symptoms that have developed are then explored and discussed on an individual basis.

3.2 Therapeutic Interventions

3.2.1 Eliciting cognitive distortions

The standard psychiatric history, including a basic personal history, was used to elicit *life events* of significance to the patient and his relatives. It was noteworthy that even markedly thought-disordered patients could frequently respond to gentle specific questioning although patience and an ability to rephrase questions was often necessary. The period prior to the development of symptoms was concentrated on, but frequently prior events and relationships dating back many years seemed to be important in determining why such events were of individual significance. With patients presenting for the first time, the events were generally easier to elicit. But even with those who had been ill for many years, their memories or those of their relatives (and even, occasionally, clinical records) were generally sufficient to elicit events of significance. This was very frequently in terms of their own rationalization of what had occurred, e.g. overwork, marital breakdown, conscription into the army, often in combination. While such rationalizations could be very suspect, that they were considered significant suggested they were worthy of consideration.

The exploration of the events described was used in unearthing the cognitions which preceded the acceptance of delusional ideas. This, in turn, led to the identification of 'faulty cognitions' which frequently related to excessive self reference (Kaney & Bentall, 1989). Reattribution, analysis of evidence, and generation of alternative explanations were then used in attempts to modify such cognitions. Assumptive schemata were elicited from the general themes of automatic thoughts and by using the technique of inference chaining (or 'downward arrow') which essentially means following cognitions through to their conclusions.

These schemata may represent distortions of classical ones (as described by Ellis, 1962), e.g. "life should be fair", "I must be approved of", by repeated or combinations of apparently validating events. Alternatively very negative schemata may have always existed, e.g. "nobody can be trusted", "I am unlovable", which emerge through stressful circumstances. These were also presented as delusional beliefs or systems about the world, such as, that the patient was a victim of overwhelming forces over which he had no control, or that he had special powers or abilities which differentiated him from the rest of mankind. Where these beliefs were 'silent', developing a rapport and using techniques for eliciting such assumptions in neurosis and good psychiatric practice enabled them to be explored and debated.

Misinterpretations of life changes and crises and neutral events were elicited. 'Faulty cognitions', particularly, personalization ('taking things personally'), selective abstraction ('getting things out of context') and arbitrary inference ('jumping to conclusions') were frequently found and attempts were made to correct them.

3.2.2 Identity

When questions about personal identity emerged as frequently happened in the younger patients, e.g. "Who am I?", "What is the purpose of being here?", though by their nature inconclusive (and without care, protracted topics), reasoning with the patient was useful in developing rapport and rational thinking strategies. Many authors have described a fundamental deficit in schizophrenia to be a breakdown in ego boundaries. Clearly the process by which differentiation between what is internal, e.g. a thought, and what external, e.g. a 'voice' or a controlling force, is flawed, possibly by some organic neuropsychological process. Ways of attempting to reinforce this 'reality boundary' are discussed later.

3.1.4 Communication deficits

Non-verbal communication, perception of which has been described as being abnormal in schizophrenia (e.g. Cramer et al, 1989), would be discussed where it appeared that this might have contributed to the belief that thoughts or feelings were being read when they were simply being appreciated by others who had interpreted non-verbal cues. Social skills training was thus considered to be useful over and above its present, well-described, position in rehabilitation programs.

Neologisms can markedly impair communication, but appear to generally develop as hybridizations or condensations of recognized words (Scharfetter, 1980). The meanings of such neologisms were asked for rather than being allowed to pass unremarked. Further discussions - "I don't know that word, is it one of your own?" - were used with the aim of impeding the progress of neologisms into the patient's personal vocabulary. One patient, for example, spoke of 'decyanization' by which he meant that he believed people were disappearing as if they were being poisoned and dissolved by cyanide. Although it seems that they were being poisoned and dissolving, he did not specifically mean by the use of cyanide which was the apparent linguistic source of the neologism.

Where language was used in a metaphorical sense or words were used imprecisely, the patient was asked to explain if he meant exactly what he had said. Sometimes plausible alternative explanations were suggested to clarify complex statements.

Attempts were made to assist the patient in 'taking the role of the other'. Rutter (1985) has described this as a central problem in language disturbance in schizophrenia. In turn, accuracy and consistency in statements used was attempted, e.g. if a patient stated that the Mafia were trying to find him, saying that this was not the case could not strictly be stated with absolute certainty. After weighing the evidence with him, stating that such an event was very unlikely to happen was pedantic but appropriately accurate in these circumstances.

It was felt that careless, placatory answers would impair rapport as the patient's belief that his fears are being taken seriously would be undermined. Family and staff, including junior nursing and clerical staff, were advised to avoid corroboration of hallucinations and delusions. In particular emphasis was made on the importance of not 'humoring' or simply placating the patient.

3.2.4 Tactical withdrawal

Attempts to directly confront the patient with his beliefs were actively avoided, however, as it was believed that this would almost certainly be ineffective (Milton *et al*, 1978), might be distressing and possibly would even be dangerous. If discussing beliefs or delusions started to increase stress significantly, it was felt safest to withdraw and make careful attempts at a later stage, often when medication had begun to take effect, to re-engage in discussion. 'Agreement to differ' was an essential way of avoiding prolonged repetitive discussion which, while not confirming the delusional beliefs, assisted in termination of discussions, and where necessary detaining or compulsory admitting to hospital under the relevant section of the British Mental Health Act, in as amicable a way as possible. The arguments used then had time to develop and were frequently returned to at a later date by the patient.

Where symptoms did not remit, it was often still possible for a patient to accept that what seemed to be originating from outside them existed only in their mind and was a result of the illness that was called schizophrenia.

3.2.5 Anxiety management techniques

Relaxation and other anxiety management techniques were taught with the aim of reducing the marked anxiety that many of the patients experienced, and which probably exacerbated their symptoms and certainly increased their social unease. When they were able to use relaxation techniques, most reported general benefits and some reported specific improvement in psychotic symptoms. Negative reactions were not found in any case.

The physiology of anxiety was explained where misinterpretations of such symptoms appeared to be occurring. For example, one patient described a fear of going to bed at night because of someone pressing on his chest. He therefore had slept on a settee in his living-room for a number of months. A discussion of the probable cause of this feeling, being hyperventilation leading to overexpansion, and use of a hypnotic, resolved this, such that he returned to sleeping normally in his bedroom. Another patient described being drugged when this appeared in part to relate to symptoms of giddiness and depersonalization and side effects from medication.

3.2.6 Reality testing and hallucinations

Hallucinations were explained as phenomena which, although appearing to originate from external sources, arose from within the patient's own mind. They could occur in all probability, in 'normal' people ('you or I') subject to specific or excessive stress. Sleep deprivation was of particular relevance, as many patients experience nights without or with poor sleep in the period before psychotic symptoms emerge, and sleep disturbance and psychosis ratings have been demonstrated to be closely correlated (Meltzer *et al*, 1970). It was stressed that the patient's experiencing hallucinations did not mean that he was 'going out of his mind'. Insanity or psychosis was explained as more complex by definition and it was fundamental that insight would be lost. Just because the 'voice' (or other perception) appeared to come from outside the patient's mind did not mean that he inevitably had to accept that it was originating from there. It would be established in collaboration with the patient that, if a voice came from an external source to the patient, other people than the patient himself should be able to hear it. The patient would be asked to test this initial hypothesis by telling the interviewer if he could hear the voice while they were together. If the voice was heard only when the patient was with his family or a close friend, similar testing would be suggested. If the interviewer, family or friend, said they could not hear the voice, the alternative explanations developed would include: that the patient was being lied to; or the voice was being directed specifically at the patient so that others could not hear it; or it was coming from within his mind (and, possibly, related to the stress that he was experiencing). The arguments for and against each proposition could then be weighed. It was only rarely found that the voice only occurred when alone and again alternative explanations for this could be discussed.

3.2.7 Coping strategies

Homework assignments were used appropriate to the patient's capabilities, e.g. suggesting that religious voices or delusions be discussed with a hospital chaplain. Diaries of dysfunctional thoughts were sometimes kept to identify thoughts occurring before or at the onset of psychotic symptoms. They were also used to test out abnormal beliefs and study the frequency and pattern of symptoms. Generally however detailed recall at the time of the interview of occasions, i.e. inductive questioning, when psychotic symptoms occurred, was used.

The identification of situations in which specific stresses, e.g. being alone, provoked hallucinations could than be utilized in developing appropriate coping strategies (e.g. Falloon, 1987). Carr (1988) investigating such strategies described five different groups of coping methods used by patients which they could be encouraged to use; behavior control, such as switching on a radio or listening to music, or physical activity; cognitive control by redirection of attention; socialization; medical methods, e.g. temporary increase in medication; or even symptomatic behaviors involving acting in some way in accordance with the symptoms. Discussing such methods with patients assisted in identifying their own individual strategies sometimes with the use of activity schedules which could help the patient gain some feeling of 'mastery' and control (Breier & Strauss, 1983) over his symptoms.

3.2.8 Decatastrophization

Hirsch & Jolley (1989) in their study of the prodromal signs of onset of acute schizophrenic episodes demonstrated that "the subjective fear of 'going crazy' was the most frequent emergent symptom of such onset". On hearing voices for the first time, patients often express that they themselves think and fear that they must be 'going mad' (Romme & Escher, 1989). The fear also that if the patient said he was 'hearing voices' or talked about his beliefs to others, they would assume that he was 'going mad', was frequently elicited. In the patient's mind, this would then be accompanied by catastrophic cognitions of probable implications which would include being taken to a doctor who would make them see a psychiatrist. This could develop to the extreme that they would then fear being locked up, perhaps forever, in a 'lunatic asylum' where he would be assaulted and terrorized by the 'really mad' inmates. This was particularly relevant in our district, as it contained a secure 'special hospital' which predominantly accepted patients who had committed serious offenses and who were referred from the courts. Such an anxiety 'feedback loop' acts to increase the original stress and may further the emergence of psychotic symptoms.

Families frequently catastrophized to at least as great an extent as the patient, developing fears of unpredictability, embarrassment and violence. Decatastrophization of such fears was used to reduce guilt, criticism and hostility. The term schizophrenia itself required decatastrophization in its own right, as it frequently precipitated fears of 'dementia praecox' - inevitable mental degeneration. Biological explanations were used in discussion of what we do understand about the genetics and neuropathology of psychosis supporting the explanations of 'internal' causes and reenforcing the rational acceptance of medication. This medication was described as necessary to assist in improving sleep, rest and 'confusion' by sedative effects and, by less clear methods, improving hallucinations and delusions. Side effects were discussed frankly and appropriate warnings given whenever medication was commenced, however psychotic or reluctant the patient.

3.2.9 Structure of sessions

Sessions would be operated in a flexible manner with their length and timing dependent on the patient's clinical state and progress. Initially two sessions a week lasting between 15 minutes and an hour (averaging about a half hour) following the initial assessment of up to an hour would usually be offered, reducing rapidly to weekly and eventually monthly. These would be combined with standard psychiatric assessment as necessary for management of the individual and so would include discussion of medication, leave or discharge arrangements whilst an inpatient and any other elements of the person's care plan. Brief concentrated sessions, in outpatient sessions or on home visits, over a period of months and with most over a period of at least one to two years seemed most effective. Lengthy sessions were occasionally necessary in the early stages, but could sometimes be counterproductive, especially if not focused on the individual's current concerns.

3.2.10 Overall goals

A major goal set with all patients and their families was to explain and de-stigmatize confusing and frightening experiences while not losing sight of the fact that something was seriously wrong. Overall the development of a strong rapport with the patient and his relatives was deemed of paramount importance. The serious discussion of confusing hallucinatory experiences and delusional ideas seemed to be remarkably helpful in this.

3.3 Experiences in a District Psychiatric Service

3.3.1 The Context

These techniques have been used in a small district with industrialized and farming areas and with an average psychiatric morbidity. The psychiatric service to Bassetlaw, a Health District in 'middle England', was provided from Nottingham,

30 miles south of it until 1984 and was generally agreed to be markedly inadequate. This study deals with the period during which a community psychiatric service was rapidly developed, based within the district. As with most such services, the concept of normalization was central to that development, but its limitations were also accepted. Admission of acutely ill patients to a hospital environment (albeit a district general hospital) as opposed to management in the home was 'abnormal' but nevertheless essential, given the circumstances and resources available, if safe management and relief to the patient and those around him were to be offered. However, the use of an unstaffed crisis flat (Turkington *et al*, 1990) mitigated against this in appropriate circumstances. The acceptance of the need for 'asylum' for the most vulnerable led to the conversion of two houses into 'hospital hostels' (Kingdon *et al*, 1991), providing domestic care and rehabilitation for all those needing it from within the district and those returning to it from the mental hospital in Nottinghamshire which closed in 1988. A comprehensive range of residential and day care provision (Groves, 1990) including support groups (Pym, 1989) and befrienders (Kingdon *et al*, 1989) has been made available to provide support and opportunity for patients to discuss and defuse their over-valued ideas, delusions and hallucinations. Early intervention before possible 'hardening' of psychotic symptoms was felt to be critical, and rapid and easy access was made available for patients and carers to the mental health staff of the service. The use of 'normalizing' rationales would seem to have been facilitated by the provision of a 'normalizing' environment and at least adequate resources.

3.3.2 Patient sample

Over a five-year period (1984-1989), 64 patients who on retrospective casenote analysis satisfied International Classification of Diseases, draft 10th Revision research criteria for schizophrenia, were referred to one of two general adult psychiatrists serving a catchment area population of 103,000 (Kingdon & Turkington, 1991). Of these patients, 46 had previously been under the care of the service provided to the district prior to the establishment of the Bassetlaw-based service, 19 received a diagnosis of schizophrenia for the first time. All were managed using the techniques described; there was some evolution of method over the five-year period, but the essential components of a normalizing rationale and use of cognitive behavior therapy had been developed prior to its use with this group of patients.

At the end of the period, all were supported in the range of community-based accommodation, including the nursing staffed hospital hostels or their own homes. Two at that stage were current inpatients on the acute psychiatric ward in the district, recovering from acute psychotic episodes. Free of psychotic symptoms were 35 (14 of 19 diagnosed during the study period); twenty had continuing symptoms but were not markedly disabled; nine, however, remained severely affected by them. Follow-up is continuing with this group and some of this latter group have made very good progress. Negative symptoms overall were not specifically assessed, but improvements were seen in the group who was transferred into the district (Kingdon *et al*, 1991). The response of patients of general diagnosis and relatives (independently assessed) to the hospital hostels was positive (Turkington *et al*, 1990).

The opinion of local General Practitioners was also independently canvassed before the service commenced and after four years of operation, and was also positive (Ferguson, 1990). The level of aggressive behavior in the unit as a whole was low, as reported elsewhere (Kingdon & Bakewell, 1988). Nevertheless, some patients could present in very hostile and aggressive fashion, particularly where it was their first contact with the developing service. The approach used would be quite direct discussion with the patient about their predominant presenting mood; "you seem to be feeling frightened, what's wrong?", "are you feeling confused or mixed-up?" and then working through any answers elicited. No suicides have occurred in the group to date which seems an important indicator of the apparent safety of the methods appropriately applied. It does seem again necessary to stress the non-confrontational approach used and the flexibility employed. 'Leaving well alone' where a patient's progress was very slow but steady seems essential. Knowing when to stop and disengage, and how to wind down an interview such that the participants leave in a relaxed and friendly fashion are skills which also seem important. They can probably be learnt with practice and appropriate support from more experienced staff who are prepared to become actively involved, 'trouble shoot' in the treatment process where the trainee is having problems.

In this context, Beck's method of summarizing at the end of an interview and asking patients about their perceptions of it and of the interviewer's manner, and any other questions that they wish to ask, has much to commend it. The patients are continuing to be followed up where symptoms persist, and are generally referred back or self-refer where relapse occurs because of the geographical nature of the district and relationship with patients, their families and doctors. Amongst all, and particularly the newly diagnosed, improvement after periods of even years with little progress has been seen to occur.

3.4 Summary

This preliminary study describes and illustrates the use of specific cognitive behavioral techniques targeted at reduction of psychotic symptoms with an explanation of schizophrenia which also aims at destigmatization. A major task has been to reduce the possibility of 'crises turning into catastrophes', short-term stress becoming long-term disability, by decatastrophization. These techniques have proved credible and acceptable to an unselected group of patients with schizophrenia. Their use appears to be safe and in this sample has coincided, particularly in those whose clinical course has been wholly managed using them, with relatively low use of medication and hospitalization. The level of symptomatology and social adjustment is also acceptable.

An uncontrolled study can only be suggestive of efficacy. Fortunately, cognitive-behavioral techniques lend themselves readily to controlled evaluation. A pilot treatment trial of this modification of these techniques in schizophrenia has recently been completed and will be reported in due course. Controlled studies of the use of *cognitive therapy* in patients with 'treatment-resistant' schizophrenia have been funded and recently completed successfully.

The assistance of patients and members of staff of the Bassetlaw Mental Health Service is very gratefully acknowledged.

Chapter B.4

Systemic Considerations for the Inpatient Treatment of First-Episode, Acute Schizophrenic Patients

Marco C.G. Merlo and Helene Hofer

4.1 Introduction

In 1989, a systemic concept for the inpatient treatment of first-episode, acute psychotic patients was first implemented on a special ward at the Psychiatric University Hospital of Berne. There are several reasons for treating this group of patients in a special unit:
   a) patients who are hospitalized for the first time should have an extensive diagnostic assessment;
   b) these patients are usually between 16 and 25 years of age and often have close contact with their families, who also need intensive help and are eager to be involved;
   c) in general acute wards, currently increasing number of individuals with drug addiction are treated, and young schizophrenic patients might be at risk to start a career of drug-abuse;
   d) young schizophrenic patients and their families may become resigned to lack of progress when they are in direct contact with chronic mentally ill patients;
   e) the first admission has a strong impact on the extent to which patients and their significant others will develop confidence in the hospital, should further crises occur;
   f) in recent years, much effort has been made towards early rehabilitation (Bennett, 1983);
   g) research has lately focused on first-episode, first-admission schizophrenic patients (McGorry & Jackson, 1999).

Although these arguments are generally accepted, there are also some against the specialization of psychiatric units, e.g. the catchment area is necessarily larger which in some cases might mean a greater distance between hospital and home. Nevertheless, schizophrenic disorders need highly sophisticated treatments which are difficult to be implemented in general psychiatric wards.

Since psychotic decompensation is characterized by a breakdown of psychosocial and biological organization (Brenner *et al*, 1992), the complexity of this disorder calls for an equally sophisticated treatment strategy. To structure this complex treatment, the concept of our special ward is based on the social systems theory (Luhmann, 1984; Willke, 1991). Other theoretical considerations about the application of an infomedical model in organizing psychosocial intervention are described by Merlo and Gekle in chapter A.1. of this book.

The goal of the treatment program is to overcome psychotic disorganization by smoothly and gradually restructuring the biological, psychological and social domains of functioning. For this, the therapeutic alliance is of central importance (Seltzer *et al*, 1989); a close relationship must be established and a consensual sphere found between the patient, significant others, and mental health professionals (Merlo, 1989), in which common experiences help the patient to communicate his wishes and beliefs. It is a bridge to the social environment which helps the patient to get out of the isolation of acute psychosis - an autistic inner world. In this phase, professionals focus on the 'here and now'; activities on the ward should help the patient to divert his attention from chaotic and often tormenting inner experiences. It is also (of vital importance) that professionals approach the patient with as much sensitivity as possible. Patients in this state tend to feel influenced, and may react with strong negative emotions even when professionals only want to give advice. At a later point, therapy focuses on the future and on finding solutions, rather than dwelling on the past and its problems.

The therapeutic team focuses on the level of action because experiences can help the patient to see himself and others in term of reality, rather than in terms of his internal state. The goals for inpatient treatment include promoting social competence, autonomy, self-esteem, resocialization and early reintegration. The overall goal is an improvement of the patient's subjective and objective *quality of life*.

4.2 The Ward as a Social System

Interpersonal dynamics on a psychiatric ward can be interpreted with the help of the social systems theory proposed by Luhmann (1984). Comparing a patient-therapist dyad to a multidisciplinary team reveals that the latter social system is much more complex and necessitates a higher level of organization. The more a system is internally differentiated, the more it has to develop a structure for exchange of information (Willke, 1991), and the concept of our inpatient therapy program is a condensation of this structure. Like every structure in living systems, it has to be updated and adapted to new requirements, but it also has to be continuously interpreted in order to avoid too much rigidity in daily practice. Flexibility and a capacity to change are the main characteristics of good multidisciplinary teamwork (Watts & Bennett, 1983). It is important for all members to agree that it is not possible for one person alone to have all the important information about a patient, and that the team as a whole can handle the complexity of treating psychotic patients better than a single person. The latter aspect of teamwork is based on the systemic concept of 'emergence', i.e. that the totality of a system is more than the sum of its parts. Solving a problem as a team is easier to do than alone. It is interesting in this connection that families with a psychotic member have more difficulties in problem solving when together than in situations where a family member is alone (Waxler, 1974).

On a ward, there are two systems which exchange information:
a) the system of PATIENTS,
b) the system of PROFESSIONALS.

Both have their environments, which consist of 'inner' and 'outer' worlds (Willke, 1991). The 'inner' world constitutes those social functions that the members of a system have outside their system, i.e. a patient is not only a patient but also, e.g. the child of his family and a colleague at his work-place. The 'outer' world consists of those social relations which do not belong to the index system. The members of systems have to accept dependency on these environments; i.e. patients are influenced in their attitudes and convictions by their families or other relevant persons, such as professionals outside the ward. The 'inner' world of the ward professionals includes their roles inside the hospital, as well as those in private relationships. In particular, the mental health professional in charge of the ward has to face conflicts between the interests of the ward and those of the institution (Watts & Bennett, 1983).

The system of PATIENTS has its own structure. As a group, this system can have a supportive influence that is similar to self-help groups on its members. This is also important, because exchanging information about their psychotic experiences can help patients to find things they have in common and to learn new coping strategies. A patient who has recovered from psychosis and is about to leave the ward provides convincing evidence for the possibility of overcoming psychosis. For this reason, patients who are free to go off hospital grounds are asked to accompany those who are still in an acute phase but not in danger of harming themselves or others. Nevertheless, it is important that contacts between acute patients and those who have made more progress should not be forced prematurely. Since group situations cause high social stress to schizophrenic patients, they should be avoided in the very early phase of inpatient treatment (Cohen & Khan, 1990). Preliminary data from a study on the influence of the social field structure in a psychiatric ward show a relationship between the status of a patient in the group and his psychopathology (Brenner et al, 1991).

There are no empirical data as to whether interventions at the group level of a psychiatric ward affect the psychopathology of individual patients. Nevertheless, we emphasize on our ward that all team members should consider the group dynamics of the system of PATIENTS. As at other levels, professionals should be aware of extremes in the group dynamics, i.e. between excessive polarization and homogeneity. An example of excessive polarization is the role of scapegoat or the expulsion of a patient from a group's activities. The latter process was found to be typical for suicidal patients or those with non-psychotic psychopathology who had mistakenly been referred to our ward. Extreme homogeneity within the group is an obstacle to new experiences and adaptive changes. Considering group dynamics can have a certain diagnostic value in order to differentiate between psychotic and non-psychotic patients.

The system of PROFESSIONALS depends on the resources which are provided by the hospital, i.e. assignment of patients or selection and employment of team members. The organizing principle for the system of professionals is to treat patients. Therefore, the main focus of daily work on the ward is centered on the exchange of information between the system of PATIENTS and that of PROFESSIONALS. To assess the group dynamics of the system of PATIENTS, we use the Systematic Multiple Level Observation of Groups (SYMLOG method) which was developed at Harvard University for investigating the dynamics in small groups (Bales & Cohen, 1979). With SYMLOG, polarization and homogeneity of subgroups or of individuals in relation to the group can be measured. The staff is trained to evaluate the system of PATIENTS with this instrument, and the information obtained is discussed at the therapy co-ordination session every week, where strategies are devised to optimize group dynamics. Information about the ward atmosphere is also exchanged at the same session so as to be able to detect if there is emotional tension - within the system of PATIENTS, within the system of PROFESSIONALS or between the two systems.

The concept of expressed emotion (EE) has been applied to the interaction between staff members and patients (cf. Bebbington & Kuipers, 1994). There were common features between attitudes of family members and those of staff members (Herzog, 1992). Similarly, Ball *et al* (1992) found that a high-EE attitude in staff members correlated with a worse outcome in schizophrenic patients treated in a day hospital. In people who interact with schizophrenic patients, strong emotional reactions are mainly caused by uncertainty as to whether the patient's inadequate behavior can be explained by laziness or by sickness; is the patient 'bad' or 'mad' ? There is no easy answer to this question, particularly in the post-acute phase, and reactions to the behavior of schizophrenic patients are often characterized either by extreme criticism (imputing badness) or overinvolvement (imputing incapacity). The person who wants to help the patient may well become trapped in one of these extremes (see also Merlo and Gekle, chapter A.1., this book). Seltzer *et al* (1989) showed that it is important for professionals not to assume too early that every aspect of behavior evidenced by the patient is a result of willed action. On the other hand, these authors rightly emphasize that staff members should not focus all their interest on the way patients act, without considering their inner readiness to do these things. In other words, does the patient really act on an impulse of his 'I', or is his action only a consequence of the influence of another person? Podvoll (1990) considered a healthy atmosphere and a relationship to the patient that is characterized by sympathy and acceptance to be crucial for a successful therapeutic effort. The same author also stressed that professionals should avoid exercising unnecessary power over the patient. On acute psychiatric wards, this has to be continuously reflected in the team as a whole, since not everyone has the personal qualities to be able to handle aggressive situations. Therefore, the selection of staff members is crucial for the ward atmosphere. In this way, unnecessary containment of patients can be avoided.

For the system of PROFESSIONALS, three different levels of information exchange can be distinguished: direct therapeutic contact with the patient, sessions for coordinating therapeutic interventions, and those focused on the team and its members. Regular sessions provide the structure for reducing any overload of information. Therapy offered on our specialized ward includes:

(a) individual psychotherapy; (b) family therapy; (c) group therapy; (d) pharmacological treatment; (e) milieu therapy; (f) occupational therapy; (g) music therapy;

(h) physiotherapy; and (i) sociotherapy.

While dividing therapy into various components makes the system much more complex, it facilitates co-ordination. To establish a clear focus during the therapeutic sessions, it is important to separate the sessions on co-ordination of therapeutic interventions from those on co-operation between the team members or on structures like timetable of the therapeutic sessions. A team that has evolved creates its own concept of treatment as a routine basis for everyday work. If there is basic consensus among the team members, much redundancy can be avoided. One of these fundamental convictions - that solving problems in a group is much better than doing so alone (i.e. the principle of 'emergence', Willke, 1991) - should be shared by all team members. However, this principle only holds if co-ordination of different interventions is successful. Extreme polarization or unification is also possible in the system of PROFESSIONALS, whose group dynamics sometimes mirror the processes in the system of PATIENTS.

Working with patients - especially with young people - usually elicits strong emotions, which may be related to the 'inner world' of a staff member. There can be very personal reasons why a professional becomes emotionally overinvolved during the process of caring for patients (Hell, 1991), e.g. a member of the therapist's family had committed suicide and he over-reacts when a patient expresses suicidal ideation. The nursing staff is most strongly exposed to such strongly emotional situations. The help of external supervisors is necessary to keep a ward atmosphere stable, and to monitor the psychic and physical health of the team members, so that a burn-out syndrome can also be avoided (Modestin et al, 1994). Supervision should be conducted separately for each professional group, to avoid focusing on interdisciplinary discussion instead of working through situations with patients. Supervisory sessions should therefore be organized along the lines proposed by M. Balint & E. Balint (1963).

Another means of activating the team and fostering therapeutic work is to conduct sessions especially directed at exchanging new scientific data and describing important innovations.

4.3 Factors Influencing Positive Teamwork

There are several necessary ingredients for positive teamwork. First of all, the choice of collaborators is of crucial importance. Establishing a therapeutic alliance with schizophrenic patients is not only a matter of training or education. The strong emotional interactions which occur on psychiatric wards mean that staff members must be able to deal with their own emotions. In particular, the nursing staff should be able to provide an example of how to cope with emotional difficulties (Seltzer et al, 1989). Psychopathology in staff members can block all positive therapeutic efforts on the ward (Hell, 1991). Therefore, anyone who has addiction problems or other major psychiatric disorders should not be recruited for this kind of work. Any staff member who becomes sexually or physically involved with a patient should be dismissed since boundary violations have a very negative influence on the ward atmosphere. Needless to say, there should be a zero-tolerance policy for any form of sexual or physical abuse of patients.

Individual attitudes towards severely mentally ill people constitute a factor which continuously affects therapeutic work. A team member who has the tendency to exert power over patients to achieve a certain kind of behavior, poisons the ward atmosphere so that it is almost impossible for other professionals to counteract this destructive approach. Schizophrenic patients are most sensitive to manipulative or violent interactions, and consequently may develop, for instance, delusions of control. People who want to help schizophrenic patients must sympathize with them and accept them (Podvoll, 1990). They should avoid making devaluing comments about patients, even when they are not present.

Though almost every hospital has a shortage of mental health services, a specialized unit which aims at an integrated pharmacological and psychotherapeutic approach to the treatment of schizophrenic calls for an adequately sized team. On our ward with 12-14 beds and 2-3 places for day hospital treatment, we have one half-time consultant, two residents, one half-time psychologist, one half-time social worker, and ten full-time nurses. In addition, there is a half-time occupational therapist, a part-time music therapist, and a physiotherapist.

Since it is typical of schizophrenia that it elicits extreme positions from professionals, strategies to prevent them from becoming trapped in escalating situations will be discussed in detail in the following.

4.4 Between Scylla and Charybdis or How to Find a Way Between Extremes

Merlo and Gekle (chapter A.1., this book) has described how schizophrenic psychosis manifests itself with extreme variations in presentation: on the one hand, there is chaotic thinking, feeling and acting, on the other, rigid thinking (e.g. delusions), lack of feeling (e.g. anhedonia), and stereotypical behavior (mannerisms). Ideas of infatuation, dwelling on spiritual problems such as the meaning of life or evil, or participating in esoteric sessions are all extreme human experiences and involve strong emotions which are likely to overwhelm them. Psychosis can also be triggered by extreme physical stress (e.g. excessive abstinence from food or sleep). Interpersonal interactions associated with strong emotions have been conceptualized by the EE-research (high-EE: criticism, hostility, overinvolvement). This concept shows that psychopathology can be triggered not only by extreme influences of this kind, but also from extreme lack of stimulation. For example, Wing & Brown (1970) showed that overstimulation causes relapse, but that understimulation may lead to or exagerate deficit sympotms (such as institutionalism).

On a ward, therapeutic interventions should help the patient to structure activities throughout the day in order to prevent him from ruminating. On the other hand, excessive use of structure may limit the patient's sense of identity as an individual. To accept the patient as a person is more important than promoting optimal functioning (Seltzer et al, 1989).

The EE-concept also deals with extremes, and can be used to measure the attitude of staff members towards patients (see above). The conviction that the patient is 'lazy and acts out of ill-will', may be one end of an extreme attitude, the other being that he is 'completely sick and cannot act through free-will'. Staff members will react with varying levels of emotions, depending on their preconceived attributions.

Another aspect of working with extreme *emotions* is the approach which tries to 'decatastrophize' the psychotic experience as it affects patients and their significant others (Kingdon & Turkington, chapter 5). This approach diminishes the level of anxiety and reinforces active coping with the psychosis. Nevertheless, psychotic decompensation should not be minimized, as it necessitates long and intensive treatment.

The same is true with respect to reinforcing the available resources, but not overlooking the psychopathological symptoms and signs. Although psychotherapy of schizophrenic patients should focus on the 'here-and-now', and foster possible solutions for the future, psychological dysfunction should not be overlooked and the patient's capabilities should be measured in real-life situations.

With regard to overstimulation versus understimulation in vocational rehabilitation, extremes should also be avoided (Wing & Brown, 1970). This is closely connected with time-structuring, as too many changes per unit of time would involve too many stimuli, but on the other hand, too few stimuli would enhance negative symptoms (Carpenter *et al*, 1985).

Patients' relationship to significant others also has its extremes. These range from expulsion from the family to withdrawal from the peer group. Contacts with other family members, including visits home over the weekend, and periods of leave should be initiated as soon as possible. In contrast to old custodial care, modern inpatient treatment strives for the co-operation of relatives from the beginning of hospitalization. Early family intervention has shown positive results for the course of illness after discharge (Glick *et al*, 1985). Although our concept lays much importance on natural (i.e. non-professional) relationships, thereby strengthening contacts with significant others, contacts with peer-group acquaintances are given priority all the same.

Pharmacological treatment of schizophrenic patients aims at a minimal effective dose of neuroleptics. No-medication or high dosage strategies are other examples of extremes which should be avoided in the treatment of schizophrenia.

The therapist who wishes to avoid extremes aims at early interventions optimizing secondary and tertiary prophylaxis (minimizing disability and handicap).

4.5 Conclusions

Systems theory helps to structure complex systems like psychiatric wards and multidisciplinary teams, and furthers an understanding of group dynamics in these complex situations. Since schizophrenia evokes strong emotions and elicits extreme reactions, daily work on psychiatric wards, as well as other intensive treatment programs, e.g. day hospitals, should be regularly examined. It is most important to aim at helping patients and their families to cope with strong emotions in a manner that is likely to integrate the psychotic experience. This goal is easier to achieve if the patient experiences the institution as a supportive place, and not as a threatening and coercive one. A positive experience of inpatient treatment is likely to have long lasting effects for reintegration into their natural social environment .

Chapter B.5

Delusional, Cognitive and Emotional Aspects of Communication with the Psychotic Patient

Giovanni C. Zapparoli, Maria C. Gislon and Giuseppe De Luca

5.1 Introduction

In this chapter we deal with two clinical phenomena which are characteristic of psychotic states: resistance to change, and psychotic communication in its delusional, cognitive and emotional aspects. In our opinion, these aspects of psychotic communication could be used in order to modify the resistance to change, a very hard, often impossible achievement for psychotic patients.

We will start with a short premise: the clinical phenomenon of resistance to change, so typical of psychotic pathology is expressed in many cases as a resistance to those environmental interventions or requests which do not take into account the patient's specific needs. These needs, in fact, very often differ from those we attribute to the patients in accordance with our preconceived ideas, opinions and goals. They serve as the basis for planning coercive interventions, which patients react to in a negative manner.

Today there seems to be general agreement that a correct understanding of a patient's needs is the precondition for structuring effective intervention. As clinicians know, this is a very difficult task with psychotic patients due to their peculiar language and style of communication, which increase our difficulties in understanding them, and thus make us more likely to interpret their needs in an arbitrary manner.

The hypothesis we would like to present here is based on our clinical experience in therapy and rehabilitation with both in- and out-patient psychotic patients during acute phases as well as in periods of remission or in chronic states. We believe that three different levels of psychotic communication must be taken into account in order to understand the patients: the delusional, the emotional and the cognitive level, and the integrative processes between each of them. Our hypothesis implies that the delusion is one of the ways the psychotic patient communicates his needs in his own language and in his often distorted way. Thus, correct reading of psychotic language and communication provides a key to understand the patient's needs and communication style. Consequently, we experimented with an intervention in which understanding the delusional level offered guidelines to engineering adequate treatment at the other two levels. This is the only way to establish a therapeutic alliance and to avoid, whenever possible, imposed or coercive intervention, based on the therapist's needs rather than the patient's.

5.2 Case report

In order to illustrate such an approach, we will describe the treatment of a chronic psychotic patient after a panic attack, how we dealt with the acute crisis and compiled an adequate treatment program, that integrates the three aforementioned levels of communication.

The patient is a 45-year old woman who met DSM-III criteria for a diagnosis of schizophrenic disorder with a long history of delusional and hallucinatory experiences. We report a dialogue with her therapist during a session following psychotic breakdown. The therapist, a psychoanalyst, worked as a consultant in a ward for chronicle patients where the woman lived. He had been seeing her regularly for three months, three times a week, in an attempt to modify her chronic state, which was accompanied by frequent, acute episodes, an increasingly serious problem both for the family and the psychiatric team who had been treating her.

Patient: I am afraid that I must depend on mom or my brother, and that I might be involved in some terrible events, in a crime or a murder. When my father died, I was afraid that I might die too. My father came to see me the other day and told me that you hadn't killed him.

Therapist: So your father came back to tell you that it was not me who had killed him.

Patient: I didn't kill him. You did, doctor. Now that both of you are dead, I must also die.

Therapist: Then I am dead too.

Patient: Yes, I figured that you were dead because you did not come. It was already a quarter to twelve and I thought that you would not show up. I thought: "He is either dead or angry". I thought that you had not come because you had agreed with my mother and my brother to send me to doctor who might do something to me.

Therapist: Dangerous things?

Patient: Yes, maybe examining and touching me everywhere, and when they touch me it hurts and makes me want to vomit.

Therapist: What do you vomit?

Patient: I don't know, but I am afraid. I always feel sick inside, here in the stomach, and the head nurse of my ward operated on me. I know you told her to do that, and she put a little radio inside my stomach and afterwards the vomiting and pain stopped. My brother ordered a nurse to take the radio out while I was asleep at night, and now I am terrified.

On the basis of this clinical material we will analyze the three aforementioned levels of communication; more specifically we will first analyze the delusional content.

As very often in the past, the patient again expresses the delusional belief that she killed her father, who was both a persecutor and a caregiver in order to deny her own dependent needs for fear of rejection. During this last psychotic breakdown, she claimed the therapist had killed her father. In our opinion, this change in the delusional content expresses her need to test the therapist's response, specifically if he would refuse or accept the role of an actor in her delusion, i.e. if he could understand her conflict, her ambivalence and help her to cope with her direct or projected aggression. This was, in our opinion, her first message to the therapist. The second message concerned her fear of change, symbolically meaning a fear of being abandoned, of losing both her family and her therapist. To cope with this fear, she worked out the delusional belief that the therapist had put a radio in her stomach which expressed her need for a constant object, symbolizing an ever present therapist. This belief helped her to cope with both the fear of rejection and the feeling of loneliness. Accordingly, the basic desire expressed at the delusional level was that the therapist could carry out two functions: not just the passive role of a spectator, who exclusively records the patient's psychotic logic or her defense mechanisms, e.g. projection, but also the role of an actor in her psychotic experience. This means that the therapist must accept the role of the persecutor and, therefore, he had killed her father, but also the role of the protector, therefore he was the surgeon who placed the little radio in her stomach and could protect her from her dangerous, aggressive drives as well as from her persecutors.

We want to emphasize that if the therapist is able to communicate to the patient by direct participation that he can understand his needs, he fosters a therapeutic alliance, which makes further interventions possible. In fact, as a consequence of the therapist's availability to participate in her delusional world, the patient decreased her resistance to treatment, and her increasing commitment to the therapeutic alliance allowed the therapist to work through the conflictory dynamics utilizing psychoanalytic techniques. Then, he was able to carry out the intervention at the emotional level specifically focusing on the fear of being abandoned just as her dead father had done in the past. She felt that she was expected to perform in a way that was impossible for her and then felt afraid of being abandoned due to her inability to achieve the external, imposed expectations and ideals. The therapist was able, for instance, to explain to the patient her fear that she could be abandoned by her family and by himself (as once happened with her father when he died), and help her to consciously perceive the connection between her psychotic panic and the threat of being abandoned.

This process was only possible because the therapist, assuming the double role of protector-persecutor and adapting himself to her delusional modality, succeeded in communicating his ability to understand the patient's language and needs. Specifically, accepting that he was the surgeon who had inserted the radio in her stomach, the therapist met the patient's need for a constant object representing himself. In fact, the latter had to be a concrete object in her delusion because the patient was incapable of abstraction and symbolization.

At this point, we want to draw attention to another specific problem of psychotic patients. Because of the regressive dependence caused by structural deficits, psychotic patients experience a disorganizing separation anxiety not only due to actual abandonment, but also due to a simple threat. Therefore, they require an external situation which they can always rely on, and for as long as they need it. By sharing the patient's delusional experience with him, the therapist attains the fundamental goal of therapy: he becomes part of the patient's world. Consequently, he is no longer a stranger, but rather someone who is indispensable to the patient's needs like a family member, except that he has specific characteristics that differ from any of the other relatives. One of the main problems with this type of patients is that their parents might die before they attain sufficient autonomy - which is not a very easy thing to happen as experience has taught us. In a psychotic patient, this problem gives rise to a state of panic, and the failure to cope with it prevents the patient from being helped to attain a minimum level of security, and then from conducting a successful therapeutic intervention. The therapist, or in general mental health professionals, can guarantee the patient continuous presence. Contrary to family members who are not replaceable in the case of absence or death, professionals are. Therefore, only the continuous presence of the staff can provide the patient with 'the permanence of the object' as Piaget put it. In fact, patients suffering from psychotic disorder are very often unable to reach even this primitive level of permanence of the object without the real presence of external figures. This was exactly the psychological condition of our patient. We interpret the delusional belief regarding the radio as a progressive, and not as a regressive sign. It is presumably a further level in the evolution towards the permanence of the object, as it expressed the ability to transfer her need for a constant object to one of the team members, even if by means of a psychotic object. As discussed above, only a concrete object either in outer or inner reality can acquire this quality, i.e. be a constant object, because that is in accordance with her concrete level of thinking and her delusional and hallucinatory experiences. Moreover, the object must be inanimate because it can be controlled in an omnipotent way, meaning that it cannot change independent of her will. For such a patient any change would cause overwhelming separation anxiety.

This example illustrates our hypothesis that the delusion should be considered as something that has understood before being removed. In fact, it is one of the possible ways the patient communicates his needs and requests. Only if we understand the patient's message can we modify psychotic symptomatology. In this case to try to reduce or eliminate the delusion (i.e. using antipsychotic medication) before understanding its meanings, would have been a repetition of the original traumatic experience, when the caregivers had failed to understand the patient's needs, but imposed their own needs upon her. It is essential to provide the patient with a positive experience different from the previous negative interpersonal experiences characterized by the incapacity of the nurturing figures to understand the needs of the patient, as in our case the relationship with the mother who was insensitive to her signals and could not respond to them.

To comprehend the meaning of the delusion provides not only the basis for enhancing the development of a trusting relationship, but also the possibility of understanding that this patient needed two different types of intervention. First, a psychodynamic therapy fostering a greater awareness of her unconscious fears, conflicts, and defenses, but even a cognitive therapy to work with her erroneous, basic cognitive models. Given the fact that the patient's needs are different, we have to integrate different models of therapy - in this case psychodynamic and cognitive ones - which do not compete but are complementary.

The focus of the psychodynamic intervention was not only working through separation anxiety, but, as a further step, the development of attachment, and increased acceptance of dependence.

Cognitive therapy was carried out by a different therapist. The analysis at the cognitive level took place in two distinct phases - assessment and treatment. During the first phase the therapist evaluated the possibility of influencing such a serious and persistent psychopathological condition with a cognitive therapeutic intervention. In fact, the dimensions of delusional and hallucinatory experiences were predominent. The patient did not question the validity of her beliefs and conclusions, which extended to almost all areas of the patient's life and inner world, influencing her goals and interpretations of reality. The degree of bizarreness and disorganization appeared elevated. The investigation was, therefore, directed primarily at revealing:

a) the cognitive basic assumptions which caused the patient to interpret the experience of reality with reference to her delusional beliefs;
b) the roots that led to these delusions: that is, the early pathogenic experiences at the base of the dysfunctional schemata according to which the patient evaluated the reality;
c) the extent to which a restructuration could be achieved.

The basic meaning structures of the patient were characterized by the following:

a) a very negative view of herself combined with profound feelings of loneliness and helplessness;
b) others were viewed as unreliable, unavailable, with persecuting characteristics. On one hand, they threatened her, hated her, wanted to kill her, denied her things that were important for survival. On the other, they could not guarantee a constant presence in any way. Fundamental in structuring these cognitive schemata of self and others was the early and prolonged relationship with her mother, who was incapable of listening and interpreting signals from her daughter, who interfered with her activities and at the same time was absent in moments of need. Therefore, no realistic base existed to create a feeling of security. Moreover, to compensate for these dysfunctional cognitive structures of self and others, the patient resorted to highly pathological images: an image of herself as omnipotent and an image of a hyperprotective attachment figure (in the past reality her father). This predisposed her to cognitive emotional dysfunctions with a depressive-manic shift from omnipotence to impotence;
c) egocentric thinking. She was unable to recognize and differentiate between her own point of view and the views of others, continually accommodating the events of reality to her schemata.

Correcting these dysfunctional cognitive models would have meant establishing cooperation in a therapeutic alliance. Yet this proved to be an impossible mission. Over 15 years, every intervention was met with enormous resistance which manifested itself in an accumulation of delusional and hallucinatory experiences and in dangerous behavior.

For the first time it was possible to work at a cognitive level because of a continual development of new models of attachment, primarily within the relationship with the main therapist. His understanding of the meaning of the delusional content enabled him to deal with whatever needs or defenses were occurring at that moment, thereby re-establishing a therapeutic alliance whenever it was disrupted.

According to the principles of cognitive therapy, the therapist tried to devise a map of more realistic cognitive structures and working models. We will briefly describe the course of this therapy.

Attention was initially focused on the deficiencies of the metacognitive processes, working on the tendency towards selective inattention and the confusion of casual and meaningful connections. This allowed the therapist to confront egocentric thinking in a more direct way. Thereafter, the patient could consider aspects of her self that had never been discussed before. For example, instead of attributing the refusals she often received when requesting something to hostility of others, she might attribute them to her inadequate manner of communicating them. Another technique in this phase involved providing feedback on the consequences of her own activity to develop a thought process more related to feedback from reality, therefore less egocentric, based on a more correct perception of reality. This phase lasted about six months with a marked shift to less rigid and dogmatic constructions. At that point, our patient was ready to be admitted to an outpatient unit where social skills training was offered. The problems, particularly those in the interpersonal context, allowed a more careful assessment of the underlying dysfunctional beliefs with the cognitive therapist. Then, reality testing took place with the help of a psychiatric nurses of the unit. Specifically, the patient could test the threatening aspects of others' way of thinking, their hostility and their rejection, her view of herself, her weakness and vulnerability, sense of passivity and helplessness in determining both the events of her life and the reactions of others.

The results obtained can be described as follows: Firstly, there was a decrease of delusional and hallucinatory experiences. Peculiar means of communicating were substituted by more direct communication of her own needs, first in the therapeutic relationship, then more independently following the internalization of the therapist's function. Secondly, dysfunctional basic models were modified, i.e. becoming more accessible to the corrective effect of environmental feedback. Thirdly, with regard to social *handicaps* and behavior, the patient is now capable of living with her family and of attending an outpatient unit where she manages to pursue simple activities and to maintain interpersonal relationships. In short, we were able to devise an effective intervention which stopped progressive deterioration, reduced psychopathological manifestations, and improved autonomous functions and skills.

The clinical data that we would like to present in this second part of our paper will confirm the hypothesis that it is possible to use communication not only between the chronic psychotic delusional patient and the therapist, but among psychotic patients themselves to gain a better understanding of a psychotic patient.

As an example, we will use a dialogue between two psychotic, depressed patients, both long-term hospitalized cases. One of the dialogues we analyzed confirmed our hypothesis. The fact that the dialogue took place between two psychotic patients gave us a clearer picture of the characteristics of psychotic language which is inevitably less obvious when one of the two speakers is the therapist. For example, more than in the patient-therapist relationship, the need to move from the role of the actor to that of spectator and vice versa is almost constantly accomplished by means of alternation and identification. Consequently, continual exchange of roles is established and carried out both alternately and adjacently. To clarify how the messages in the dialogue between the two patients can be used as a basis for a treatment program, we will quote the more significant parts of this long, recorded dialogue between these two patients. This treatment program includes integrated interventions from different theoretical models, if it is required by the patient's needs.

On the delusional level, we noted the presence of a pathological sense of guilt, impossible to be corrected due to the patients' convictions of a reparative activity. This happens because the sense of guilt is not due to a 'human' cause: "If I had stolen something, I could make up for it", but rather by 'inhuman' causes: "One's own inability to love, indifference towards others, total selfishness even where one's own family is concerned".

On the emotional level, we found the following main themes: a feeling of helplessness towards making progress; the inability to find a place and a solution, "the idea of staying in the hospital is killing me, but so is the idea of going home"; the need to defend oneself by denying fear and panic caused by changes in emotion, and emptiness due to the lack of motivation and repetition; the fear of boredom and of inducing it in others.

On the cognitive level, we noted:

a) the presence of negative automatic thoughts; a negative view of the self: "Complete helplessness when faced with positive qualities: love, giving oneself to others, belief in God, etc."; a negative view of the world: "Others are incapable of giving assistance, not even God can help", and a negative view of the future: "The thought of living drives me mad", "I shall have to live forever if I am to make amends for my guilt";

b) the presence of systematically faulty logic arbitrary inference: "The doctor did not say hello; he wanted me to know that I did not deserve it"; generalization: "Only unpleasant things come to my mind. My wife screamed at me that our neighbor had died and I said I could not care less. I have been tormenting myself about it ever since", minimization: "I have worked all my life, it was not worth it", and above all, dichotomous thinking: "Not even God can make me well again. I am possessed by the devil";

c) the depressogenic *schemata* which influence the evaluation of information about experience in a negative way, e.g. exaggeration of the acceptance of the past resulted in an incapability to learn from the present; the interpretation of experiences was only with reference to their guilt;

d) egocentric thinking: the total incapacity to modify and test schemata and points of view; e.g. the inability to be critical of the origin of guilt and the conviction that there can be no redemption for it;

e) the dimensional aspects which are characteristic of delusional experience were present: the conviction of the validity of their beliefs was absolute, most of their time was spent in ruminating over their various delusional worries, there was a bizarre quality in the negative contents of their thoughts, especially where the cause of their inhuman sense of guilt was concerned.

We continue with a description of phenomena which, from a clinical point of view, appeared to be more relevant and significant within the interaction of the two patients. These are grouped into three areas:

a) The phenomenon of sameness through a double identification modality: each one of the two patients repeatedly recognized himself in what the other was saying.

Rose: "I do not love my children. It is agony. They adore me and I cannot feel anything. I just cannot believe in God's mercy".

George: "Me neither, I have a feeling of sorrow for my son. He is really an orphan. I have no God".

George: "I have always thought only about myself. I have always considered my wife as an object to be used".

Rose: "Me, too; me, too; I am just the same, just the same, I never loved my husband. I always did things for my own good, not his".

b) In the second area we can recognize a different modality:

George: "I think about suicide, but I am scared of dying".

Rose: "I am not. I would like to go to sleep and never wake up again. If I die of natural causes, I do not think I will go to hell".

George: "Not me. I know I will be damned even if I die a natural death".

George: "But, look, your desperation began when your husband died. I already had mine even before my son died".

Rose: "I am still in the same position but I am worse off than you. You have got a wife. You still have a chance to do something for her".

From this dialogue, differentiation, contrast, recovering identity and individuality have started to emerge.

c) The phenomenon of fear of change and the phenomenon of boredom:

Rose: "I would like an anesthetic which would shut out everything, which would make me stay as I am".

George: "I do not know what to do. I know I have bored you".

Rose: "I keep on repeating the same things; the same old problems come into my head. There is no solution. I know I have been boring".

Here the fear of possible change emerges together with a tendency to repeat oneself which generates boredom, but which is one of the consequences of the defense mechanisms against change (everything must remain as it is).

Let us consider how the understanding of the patient's needs can be one of the means of establishing a therapeutic alliance, thus overcoming typical resistance present in the treatment of psychotic patients.

The phenomenon of sameness is correlated with the need to identify oneself with others: finding a common defense mechanism enhances the feeling of having strengthened each other's defenses and, therefore, the illusion that they work better.

The phenomenon of contrast is linked to a search for the personal, original, yet not collective defense mechanism and expresses the need to differentiate oneself from others, avoiding a dangerous loss of one's sense of individuality and identity.

Finally, the message expressing the fear of change appears explainable as a fear of modification of a protective position, in this case bound up with pain and with refusal of a condition of 'pleasure' felt to be threatening. But this would be too complex to be analyzed here.

With these two patients, as with the patient of the first example, we utilized what we could comprehend through the analysis of the delusional content during the course of treatment. For instance, in certain periods we encouraged the identification with others, i.e. a collective aspect; in other periods we encouraged a process of individuation, i.e. a personal aspect; in further periods we accepted their need of a repetitive situation, as they needed protection from the fear of change equated by them to abandonment and to loss of security. This flexible attitude became the basis for the therapeutic alliance which enabled us to carry out the successive interventions focused on the final reduction of the conflict between the patients' inner delusional reality and the outer reality.

5.3 Conclusion

To establish a therapeutic alliance with patients and, therefore the possibility of success in any intervention, we must take into account that the needs of the patients are not only multiple, but also contradictory, and change over time. Consequently, a flexible attitude is an essential condition to developing a feeling of trust and security in the relationship with mental health professionals, who must continuously adapt their interventions to the different and changing needs of their patients. Such an attitude must also be used with psychotic patients even though it is much more dependent on our capacity to understand psychotic language characterized by delusions and hallucinations.

This approach appears to be the most meaningful guide to understanding the patients' real problems, to avoiding the risk of projecting on them our expectations or of attributing to them our ideals, goals or needs. The best evidence for this is that in this way the patient stimulates the therapist to drop dogmatic and rigid attitudes in his theoretical perspective and to tailor a model of intervention to the actual needs of the patients.

Chapter B.6

Why is Individual Psychotherapy Contraindicated in Schizophrenia? - Theoretical Reflections from a Constructivist Point of View

Giovanni Liotti and Mario A. Reda

6.1 Introduction

A mature theory of psychotherapy should be able to explain the reasons for its techniques being indicated or contra-indicated in particular disorders and in particular settings. A psychoanalyst, for instance, may explain the relative contra-indication of individual settings in the psychotherapy of schizophrenia through the use of such concepts as 'omnipotence of thought' and 'unconscious fear of dependency'. He can state that a schizophrenic will fight against the feelings of dependency that are unavoidable in individual psychotherapy, because to accept depending on the therapist implies the relinquishment of unconscious fantasies of omnipotence. According to psychoanalytic speculations, these fantasies underlay schizophrenic thought disturbances (Searles, 1955). In group settings it can be easier both to avoid feelings of dependency and correct fantasies of omnipotence.

Most cognitive psychotherapists would subscribe to the opinion that group, community (Perris, 1989) or family (Falloon *et al*, 1984, 1987) settings seem more suited to the psychological treatment of schizophrenics than individual settings. Is there any theoretical reason within the cognitive theory of psychotherapy for regarding the individual setting as relatively contra-indicated in the treatment of schizophrenia?

In this chapter, we shall approach this theoretical problem from a constructivist point of view. In the first section, we shall apply the constructivist theory to a cognitive-developmental analysis of autism, cognitive impairments, patterns of attachment and interpersonal schemata in schizophrenia. In the second section, we shall discuss, from a constructivist point of view, the results of a recent experimental study of the psychophysiological reactions of schizophrenics in the individual setting of training in muscular relaxation. The lines of reasoning that will be developed in both sections explain well why cognitive and behavioral techniques are more likely to fail in the treatment of schizophrenia, if they are applied in a classic, outpatient, individual setting.

6.2 Autism and Cognitive Impairments in Schizophrenia: A Constructivist Analysis

The practical reasons for avoiding individual psychotherapy in schizophrenia are obvious and are related to the patient's two basic disturbances: autism, and cognitive impairments (e.g. attention impairments) or distortions (e.g. delusions). Because of autism, schizophrenics cannot commit themselves to interpersonal relationships such as the therapeutic one. On the other hand, the schizophrenics' cognitive impairments and distortions hinder or even prohibit any meaningful therapeutic dialogue. Psychotherapists dealing individually with schizophrenics have observed that the intensity of autistic and cognitive impairments during treatment alternates when the patient is more autistic or his cognitive impairments are less severe, whereas hallucinations and delusions reappear in full intensity when the patient - thanks to therapeutic efforts aimed at reducing the autistic attitude -establishes a closer relationship with the therapist (Arieti, 1974; Scheflen, 1981).

Attachment theory (Bretherton, 1985; Bowlby, 1982) and the constructivist view of cognitive development (Rosen, 1985) provide a simple theoretical explanation of the oscillation between autism and cognitive impairments during the individual psychotherapy of schizophrenia.

Autism may be theoretically related to the extreme inhibition of the behavioral-motivational system mediating attachment. The following line of reasoning supports this hypothesis:

Both neurophysiological inborn defects and early interpersonal influences are theoretically able to bring on the inhibition of the attachment system. This inhibition has been observed and empirically studied: one-year olds, for instance, have been observed to avoid the attachment figure in situations usually eliciting attachment behavior in infants (Main & Weston, 1982). The child's avoidance of the attachment figure is statistically related to the caregiver's rejecting or neglecting the child (Bretherton, 1985). Our knowledge of behavioral abnormalities in parents of schizophrenics and of disturbed communication in their families (Lidz, 1973; Mednick, 1973; Falloon et al, 1984) allows for the hypothesis that adult schizophrenics may have been seriously neglected, rejected or abused by their parents since their infancy.

All these considerations make it reasonable to believe that adult schizophrenics have developed their representational models of self and others (interpersonal schemata: Safran, 1990) stemming from a particularly severe and protracted experience of inhibited attachment. If this is the case, from a constructivist point of view we can expect that their relinquishment of autism within the setting of individual psychotherapy is accompanied by an increased risk for delusions, hallucinations and other cognitive impairments (Liotti & Onofri, 1987).

To explain this statement, it is necessary, first, to dwell on the *emotions* implied in the functioning of the control system mediating attachment behavior. These *emotions* may be regarded as felt phases of the operations of the control system, while the system governs explicit behavior in accordance with the environmental contingencies (Bowlby, 1982). When proximity to the attachment figure is achieved (the goal of the attachment control system once it is activated), the person feels secure. When separation from the attachment figure is threatened, the person is angry and/or afraid. Sadness is the consequence of the protracted failure to attain the goal of the attachment system. Prolonged separations from the attachment figure are accompanied by the experience of despair. If the goal of the attachment system seems unattainable (e.g. because of the consistent unavailability of the attachment figure), the system is actively inhibited with the accompanying subjective experience of emotional detachment and emptiness.

In the development of schizophrenia, we have hypothesized that the basic interpersonal schemata are constructed stemming from the inhibition of the attachment system. This means that no emotion of attachment is experienced in interpersonal situations after the inhibition has been brought over, and no such emotion enters into the patient's memory schemata. The cognitive processes canalized by interpersonal schemata, that have been developed within such an atmosphere of emotional detachment, are scarcely efficient when one comes to deal with the various emotions implied by the reactivation of the attachment system. Feeling secure in the company of a protective person; feeling angry when something or somebody threatens this relationship; being afraid of the loss of, or sad because of the separation from this person: the interpersonal schemata developed within an atmosphere of detachment are unfit for the *attribution* of proper meaning to all these emotional experiences. When autism is overcome within the warm, protective atmosphere of individual therapeutic alliances - that is to say, when the schizophrenic's attachment system is reactivated and directed toward the therapist with the accompanying flow of emotions - then the patient's cognitive processes go astray.

The patient, not severely autistic any more, may appear distracted, perplexed, confused. His interpersonal schemata prove to be unfit for attributing meaning to his ongoing emotional-interpersonal experiences and for assimilating these experiences. When the schemata of semantic memory fail to assimilate an experience (interpersonal schemata are part of semantic memory: Tulving, 1972; Bowlby, 1980, 1985), episodic memories pertaining to the closest meaning domains are automatically summoned. Episodic memories related to early, traumatic experiences of attachment (i.e. experiences that precede and cause the inhibition of the attachment system) may be evoked in the automatic effort of finding the meaning of one's changing interpersonal experience within the therapeutic alliance. These episodic memories are likely to convey the re-enactment of experiences of rejection, neglect, abuse or hostility of sufficient severity to justify the inhibition of the attachment system that has followed them. The re-enactment of these painful episodic memories is, however, unrelatable to the explicit self-description allowed for by interpersonal schemata that have been developed on the basis of an inhibited attachment. Memories that cannot be related to a self-schema could be the basis for developing hallucinations and delusions (Bliss, 1986; Horowitz, 1975; Zigler & Levine, 1983). The process that has been initiated by the schizophrenic's relinquishment of autism, i.e. reactivation of the attachment system ends with the facilitation of hallucinations and delusions.

This explanation of the oscillation between autism and cognitive impairments of schizophrenics engaged in individual psychotherapy is coherent with cognitive-developmental approaches to psychopathology and psychotherapy. It is, of course, a highly theoretical and speculative explanation, although it is compatible both with what we know about the family environment in which schizophrenics have often developed since infancy, and with the hypothesis that genetic deficits can mediate the easy inhibition of the attachment system and/or abnormally influence the processing of cognitive-emotional information in schizophrenics.

Experimental support to the above cognitive-developmental (constructivist) explanation of the relative contra-indication of individual settings in the psychotherapy of schizophrenia may be found in a recent psychophysiological study. This study (Blanco et al, 1990) is concerned with the psychophysiological aspects of the emotional reactions of schizophrenics in the setting of an individual treatment based on biofeedback-assisted muscular relaxation training.

6.3 Emotional Correlates of Muscular Relaxation in Schizophrenics Treated in an Individual Setting

Three groups of subjects have been trained in muscular relaxation with the help of a biofeedback apparatus by the same therapist and in the same individual setting. The first group was composed of 30 persons free from any sign of psychopathology, the second of 37 agoraphobic patients and the third of 31 schizophrenic patients. The three groups were similar as far as age, sex and socio-cultural characteristics were concerned. Each subject in the three groups participated in 30 to 60 sessions, one every two weeks, each session lasting about 30 minutes. During each session, the electromyogram (EMG), the skin conductance level (SCL) and the skin temperature (ST) were registered (Blanco et al, 1990).

It is well known that, while muscular tension is related to anxiety, muscular relaxation normally reflects a state of emotional relaxation, i.e. feeling calm and secure. Emotional relaxation, in turn, is related to increased ST and to decreased SCL. Therefore, we should expect that if cognitive processes related to self-knowledge (self-perception, appraisal of emotions in self and others) do not interfere in the whole physiological-emotional process, the EMG ratings should be positively related to SCL ratings and negatively related to ST ratings during the training in muscular relaxation. This, indeed, was the case in the group of normal subjects (Figure 1).

In the group of agoraphobics (Figure 2) during the first sessions, the correlation between SCL ratings and EMG ratings is inverted: muscular relaxation reflects an increased emotional tension, as indicated by an increased SCL (Blanco et al, 1984). Only in the second half of training were muscular relaxation and emotional relaxation (EMG and SCL ratings) positively correlated as in normal subjects.

This pattern of relationships between muscular and emotional relaxation in agoraphobics can be explained in terms of the agoraphobic cognitive organization (Guidano & Liotti, 1983; Liotti, 1986). Agoraphobics are extremely afraid of losing control, both when they are alone and when they are in the presence of strangers. They appraise the feelings of muscular relaxation as signs of impending loss of control. Only when they become convinced that this appraisal is wrong, and/or when

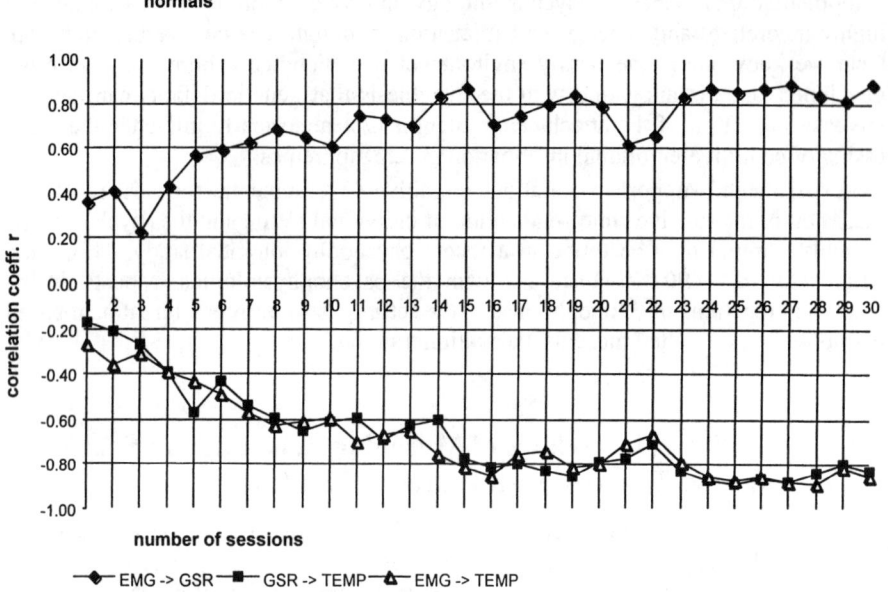

Figure 1. Group of normals.

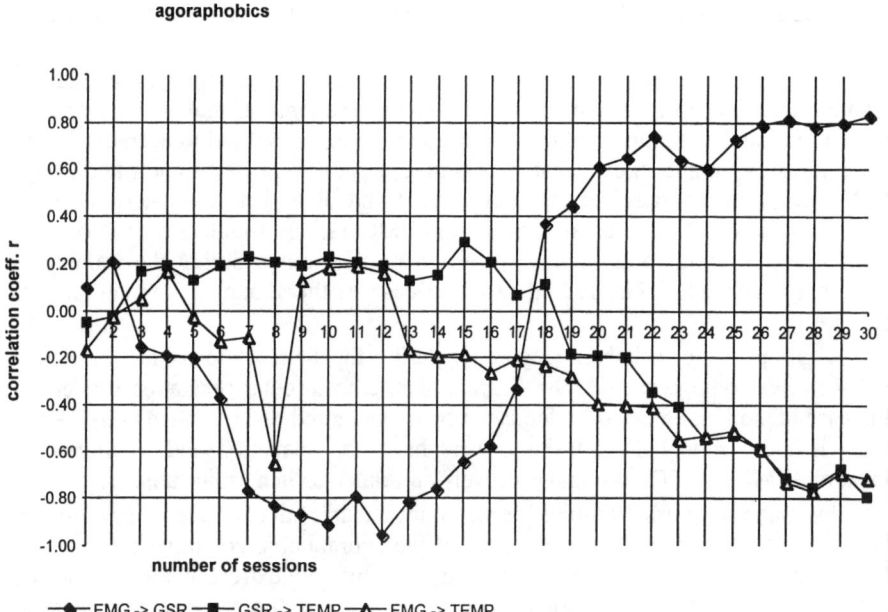

Figure 2. Group of agoraphobics.

they get to know their therapist well and deeply trust him or her, they begin to relax emotionally while relaxing their muscles. It is important to notice that, although initially inverted with respect to the norm, there is, **from the beginning of training**, a stable, consistent relation in agoraphobics between (a) the experience of relaxing one's muscles in front of a therapist and (b) the feeling tone along the dimension of anxiety-security. This relation is easily understandable in terms of the agoraphobics' interpersonal schemata, i.e. of their way of attributing meaning to their own feelings in interpersonal situations.

The schizophrenics in the experiment showed quite a different pattern of emotional-physiological reactions during the relaxation training from both normal and agoraphobic subjects. In the first part of treatment, there was no correlation between muscular relaxation and the physiological signs of emotional arousal (SCL and ST) in our group of schizophrenics. This fact points to the possibility that schizophrenics are unable to make any sense of the experience of being physically relaxed in front of another person. They cannot assimilate this experience to interpersonal schemata of the kind developed in secure attachments, i.e. they cannot perceive themselves as being properly cared for and the therapist as a helpful, trustworthy person: therefore,

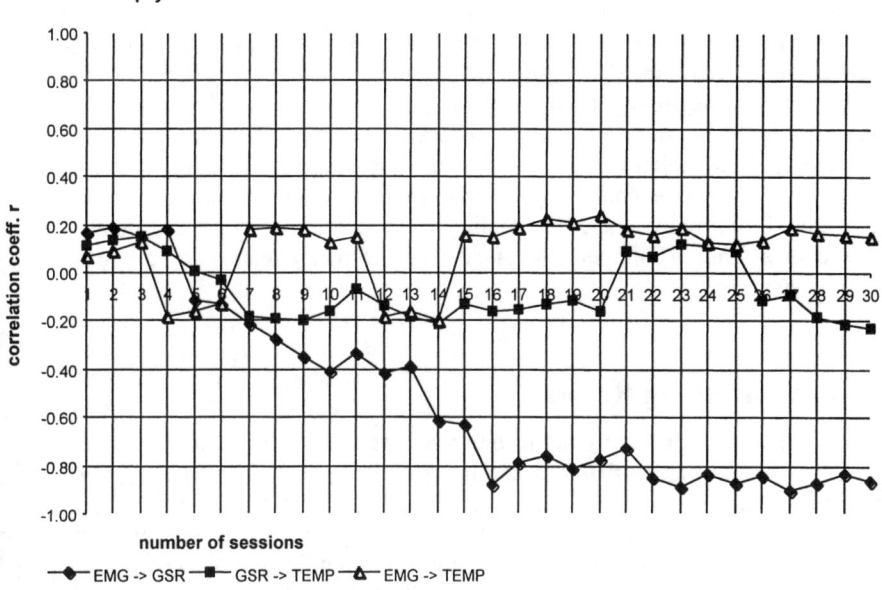

Figure 3. Group of psychotics.

they cannot feel secure and calm in the interpersonal situation of relaxation training. Neither can they assimilate this situation to the schemata developed within anxious attachments of the kind related to the vulnerability to agoraphobia (Guidano & Liotti, 1983; Liotti, 1986, 1991): therefore, they cannot consistently appraise being relaxed in front of the therapist as a sign of potential danger. Their appraisal of the feeling of muscular relaxation in the particular interpersonal setting of training is extremely haphazard and does not seem relatable to the consistent operations of any kind of interpersonal schema. As has been stated in the first section of this paper, this is exactly the situation we can expect to meet with when the early interpersonal schemata have been developed stemming from an extreme inhibition of the behavioral system mediating attachment. Feelings of relaxation experienced in interpersonal situations that normally imply the activation of the attachment system do not find any correspondence in memory schemata constructed out of the experience of extreme emotional detachment. When matched with the schemata of an autistic, emotionally detached patient, the feelings experienced while the muscles relax during training would, then, appear meaningless. These feelings may be interpreted in continuously changing ways, until the attachment system is activated again. Thanks to prolonged exposure to the situation of being cared for by a concerned person, a patient's usually inhibited attachment system can be reactivated: this is what happens, as psychoanalysts engaged in individual treatments of schizophrenics testify (Arieti, 1974; Searles, 1955), when transference develops. The reactivation of the attachment system as we have argued above, is likely to evoke episodic memories related to experiences of attachment preceding the inhibition of the system. These memories are certainly painful, if we assume that they are related to motives for inhibiting the attachment system We could, then, expect that in the second part of relaxation training: (a) the schizophrenic's attachment system is reactivated; (b) painful memories tend to be evoked; (c) the physiological correlates of these memories (increased SCL) appear together with the signs of muscular relaxation. Indeed, in the second half of training the correlations between the EMG and SCL ratings of schizophrenics resembled those of agoraphobics at the beginning of training (Figure 3). When schizophrenics become familial with the interpersonal situation of training, they **begin** to attribute consistent meaning to their feelings of muscular relaxation, but this meaning is exactly the opposite of what one could expect both from a psychophysiological (muscular relaxation is normally related to feeling calm) and from a psychosocial (being relaxed in a familial interpersonal situation is normally related to feeling secure) point of view.

6.4 Concluding Remark

The fact that agoraphobics react to muscular relaxation with emotional stress only when they are still unfamiliar with the interpersonal situation in training, while it is familiarity with this interpersonal context that coincides with the schizophrenics' emotional uneasiness, is a particularly interesting finding. It supports our constructivist view of the reasons for the relative contraindication of individual settings in the psychotherapy of schizophrenia, while these settings are suitable for the treatment of 'neurotic' disturbances such as agoraphobia. The different organization of attachment-related interpersonal schemata in schizophrenics and agoraphobics explains why it is undesirable in one case and desirable in the other that the attachment system is activated during the therapeutic restructuring of interpersonal cognitions. Community, group and family settings are less likely to bring about the activity of the attachment system than individual settings (Bowlby, 1982). These settings allow for a correction of schizophrenics' social-cognitive impairments (Falloon *et al*, 1984; Perris, 1989) while the patients' attachment system is not yet strongly activated, and they are, therefore, free from emotional experiences to which their interpersonal schemata cannot attribute any proper meaning. In individual settings, the reactivation of an attachment system that has been inhibited for the greater part of the patient's life may evoke intense emotions (and prime early, painful memories) before the patient's cognitive impairments can be at least partially corrected and therefore make it possible to attribute a manageable, if not a rational meaning to what is going on in the therapeutic alliance.

C. Empirical Evaluation

Chapter C.1

Social Skills Training Programmes for Schizophrenic Patients: What Works and How can it be Improved?

Peter Zorn and Volker Roder

1.1 Current Treatment Approaches Based on Biopsychosocial Models of Schizophrenia

Over the past decade, our understanding of schizophrenia has been profoundly influenced by vulnerability-stress models of this major mental disorder (Nuechterlein & Dawson, 1984a). The basis of these models is a conceptual blueprint that presents schizophrenia as a complex disorder involving psychological, biological and social factors, which interact in aetiology, outcome and treatment (Zubin & Spring, 1977). The results of recent empirical research substantiate this multidimensional and interactional view of schizophrenia (Brenner *et al*, 1997).

Within this framework for understanding the variability in schizophrenic disorders, various researchers have developed clinical concepts for the integrative treatment of schizophrenic patients. For example, as early as 1988, Häfner (1988) called for a broad concept of extramural care for this group of patients to address their various needs and deficits in biophysiological and psychological domains of functioning. According to Häfner, the following therapy methods should be offered: (neuroleptic) medication; psychological therapy directed at specific disorders; individual supportive psychotherapy; family therapy; family management and education. In addition, rehabilitation methods specifically aimed at reducing deficits in social and independent functioning, which have emerged in the course of illness should be provided. These rehabilitation methods should equip patients with the requisite skills, such as those associated with residential, vocational and recreational areas, in order to enable them to lead satisfying lives and promote reintegration in the community. The need for this multidimensional approach to treatment and rehabilitation in schizophrenia, and for residential, vocational and recreational skills training in particular, has been emphasised by other authors as well (Gmür 1991; Liberman *et al*, 1993; Möller 1993). The importance of community skills training for schizophrenic patients has been noted in clinical practice for several reasons: it enables them to lead independent lives outside the confines of psychiatric institutions for longer periods of time; it fosters social integration; and it raises social compe tence in the natural environment. As a result, such interventions seem to have a beneficial effect on both psychological stability and relapse prevention (Roder *et al*, 1997).

The efficacy of comprehensive treatment programmes in clinical practice has been confirmed by the status of research as well. First, there is adequate empirical support that the judicious use of neuroleptic medication embedded in an integrative treatment approach has a positive effect on both the outcome of illness and relapse prevention (e.g., Kane & Marder, 1993; Soni *et al*, 1994). Second, the efficacy of focused psychological intervention has repeatedly been demonstrated. Empirically-based, behavior therapies are successful methods of treating the basic areas of dysfunction in schizophrenia (Möller, 1993). In the interim, the efficacy of various forms of behavior therapy has been well documented (e.g., Brenner *et al*, 1992; Bellack & Mueser; 1993; Lehman *et al*, 1995; Penn & Mueser, 1996; Roder *et al*, 1997). These include behavioral family therapy (e.g., Hogarty *et al*, 1986, 1991; Mueser *et al*, 1994; Dixon & Lehman, 1995; Hahlweg *et al*, 1995); cognitive training and therapy (e.g., Olbrich & Mussgay, 1990; Brenner *et al*, 1992; Delahunty *et al*, 1993; Vauth & Stieglitz, 1993; Chadwick & Birchwood, 1994; Roder *et al*, 1997); and social skills training (e.g., Liberman *et al*, 1985, 1993; Roder *et al*, 1990; Brenner *et al*, 1992; Wallace *et al*, 1992). On the other hand, the current status of research on rehabilitation in general, and on residential, vocational and recreational rehabilitation in particular, is unsatisfactory. Although the literature has highlighted schizophrenic patients' need for specific community skills training, there is a limited amount of research available on these issues, and a lack of empirical data to evaluate the efficacy of such measures in terms of outcome and relapse prevention in particular.

1.2 The Relevance of Residential, Vocational and Recreational Rehabilitation for Schizophrenic Patients

The need for residential, vocational and recreational rehabilitation has been substantiated by sound empirical evidence of deficits in these areas of functioning. For example, Möller and von Zerssen (1986) conducted a prospective, long-term study to investigate the course of illness in 81 schizophrenic patients over a period of five years. The data obtained showed that 46% of the sample had severe job problems, whereas 18% had moderate ones. While 44% of the patients reported rarely pursuing any hobbies, 17% reported not having any. An observer rating showed that 30% of the patients failed to engage in any recreational activities. Similar results were obtained in a longitudinal study on the course of illness in 92 schizophrenic patients (half of them were night clinic patients, and half of them were in-patients) using both a prospective and a retrospective design (Gmür, 1987). At follow-up, 31% of the night clinic patients and 16% of the in-patients reported being bored in their free-time. Nearly 30% of the patients in both cohorts indicated having no hobbies at all. In regard to employment at follow-up, only 35% of all the patients had a regular job, whereas 66% had neither a steady nor a free-lance job. After having been discharged from the hospital, about one-third of the patients moved to unsupervised domiciles, another third were placed in supervised residential facilities, and the other patients stayed in the hospital. Ciompi and Müller (1976) reported even worse outcomes in their retrospective study of 289 patients assessed for an average of 37 years. While only 12% of the patients had unsupervised accommodation at the last follow-up point, the remaining patients (68%) were either hospitalised or in family care (either their own family or a foster home). Ciompi and Müller attributed these discouraging findings to a severe lack of self-reliance and social contact in schizophrenic patients.

Comparably poor adjustment in vocational and recreational areas of functioning have also been noted by other authors. According to Rittmannsberger and co-workers (1996), these patients less often succeeded in obtaining employment on the competitive job market than other nosological groups (14% v. 34%). Indeed, most of the former were unable to find a job at all (68% v. 35% for other nosological groups) and became financially dependent on disability compensation payments. With regard to residential placement, Hirschberg (1988) reported that 30% of the patients in treatment for the first time lived alone, and about 50% lived with their parents. Even though these outcomes remain relatively stable in the course of illness, there is an increase in the number of schizophrenic patients who move into supervised residential arrangements. These findings have been supported by other studies (e.g., Angst 1988, for a review of pertinent studies conducted in Europe, and McGlashan, 1988, for those conducted in the United States).

The fact remains that most of the rehabilitation interventions currently in practice in the residential, vocational and recreational areas are not designed within a coherent conceptual framework and therefore lack a common focus of training. This has proved an obstacle for the evaluation of their efficacy. The effects of such rehabilitation approaches have been inferred based on a very limited body of well controlled studies. Although there is no data available on the outcome of recreational skills training programmes, there are some controlled empirical studies on residential and vocational rehabilitation. For example, Ciompi and colleagues (1991, 1993) compared a group of 22 acute schizophrenic patients who received milieu therapy and low-dose neuroleptic medication at the "Soteria Bern", a supervised half-way house, with a matched group of patients who were offered traditional standard therapy (i.e. primarily medication). At two-year follow-up, there were no significant differences between the two groups in either vocational or residential outcomes. In the area of residential rehabilitation, for example, Vaitl and colleagues (1987) developed specific training programmes. Findings demonstrated that during a catamnestic period of three years, 50% of the patients achieved the rehabilitation goal of moving into a collective. Similar findings were described by Eikelmann and Reker (1991): 50% of the schizophrenic patients surveyed improved their residential situation (transitional residential placement) as a result of rehabilitation efforts. These patients showed a low level of psychopathology. Social integration proved to be another predictor of successful residential rehabilitation). Vaitl and colleagues also demonstrated in 1987 (Vaitl et al, 1987) that psychopathology and social variables have an impact on the outcome of rehabilitation. They noted therapy gains in residential rehabilitation in only 14% of a sample of severely disturbed and socially maladjusted chronic schizophrenic patients residing in half-way houses (average duration of hospitalisation: 7.4 years) in contrast to substantial deterioration in 12%. Reker and Eikelmann (1993, 1994) assessed the outcomes of vocational rehabilitation. They found that it had a positive impact on the employment status of 21% of a total of 126 patients (72.2% of them had been diagnosed as schizophrenic), no impact on 60.5%, and a detrimental effect on 18.5%. Psychopathology and social parameters predicted employment status in this study as well. The duration of illness and hospitalisation was significantly shorter and the level of social adjustment was significantly higher in patients with successful outcomes. Lewandowski and collaborators (1992) even reported successful vocational outcomes in 33% of a sample of schizophrenic patients. Predictors of a favourable course of rehabilitation also included reduced residual symptoms and active social behavior. These findings have been confirmed by various other authors (Lysaker & Bell, 1995; Lysaker et al, 1995).

A lack of empirical studies specifically designed to assess the effects of residential, vocational and recreational rehabilitation on relapse prevention has led some investigators to infer success on the strength of studies on variables that predict the course of illness. The only measure of community tenure that has been shown to have an effect on relapse prevention is employment. A number of studies that were based on the hypothesis that increased ego strength, self-reliance, daily structure, and social integration have a therapeutic effect (Häfner, 1988) have demonstrated that employment stabilises psychiatric patients and contributes to enhanced psychological well-being (Watts & Bennett, 1983; Cohen, 1990; Rudas, 1990). Studies based on the construct of Expressed Emotion (EE: Leff & Vaughn, 1985) seem to be particularly suited to examine the relationship between residential placement and relapse prevention. A number of them have demonstrated that patients residing in low-EE households were socially more well-adjusted and better integrated in the community in the longer term than those living in high-EE environments (e.g., Hogarty et al, 1987). However, doubt has been cast on the prognostic utility of the EE concept for relapse prevention (Jenkins & Karno, 1992). Instead, it has been noted that the patients' poor social competence contributes to the negative interaction patterns characteristic of high-EE environments (Bellack, 1992). Nevertheless, the body of empirical data available to date suggests the association between a nonaffectively charged, socially reinforcing family environment and the reduced likelihood of relapse (Buchkremer et al, 1991; Hahlweg et al, 1995). Owing to the fact that recreational activities are one aspect of psychosocial adjustment and serve as a buffer against negative symptoms such as loss of energy and initiative, sluggishness, and social withdrawal (Klosterkötter et al, 1994), it should be possible to determine the utility of recreational skills training in preventing relapse. The relationship between the positive effect of a high level of psychosocial adjustment and a favourable course of illness has been well documented in the literature (e.g., Rey & Bailer, 1996). In the same vein, numerous studies have provided empirical support for the relationship between marked negative symptoms and a negative course of illness (Deister & Marneros, 1994). Consequently, positive residential, vocational and recreational adjustment can override stress and vulnera-bility by improving psychosocial functioning. These protective factors might contri-bute to relapse prevention in schizophrenia.

The status of research on residential, vocational and recreational skills training in the rehabilitation of schizophrenic patients may be summarised as follows: (1) The crucial need for residential, vocational and recreational rehabilitation has been inferred from the evidence of substantial deterioration in these central domains of community living in longitudinal studies. (2) The measures of rehabilitation in use today seem to be either incomplete (recreational rehabilitation) or not overly successful (vocational and residential areas of functioning). Despite some positive outcomes, substantially negative ones have also been reported. (3) In the available service delivery system, the efficacy of vocational and residential rehabilitation seems to be primarily dependent on psychopathology and social parameters. There is a link between severity of impairment and a decrease in the likelihood of rehabilitation success. (4) Studies on the predictors of the course of the disorder indicate the importance of training community skills, in particular job skills, in preventing relapse. The third point merits special attention when designing efficacious therapeutic and rehabilitative techniques in the future. Social skills training procedures connected with general rehabilitation topics, especially those focused on residential, vocational and recreational areas of functioning, could foster community adaptation, and thereby contribute to relapse prevention. This indicates that general rehabilitation topics should form an integral part of psychotherapy (i.e. cognitive behavior therapy). However, modification of the rehabilitative measures that have been implemented to date does not seem to be a very promising strategy due to the lack of both a common therapeutic focus and a sound conceptual basis guiding therapeutic action. Therefore, new behavior therapy interventions directed at residential, vocational and recreational topics are imperative for successful treatment. Against this background, we have developed three specific cognitive-behavior therapy programmes for the treatment of residential, vocational and recreational functioning (Roder et al, 1998). These new programmes are a further elaboration of Integrated Psychological Therapy (IPT).

1.3   Integrated Psychological Therapy (IPT)

IPT (Integrated Psychological Therapy) for schizophrenic patients is a cognitive-oriented group format treatment programme that has been developed by our group and widely disseminated over the past few years (Brenner et al, 1994; Roder et al, 1997). It is based on the underlying assumption that elementary attentional-perceptual and cognitive deficits have a pervasive effect on higher levels of behavioral organisation, and that there are vicious circles between these various interacting levels of behavior (Pervasiveness hypothesis: Brenner, 1987). IPT attempts to improve cognitive, social and problem-solving skills in a series of incremental steps. Whereas the focus of the first and second subprograms ("Cognitive Differentiation" and "Social Perception") is on improving cognitive and perceptual skills (i.e. the more elementary levels of functioning), the fourth and fifth subprograms ("Social Skills" and "Interpersonal Problem Solving") address deficits in social functioning and problem solving. The third subprogramme ("Verbal Communication") serves as an intermediary. In the interim, various evaluative studies with more than 900 patients have been conducted on IPT by different research groups (reviews in Mussgay & Olbrich 1988, and Theilemann & Peter, 1994). Although these studies have demonstrated that therapy has a positive effect on cognitive functioning and on psychopathology in subacute and chronic schizophrenic patients in particular, there is a lack of conclusive evidence for improvements in the domain of social functioning and for transfer and generalisation of therapy gains (Roder et al, 1995). Furthermore, the majority of data obtained in these studies and more recent research on the mechanisms of IPT effects (Roder & Brenner, 1990) do not lend support to the assumption that improvements in cognitive functions have a pervasive effect on more complex levels of behavioral organisation as postulated in the original version of Brenner's pervasiveness hypothesis (Brenner, 1987). Improved cognitive functioning seems to be a necessary, yet in itself insufficient prerequisite for social competence in schizophrenic patients.

These results and considerations prompted the need to expand the scope of Integrated Psychological Therapy (IPT). Several years ago, our group started a new project to improve the therapeutic efficacy of IPT social skills training. Studies conducted by Liberman's research team have confirmed the relationship between such a specific social skills training procedure and substantial improvement in various domains of social functioning. In addition, better results in the maintenance and generalisation of therapy effects were shown (Liberman et al, 1993; Mueser et al, 1995; Marder et al, 1996). Although these approaches have been shown to be superior to non-specific social skills training procedures, they strongly reflect particularities of the North American culture and are thus not applicable to conditions in Europe. Criticism that has been voiced on IPT might thus be deflected by specifying and differentiating the issues to be targeted in training.

1.4 Cognitive behavior therapy programmes in the residential, vocational and recreational areas (WAF[1])

Encouraged by the research results described above, our research team has recently devised specific, group-format cognitive behavior therapy programmes for schizophrenic patients in the residential, vocational and recreational areas ("WAF"). These novel programmes have much in common with Integrated Psychological Therapy (IPT): they are based on vulnerability-stress models use cognitive-oriented procedures, and they employ basic behavioral techniques. However, those programmes differ from IPT in the greater emphasis placed on the acquisition of circumscribed social skills (Roder et al, 1995, 1997). Based on the considerations outlined above, the focus of training is on the three central domains of community living - housing, work, and recreation. Consequently, training is provided in specific behavioral competencies in order to equip patients with the necessary skills to be able to find an adequate job or place to live and to maintain these for a longer period of time, or to make use of their free time in a more active manner. Cognitive disturbances are treated indirectly by teaching patients action-oriented skills. Thus, the integration of rehabilitation and behavior therapy can be achieved as called for above. Provided in conjunction with rehabilitative measures currently in use, the three new therapy programmes should improve community tenure in the targeted areas of functioning. Furthermore, they are expected to improve cognitive functioning and promote generalisation to overall social competence. Detailed and highly standardised therapy manuals are available for all three therapy programmes. Each of

---

[1] The german abbreviation (Wohnen - Arbeit - Freizeit; "WAF") has been retained throughout

the new cognitive behavior therapy programmes focuses on: (1) sensitising the patients to their needs, options and skills (cognitive and emotional skills training); (2) helping them to make a decision in any one of these three areas; (3) providing support in putting the decision into action (practical implementation of skills); (4) teaching them how to anticipate difficulties and to solve concrete problems, which might occur in the new residential, vocational or leisure-time situation. Applying a problem-solving strategy to problems in the patient's own life should ensure the acquisition and generalisation of problem-solving skills.

The programmes can be tailored to meet the individual needs of those participating in therapy. Based on problem analysis (Roder, 1989), the therapists designate which of the theme-oriented therapy units specified in the therapy manuals are to be addressed in the therapy group and also decide which issues require increased or decreased attention. The therapy units consist of a series of incremental steps designed to meet therapeutic demands. While the first step focuses on the acquisition of action-oriented cognitive skills ("Cognitive Processing", CP), the second step is directed at the "Practical Implementation" (PI) of these skills. Problems that arise in the course of working towards individual goals and maintaining these outcomes in the longer term are dealt with in the third step described above ("Problem Solving", PS). The same or similar (cognitive) behavioral techniques are employed as in IPT. These include problem and behavior analysis, modelling, role playing, cognitive restructuring, problem solving, brainstorming, decision training, positive reinforcement, positive connotation, structuring, covert learning, self-control, self-verbalisation and self-reinforcement, cognitive rehearsal, coaching, coping techniques, etc. Four different formats of therapeutic intervention can be distinguished in the new therapy programmes: group therapy in the hospital (G-format); individual sessions (I-format); group activities that take place outside the confines of the treatment site (A-format); and homework assignments (H-format). The new programmes also include two addendums to IPT procedures. Individual sessions were added, as clinical experience has shown that schizophrenic patients generally have a great deal of trouble discussing personal problems in a problem-focused manner in a group setting. In addition, external group activities were included to improve transfer and generalisation of therapy effects ("in vivo" exercises, therapeutic activities) and to enhance group cohesion (motivational activities).

1.4.1. Pilot studies on the three new cognitive behavior therapy programmes (WAF)

Pilot studies on the therapy programmes for residential, vocational and recreational rehabilitation were started in the 1990s (Roder, 1993; Roder et al 1998). Because this marked the first clinical use of the programmes, the main objective of the pilot studies was to determine the clinical utility and appropriateness of these programmes. Consequently, evaluation was designed to clarify whether they fulfilled their purpose, i.e. whether the issues targeted in therapy were relevant to the patients' needs and were easy to understand. In addition, evaluation was performed to clarify whether the therapy programmes helped patients to gain greater confidence in their ability to handle the problem areas focused on in therapy (expectancy of competence) and to actually become more competent in coping with these tasks (appraisal of competence), and whether there were any concrete changes in their residential, vocational or recreational situation. Evaluation of therapy effects was undertaken using an A-B-A intragroup design with a one-month baseline, a two-month treatment phase and a one-month follow-up. In view of the questions to be addressed in this study, new rating scales, developed especially for this purpose were administered rather than standardised measures. These included the Questionnaire on Competence and Relevance (FKKR); Group Participation Form (BT); Group Content Form (BAB); and Scale on Interpersonal Functioning (BIG). A total of 22 patients presenting a schizophrenic disorder according to DSM-IV/ICD-10 criteria and a need for residential, vocational or recreational rehabilitation were selected for the study. Complete data sets were obtained for 18 participants (six patients for each therapy group).

The recreational group showed changes in the following variables: expectancy of competence, appraisal of competence, and relevance of the issues targeted. Five of the six patients participating in this programme rated their expectancy of competence higher at the end of therapy than at the beginning. On the other hand, they rated "relevance" of the issues targeted in therapy significantly higher at the beginning of therapy than at the end. This outcome is congruent with the objective of intervention: the more a problem is worked on, the better it can be handled, and the less cause for concern it is. Similar treatment effects were recorded in the residential and vocational therapy groups. In addition, the patients showed improved adjustments in the area of targeted community functioning. Half of the patients took up a hobby in the course of recreational therapy, which they continued to pursue at follow-up. Four of the six patients relocated during residential therapy or follow-up. Although four patients applied for new jobs, only one patient was actually hired in the course of vocational therapy programme. These results also seem to be important considering that none of the patients had had any concrete goals in the respective rehabilitation area prior to the onset of therapy.

In summary, the results from all three pilot studies show that the therapy programmes bear relevance to the patients' needs and assets, that they are easy to use, and that they encourage active participation in the therapy group. Similar positive results were obtained in the categories of expectancy and appraisal of competence. In spite of these positive outcomes, the therapy manuals seemed to warrant certain modifications. For example, alternatives varying in the level of complexity and difficulty for each therapy issue had to be developed so that personalised treatment plans could be devised for each patient and each therapy group. In addition, the experience gathered predominantly in the vocational and residential therapy programmes pointed to the importance of prolonging therapy to ensure a lasting change in the areas targeted. The three therapy programmes have been since revised to reflect the results obtained in the pilot studies.

1.4.2. Multicenter study on the three new cognitive behavior therapy programmes (WAF)

The objective of the ongoing multicenter study[2] is to evaluate the efficacy of the three new therapy programmes for residential, vocational and recreational rehabi-

---

[2] This project was supported by Grant No. 32-45577.95 Swiss National Science Foundation and by Stanley Thomas Johnson Foundation.

litation (WAF) using a larger sample of patients. Participants in the study were recruited from eight psychiatric institutions, all of which offer a comparable standard of care in the areas of psychopharmacotherapy, sociotherapy and work therapy (in Switzerland: University Psychiatric Services, Mid and West Sectors, Berne; Psychiatric University Hospital Zurich; Psychiatric Hospital Wil; Psychiatric Hospital Rheinau; Out-Patient Psychiatric Services Liestal; in Germany: Psychiatric Hospital Haar/Munich; Private Psychiatric Hospital Dr. med Kurt Fontheim Liebenburg; in Austria: Institute of Psychotherapy Vienna). The participants were selected according to the following criteria: (1) diagnosis of a schizophrenic or a schizoaffective disorder according to ICD-10 (World Health Organisation, 1993); (2) history of three or more previous hospitalisations; (3) age between 20 and 50 years; (4) average intelligence according to WIP (Dahl, 1986); (5) continuous deterioration in the following areas of psychosocial functioning over the preceding 24 months: housing, work, leisure, and social skills (GAF, DSM-IV, American Psychiatric Association 1994); (6) need for therapy and rehabilitation in housing, work, leisure, and social skills. Patients were excluded from the study if they showed evidence of excessive substance abuse or organic brain syndrome (double-diagnosis patients). The study follows an intergroup design and is aimed at the evaluation of treatment effects by using repeated measurements. The experimental groups receive one of the three new programmes (specific residential, vocational or recreational skills training), while the control group is offered non-specific social skills training according to IPT. Subjects were assigned to the different treatment groups according to rehabilitation necessities. Each group was offered a three-month treatment phase with two group sessions (90 minutes each) and one individual session (30 minutes) a week, followed by a three-month aftercare phase with one group session a week and one bi-weekly individual session. The follow-up intervals are one and two years after entry in the study. As depicted in Figure 1, assessment instruments were applied at four different intervals: before and after treatment (T1 and T2), at the end of the aftercare phase (T3), and after the first follow-up (T4). Additionally, for the

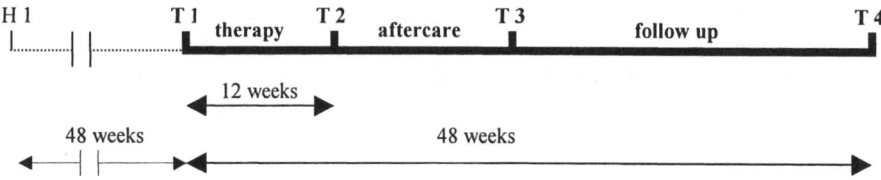

Figure 1. Multi-centre study: Points of assessment

experimental and the control group inpatient hospitalisations (number of days hospitalised) and relapses have been recorded during treatment and at both of the follow up-phases. Corresponding assessments were also carried out retrospectively for the two-year phase before treatment onset, based on patients' history. Therefore, hospitalisation rates of the subjects were recorded for a total period of approximately four years.

We hypothesise that better results will be achieved in the experimental groups (WAF) in regard to improved general social abilities and psychopathology. In addition, we expect better generalisation effects in the experimental groups in specific areas of social functioning such as housing, work and leisure. The new therapy programmes (WAF) and non-specific social skills-training are expected to be equally effective in the cognitive parameters.

The assessment instruments used in the study can be classified into measures of social functioning, psychopathology and cognitive abilities. Measures of social functioning include: Global Assessment of Functioning Scale, GAF (DSM-IV, American Psychiatric Association 1994, expert rating) to assess the general level of psychosocial functioning (psychological, social and vocational level of functioning, social behavior, social adjustment); Social Interview Schedule, SIS (Clare & Cairns 1978; Hecht et al, 1987: self-rating) to assess psychosocial adjustment and social behavior (areas: residential and job adjustment, economic situation, leisure and recreational behavior, contacts in- and outside the family). Assessment covers the following aspects for each area: real-life situations; satisfaction with different social roles; role performance; Disability Assessment Schedule, DAS (World Health Organisation, 1988: expert rating) to assess social impairment (residential, vocational and recreational adjustment, general social behavior). Intentionality Rating Scale, InSka, Subscales I, and V (Mundt et al, 1985: expert rating) to assess initiative, motivation, and general social behavior. Psychopathology was measured by the following instruments: Brief Psychiatric Rating Scale, BPRS (Overall & Gorham 1962; CIPS 1981: expert rating) to assess psychopathological symptoms; Scale for the Assessment of Negative Symptoms, SANS (Andreasen 1981: expert rating) to assess negative symptoms. Scale for the Assessment of Well-Being, BF-S (von Zerssen 1976: self-rating) to assess well-being as perceived by the patient. Cognitive abilities were evaluated by Number Connecting Test, ZVT (Oswald & Roth, 1978: test) to assess speed of cognitive performance; Continuous Concentration Test, KVT (Abels, 1974: test) to assess sustained concentration over a longer period of time; Attention-Stress Test, d2 (Brickenkamp, 1981: test) to assess discrimination task performance and speed of information processing. Motivation for participation in the group and motivational influences during therapy were measured by the Therapy Motivation Questionaire, FPTM (Schulz et al, 1995: self-rating). Furthermore, the Wisconsin Card Sorting Test, WCST was used with the aim of measuring and controlling the influence of individual learning capacity (concept formation, concept attainment, concept shift, perseverations) as a possible moderator variable. Data analysis was performed both on these measures and on the neuroleptic and anticholinergic medication prescribed in the course of the study. For reasons of comparability, medication doses were converted into chlor-promazine equivalents.

103 subjects participating in either a recreational or vocational group as well as 40 controls (IPT) have been included in data analysis. The following discussion of

the results is therefore based on a total sample of 112 subjects. Up to now not enough data is available for either the residential group or the follow-up measurements. A more detailed representation and discussion of the results will follow in other publications. Demographic and clinical characteristics are presented in Table 1.

Table 1. Overview of patient characteristics (n=143)

	Experimental groups (n = 103)		Control groups (n = 40)	
	Recreational (n = 44) M ± SD	Vocational (n = 29) M ± SD	Residential (n = 30) M ± SD	IPT (n = 40) M ± SD
Age	35.8 ± 7.7	33.3 ± 7.1	35.7 ± 9.1	31.2 ± 7.3
IQ (WIP)	102.5 ± 15.9	102.4 ± 10.8	99.8 ± 12.0	101.3 ± 8.7
Duration of hospitalisation (months)	19.5 ± 32.0	8.3 ± 10.3	17.3 ± 11.9	15.2 ± 17.9
Duration of illness (years)	9.5 ± 6.1	5.8 ± 3.9	7.1 ± 5.6	5.9 ± 5.4
Daily dose of neuroleptics (chlorpromazine values)	593.4 ± 776.4	241.1 ± 281.1	567.6 ± 474.8	345.8 ± 298.2
Psychopathology (BPRS/SANS, z-values)	0.05 ± 0.87	0.11 ± 0.86	0.13 ± 0.52	-0.24 ± 0.83
Motivation (FPTM, means)	2.76 0.30	2.79 ± 0.25	2.63 ± 0.25	2.60 ± 0.33

Data analysis covered four main steps: (1) Data reduction: By means of factor analysis, we empirically investigated the theoretical demarcation of three levels of deficits common in schizophrenia patients (i.e. psychopathology, cognitive and social deficits). We then exploratively combined the 16 corresponding dependent variables to factors. (2) Effect sizes: These were calculated for all factors as dependent variables in order to describe the course over the four measurement points. (3) Inferential statistics: For inferential statistics, the results of each of the 16 dependent variables distributed over the factors were transformed into standardised z-values, and the mean z-values were built for each factor. The course over the measurement points (T1 to T4) was analysed for significant main effects and interactions by two-tailled repeated measures ANOVAs. (4) Differential analysis of social skills acquisition: To obtain a more detailed picture of the changes in social functioning of each group, we analysed the items of the two dimensions "management/coping" and "satisfaction" of the Social Interview Shedule (SIS) by paired-samples T-tests. (5) Moderator variables: An assessment of the impact of potential moderator variables such as medication or therapy motivation on outcome was performed.

In the present data evaluation, improvements in social functioning were found for both non-specific social-skills training (IPT, control group), and for the newly developed specific social-skills training programmes (WAF, programmes: residential, vocational and recreational areas). Social functioning improved both during therapy and aftercare phase, so that six months after beginning treatment we obtained moderate to high effects for all groups on this level. Results indicate improvements in social interest and social integration primarily for patients in the recreational and IPT groups. Moreover, results indicate better social coping and social well-being for those patients who participated in an experimental group. Notable results were also obtained in the differential analysis of social behavior. These point to a generalisation to daily life of the improved social skills acquired in all treatment groups (WAF). In regard to psychopathology, patients participating in the newly developed specific social-skills training programmes (WAF) showed a significant reduction of negative symptoms. This symptom reduction could have been a supporting factor with regard to the obtained generalisation effects of these patients. For all three experimental groups we also found high treatment effects in the reduction of positive symptoms, for the treatment as well as the aftercare phase. The control group showed only a small reduction at the end of the aftercare phase. We assume that these positive effects in the experimental groups can be ascribed to the direct and focused way of dealing with specific goal-oriented issues highly relevant to daily life. Placing increased emphasis on such highly focused and relevant issues could serve to reduce symptoms. Furthermore, we found positive effects on the level of cognitive functioning. Attentional tests revealed small to medium improvements in all treatment groups (WAF and IPT) up to the end of the aftercare phase. However, our data also yielded qualitative differences between the control- and the experimental groups, mainly with regard to the comparison of IPT and the vocational group. For example, the control group improved markedly in speed, whereas the vocational group showed corresponding improvements in concentration. It may be assumed that enhanced concentration counteracts disorganized cognitive structures. However, a comparable benefit may not be assumed to derive from enhanced speed performance. These considerations could further elucidate the results obtained on the psychopathological level. Finally, significant results were obtained in regard to medication. The findings suggest that patients receiving atypical neuroleptics are better capable of maintaining concentration. This result accords with previous studies (e.g., Meltzer & McGurk, 1999), which indicate a favourable influence of atypical neuroleptic medi-cation on the cognitive level.

In summary, we found higher global treatment effects on all dependent variables for all experimental groups compared to the control group, and most especially for the treatment phase. Global treatment effects further increased during the aftercare phase in all groups. These results indicate that specific social-skills training in narrowly defined areas can more rapidly lead to improvements in social, cognitive and psychopathological parameters. The newly developed specific social-skills training programmes (WAF) may contribute valuable therapy formats to the more conventional forms of non-specific social-skills training. In specific areas of rehabilitation, such as residential, vocational and recreational, these new programmes could represent promising extensions within multimodal treatment approaches for schizophrenic patients.

Chapter C.2

Cognitive Changes in the Course of Psychiatric Rehabilitation

Will Spaulding, David Penn and Calvin Garbin

2.1 Introduction

This chapter addresses some of the particulars of using cognitive assessment techniques in psychiatric rehabilitation of schizophrenia and related disorders. The focus is on use of laboratory cognitive measures to understand patients' response to the rehabilitation milieu. Other chapters in this volume and elsewhere give a conceptual overview of clinically applied cognitive psychology, and provide theoretical and empirical evidence of the value of developing our technology for this purpose. This chapter describes intermediate steps in technological development, those which lie between conceptual formulation and construction of a comprehensive approach. In that sense, the work described here presumes the theoretical and empirical value of cognitive treatment of schizophrenia, and lays the foundation for a working technology.

The theoretical ideas and experimental findings which relate cognitive factors to assessment and treatment of schizophrenia have been promising and intellectually exhilarating. However, actual development of a technology, after the theoretical groundwork and initial empirical validation, becomes a gradual and sometimes even tedious working out of specific quantitative relationships between measures in various domains of interest. Developing a cognitive technology for treating schizophrenia has certainly been a gradual process, but it is not tedious. As quantitative relationships are clarified, theoretical assumptions are corroborated in some cases, and called into question in others. For the most part, the findings have been surprisingly congruent with expectations generated by theories of schizophrenic cognition. This ongoing relationship between psychopathological theory and development of the nascent applied technology lends excitement to what might otherwise be an uninteresting process of quantitative analysis.

2.2 Background of the Present Analyses

The analyses described here are part of a research program of over 12 years' duration, whose focus has been application of the principles and technologies of experimental psychopathology in clinical treatment and assessment. The main site for the research program is the Extended Care Unit (ECU), an inpatient psychiatric rehabilitation unit located in a public psychiatric hospital in Nebraska. The ECU is a referral unit which treats the most chronic, treatment resistance patients in the mental health system who do not need a high security environment. Schizophrenia is the overwhelmingly predominant diagnosis in this population, but due to the chronicity of the population and their history of nonresponse to conventional treatment, diagnosis is generally more equivocal than in other psychiatric populations. The average age of the population is about 31, with about 10 years elapsed since onset of the disorder. About 60% are male. As with other chronic schizophrenic populations, most patients have secondary substance abuse problems and/or personality disorders. For many of the patients, their most recent hospitalization was occasioned by a psychotic relapse. However, such patients spend 3 or more months in the hospital receiving unit before being referred to ECU. By this time they are judged to be optimally medicated and neurophysiologically stabilized. Thus, in contrast to most inpatient situations, the first several weeks on ECU is not dominated by recompensation following an acute psychotic episode. Patients come to the ECU either because their functioning while optimally medicated is still too poor to permit community living, or because their history of extreme recidivism indicates a need for rehabilitation.

The ECU's rehabilitation approach was first implemented in 1982, based primarily on a comprehensive model developed by Gordon Paul (Paul & Lentz, 1977). The model is generally characterized as a 'social learning' approach, emphasizing behavioral contingency management combined with training in interpersonal and daily living skills. Over the years the ECU has also incorporated technologies from other models, most notably the highly developed social skills training techniques produced by the UCLA Clinical Research Center for Schizophrenia (Liberman *et al*, 1986), and the Integrated Psychological Therapy for Schizophrenic Patients approach developed at the University of Berne, Switzerland (Brenner, 1987). Thus, the ECU provides ideal opportunities for study of patients undergoing rehabilitation that directly and indirectly addresses their cognitive functioning.

One of the first steps in the research program was to develop an assessment instrument appropriate for study of cognition in schizophrenia. A computer-administered test battery was constructed, called COGLAB and large-scale multivariate studies were conducted to determine the battery's psychometric properties in normal and patient populations (Spaulding *et al*, 1981, 1989a and 1989b). COGLAB consists of six tasks, all borrowed from the traditional psychopathology literature on schizophrenia: an 85-trial reaction time protocol similar to Steffy's 'embedded sets' task (Bellissimo & Steffy, 1972), a perceptual task based on the well-known Meuller-Lyer illusion, a size estimation task (Strauss *et al*, 1974), a backward-masking task (Saccuzzo & Miller, 1977), a combined vigilance and span of apprehension task (Asarnow & MacCrimmon, 1978), and a concept manipulation task similar to the Wisconsin Card Sorting Test (Wagman & Wagman, 1992). The entire battery can be administered in 50 to 60 minutes to all but the most severely dilapidated or noncompliant chronic schizophrenic patients. The various tasks and measures have been described in detail elsewhere (Spaulding *et al*, 1981; 1989a; 1989b), so descriptions here will be limited to those necessary for interpreting the results of the analyses.

Thirteen primary and derived measures of cognitive performance can be analyzed with COGLAB data. The initial analyses of its psychometric properties indicate it has a fairly differentiated factor structure in normals, which 'collapses' into a single factor in chronic schizophrenia patients (Spaulding et al, 1989a). This probably means that in these patients overall performance is pervasively influenced by a single general impairment factor. However, the single factor in patients only accounts for about 30% of the total variance across the battery. This means that there is considerable heterogeneity of performance within patients. In other words, patients have individually different performance profiles across the tasks in the battery, even

Table 1. Subscale item composition of the NOSIE-30.

Social Competence (COM)
11. Refuses to do ordinary things expected of him.
13. Has trouble remembering.
21. Has to be reminded what to do.
24. Has to be told to follow hospital routine.
25. Has difficulty completing simple tasks on his own.

Social Interest (INT)
4. Shows interest in activities around him.
9. Tries to be friendly with others.
15. Laughs or smiles at funny comments or events.
19. Talks about his interests.

Neatness (NEA)
1. Is sloppy.
8. Keeps his cloths neat.
16. Is messy in his sleeping habits.
30. Keeps himself clean.

Irritability (IRR)
2. Is impatient.
6. Gets angry or easily annoyed.
10. Becomes upset easily if something doesn't suit him.
12. Is irritable or grouchy.
29. Is quick to fly off the handle.

Psychoticism (PSY)
7. Hears things that are not there.
20. Sees things that are not there.
26. Talks, mutters or mumbles to himself.
28. Giggles or smiles to himself for no apparent reason.

Retardation (RET)
5. Sits, unless directed to activity.
22. Sleeps, unless directed to activity.
27. Is slow-moving or sluggish.

Unscored items
3. Cries.
14. Refuses to speak.
18. Says he feels blue or depressed.
23. Says he feels no good.

though there is also a weak-to-moderate dimension of impairment which pervades performance on most of the tasks.

Having established some of the properties of the cognitive assessment itself, the next step is to determine whether these properties have any relationship to important factors in other domains, such as symptomatology, personal and social functioning or response to rehabilitation interventions. The analyses reported here address the relationship between COGLAB performance and ambient social behavior in the rehabilitation milieu, as measured by the Nurses' Observational Scale for Inpatient Evaluation, 30-item version (NOSIE-30; Honigfeld et al, 1966).

The NOSIE-30 was developed in the 1960's and initially proved very useful in assessment of antipsychotic medication effects. It has since become a popular instrument for assessing a variety of psychiatric treatments. As its name implies, the NOSIE-30 is a behavioral checklist completed by one or more nursing personnel, based on direct observation of patients' behavior over a period of at least 72 hours.

The items are behavioral descriptors scored on a 5-point Likert type frequency scale, ranging from 'never' to 'always'. Scoring the NOSIE-30 items requires a minimal amount of inference from directly observable behavior. As a result, nursing personnel can be trained to acceptable levels of interrater reliability with a fairly modest investment of time and energy. Spot checks of the NOSIE-30 data reported here yielded interrater reliability figures ranging from $r = .68$ to $r = .72$.

The NOSIE-30 has six empirically-derived subscales and a composite Total Assets scale. Three of the subscales reflect behavioral assets, named Social Competence, Social Interest and Neatness. The other three reflect behavioral liabilities, named Irritability, Psychoticism and Psychomotor Retardation. The specific items associated with each subscale are listed in Table 1.

Routine collection of NOSIE-30 data on the ECU began at about the same time as routine collection of COGLAB data, in 1983. After 10 years, a large data archive had accumulated, making possible analysis of large numbers of carefully selected cases. For the purposes of this study, cases were selected for which there were two occasions of COGLAB assessment six months apart, with continuous treatment on the ECU and continuous NOSIE-30 assessment during the same period, and no unusual or cataclysmic events which disrupted rehabilitation during that period (e.g. severe psychotic relapse, elopement from the hospital or serious physical injury). This selection process resulted in a study cohort of 112 patients.

The date of the first COGLAB assessment is hereafter designated Time 1, the second Time 2. The NOSIE-30 scores for Time 1 and Time 2 are the average weekly NOSIE-30 scores for the month the COGLAB was administered; thus, the NOSIE-30 score used in the analysis is actually the average of four weekly scores.

In this study cohort, the beginning of a subject's six-month study period is generally within a month or so of actual transfer to the ECU, and in that sense reflects the 'beginning' of rehabilitation. However, due to the heterogeneity of the population, no two patients experience the same pace and sequence of treatment, either before or after their arrival at ECU. Also, some of the patients had been resident of ECU before 1982, when it had been a custodial ward with minimal treatment and no rehabilitation. Thus, for many cases it is problematic to determine exactly when rehabilitation really began, and in that sense the designation of Time 1 is somewhat arbitrary. Nevertheless, it is fair to say that between Time 1 and Time 2 there was invariably six months of intensive, individualized psychiatric treatment and rehabilitation in the ECU.

A series of questions was addressed in the data analyses: 1) What relationships exist between cognitive functioning measured by COGLAB and social behavior measured by NOSIE-30? 2) Do these relationships change over time and the course of 5 months' treatment? 3) What changes in social functioning reflect changes in cognitive functioning? 4) Does cognitive functioning predict anything about changes in social functioning over the next six months? To answer these questions, the data was analyzed in a series of multiple regression analyses. Multiple regression is a statistical technique wherein a group of measures can be assessed for their collective relationship to a criterion measure. The former measures are termed independent or predictor variables[1], and the latter is termed the criterion, dependent or target variable. In this study the predictor variables are COGLAB measures, and the target variables are the respective NOSIE-30 subscale and Total Assets scores.

Multiple regression solution using linear regression models (i.e. models wherein all expressions have an exponential value of 1) have the following general structure:

$$T = C + ß_1P_1 + ß_2P_2 + ß_3P_3... \text{ etc.},$$

Where T is a standardized value (i.e. a Z score) of the target variable, P_n are standardized values of the respective predictor values, C is a constant, and $ß$ ('beta') is a standardized coefficient that reflects the weight of its respective predictor variable in determining the value of T. The overall accuracy of the formula in predicting values of T can be expressed as a multiple regression coefficient, R. R is analogous to r, the bivariate correlation coefficient. As with bivariate correlations, R is the square root of the proportion of the target variable's variance accounted for by the predictor variables; thus $R = .30$ means that 9% of the total variance of T is accounted for by the set of predictor variables in the equation ($R^2 = 0.9$). For any R an F can be computed which indicates the probability that the observed R is really 0. This provides some assurance that a particular solution is not simply the result of chance relationships in the data.

Because multiple regression analytic procedures are designed to take advantage of all relationships in the data, whether chance or real, the R of a solution will be larger than the 'true' value of R by a mathematically predictable amount. The 'true' value can be computed and is usually expressed as adjusted R^2, a more accurate reflection of the association between the target variable and the predictor set.

There are several alternative approaches to multiple regression analysis, each designed for different purposes. The analyses in this study use two approaches, Full Model and Stepwise. A Full Model solution is designed to characterize the collective contributions of an entire set of predictors. The respective $ß$ coefficients can be thought of as analogous to factor loadings, expressing the association of each predictor variable to a single hypothetical factor that predicts the criterion. Each $ß$ is distributed according to an F distribution, so each can be assessed with respect to the probability that it is really 0. One way to interpret a Full Model solution is to

---

[1] Note that the terms "predictor" and "prediction" are used here in a special statistical sense, expressing a quantitative association between two or more variables, but not necessarily a causal relationship or a particular order over time. When "prediction" is used here to mean measures at one time predicting measures at a later time, the term "prognostic" will also be used.

characterize the nature of the single hypothetical factor by observing which predictor variables are most closely associated with it.

The purpose of a Stepwise solution is to identify the most efficient combination of predictors necessary to predict the target. The aim is not to characterize an underlying hypothetical factor, but to determine which predictor variables best capture it. This is done by incrementally adding (step forward) or subtracting (step backward) variables to or from the predictor set, and evaluating at each step whether the change has improved the solution's predictive accuracy. A Stepwise solution reveals less than a Full Model solution about the nature of underlying factors, but reveals more about whether a prediction involves more than one source of variance among the predictor set.

In this study, Full Model solutions are presented along with Stepwise solutions, because each contributes to interpreting relationships among cognitive and behavioral measures. This applies to one particularly important issue which pervades experimental psychopathology, the question of global vs. specific cognitive impairments. It is extremely difficult to establish that the plethora of cognitive impairments observed in schizophrenia are really separate deficits, rather than the result of a single global cognitive impairment pervasively affecting performance (Knight, 1984). Even when there appear to be significant quantitative differences in the severity of different deficits, this could be due to the different psychometric properties of the measures involved. This problem applies to the relationship between cognitive and behavioral expressions of the disorder as well. Joint examination of Full Model and Stepwise regression solutions can help resolve the question of whether cognitive effects on behavior are due to a single pervasive cognitive impairment, or to the combined operation of processes which are meaningfully separate from each other.

All the following analyses began with computation of the bivariate correlations between 13 COGLAB measures and the NOSIE-30 Total Assets scale and the six subscales. Only those COGLAB measures showing a significant bivariate relationship with the respective NOSIE-30 scale were used in the subsequent multiple regression analyses. In all cases, the sign of the correlation coefficient and the ß coefficient is positive for intuitively congruent relationships and negative for counterintuitive relationships. In other words, a positive correlation and ß indicate good or improving cognitive performance related to good or improving social behavior, and a negative sign indicates good or improving cognitive performance related to poor or deteriorating social behavior.

2.3 Relationships Between Cognitive and Social-Behavioral Functioning

In the first set of analyses, the cross-sectional relationship between COGLAB and NOSIE-30 measures at Time 1 (N=112) were evaluated, with Time 1 COGLAB measures in the predictor set and each Time 1 NOSIE-30 scale in turn as the target variable. The results of the Full Model and Stepwise multiple regression analyses are summarized in Table 2. In the Full Model solution, the NOSIE-30 Total Assets scale was predicted at a statistically significant level by 5 COGLAB measures,

Table 2. Cross-sectional relationships of NOSIE scores with COGLAB measures at Time 1.

Full Model				Stepwise			
1. NOSIE Social Competence (COM)							
R = .47	$R^2 = .22$		AdjR² = .16	R = .39	$R^2 = .15$		AdjR² = .14
F = 3.78			p < .002	F = 15.15			p < .0002
var	r	beta	F of Beta	var	r	beta	F of Beta
RT trials > 1 sec	.27	.27	.073	RT Avg	.39	.391	15.15***
Vig Fls Alarms	.29	.29	.190				
Masking funct	.23	.23	.050				
RT anticip err	.26	.26	.154				
Vig Hits	.24	.24	.083				
RT Avg	.39	.39	.196				
2. NOSIE Social Interest (INT)							
R = .16	$R^2 = .03$		AdjR² = .02				
F = 2.98			NS	(no variables entered)			
var	r	beta	F of Beta				
Sorting 3rd mod	.16	.165	2.98				
3. NOSIE Neatness (NEA)							
R = ..53	$R^2 = .30$		AdjR² = .19	R = .48	$R^2 = .23$		AdjR² = .21
F = 3.27			p < .002	F = 12.56			p < .0001
var	r	beta	F of Beta	var	r	beta	F of Beta
Sorting Tot err	.20	.188	.63	RT Avg	.43	.368	13.46***
RT anticip err	.21	.086	.41	Vig Fls Alarms	.33	.223	4.95*
Vig Fls Alarms	.33	.256	5.55*				
Vig Hits	.21	.011	.01				
RT trials > 1 sec	.33	.162	1.53				
Masking Tot	.19	.055	.23				
Masking funct	.22	.030	.07				
RT Avg	.43	.213	1.98				
Sorting rndm err	.21	-.021	.01				
4. NOSIE Irritability (IRR)							
R = .38	$R^2 = .14$		AdjR² = .12	R = .33	$R^2 = .11$		AdjR² = .10
F = 5.35			p < .0019	F = 11.8			p < .0009
var	r	beta	F of Beta	var	r	beta	F of Beta
RT trials > 1 sec	.33	.229	3.54	RT trials > 1 sec	.33	.329	11.80***
Vig Hits	.22	.139	1.86				
RT Avg	.31	.121	.89				
5. NOSIE Psychoticism (PSY)							
R = .54	$R^2 = .29$		AdjR² = .25	R = .49	$R^2 = .25$		AdjR² = .24
F = 7.58			p < .0001	F = 31.60			p < .0001
var	r	beta	F of Beta	var	r	beta	F of Beta
Sorting 3rd mod	-.20	-.117	1.72	RT trials > 1 sec	.50	.50	31.60***
RT Crossover	-.21	-.092	1.02				
Vig Hits	.21	.078	.70				
RT trials > 1 sec	.50	.375	10.56***				
RT Avg	.41	.110	.36				
6. NOSIE Motor Retardation (RET)							
R = .35	$R^2 = .12$		AdjR² = .09	R = .29	$R^2 = .09$		AdjR² = .07
F = 3.35			p < .013	F = 4.77			p < .011
var	r	beta	F of Beta	var	r	beta	F of Beta
Sorting 3rd mod	.18	.244	6.14**	RT Avg	.20	.24	5.97**
RT Anticip err	.18	.135	1.79	Sorting 3rd mod	.18	.23	5.43*
Vig Hits	.18	.148	2.04				
RT Avg	.20	.149	1.85				
7. NOSIE Total Assets (TOT)							
R = .47	$R^2 = .22$		AdjR² = .17	R = .41	$R^2 = .17$		AdjR² = .16
F = 5.14			p < .0003	F = 19.80			p < .0001
var	r	beta	F of Beta	var	r	beta	F of Beta
RT trials > 1 sec	.33	.136	1.31	RT Avg	.41	.412	19.80***
Vig Fls Alarms	.24	.132	1.85				
RT Anticip err	.19	.072	.55				
Vig Hits	.27	.134	1.82				
RT Avg	.41	.218	2.79				

which accounted for 17% (adjusted $R^2 = .17$) of the target variable's variance. The Stepwise solution indicates only a very slight reduction in accuracy (1% of the target variance) for an equation that includes only a single measure, Reaction Time average latency (RT Avg.). Inspection of the Full Model predictor set reveals that three are also Reaction Time measures, and two are measures of relatively molecular cognitive functions derived from the COGLAB vigilance/span task. Reaction time trials exceeding one second (RT trials > 1 sec) is the number of trials for which latency was greater than 1 second, indicating a gross lapse of attention to the task. Anticipatory errors (RT Anticip err) is the number of times the subjects responded (or inadvertently lifted their finger) before the imperative signal. False alarms in the vigilance/span of apprehension task (Vig Fls alarms) is the total errors of commission, and hits on that task (Vig hits) is the total correct responses. This pattern of results suggests that there is a single cognitive factor, representing molecular attentional processes which operate within a 1 second time frame, which is associated with patients' overall social and behavioral functioning. All the predictive relationships are in the expected direction, i.e. poorer cognitive performance predicting poorer NOSIE-30 Total Assets.

The results of the NOSIE-30 subscale analyses do little to modify this conclusion. The Social Competence Full Model solution is almost identical to the Total Assets solution, with the addition of the backward masking effect (Masking funct.). The Stepwise solution shows a comparable reduction to a single variable, RT Avg. Prediction of Social Interest does not reach statistical significance, indicated by the low overall **F**. The Neatness subscale shows several additional bivariate correlations, including total errors on the sorting task (Sorting Tot err), the total masking score (Masking Tot) and random errors on the sorting task (Sorting rndm err), and the Stepwise solution identifies two separate sources of predictive variance, RT avg and Vig Fls alarms. Interestingly, in the Full Model Sorting rndm err shows a positive bivariate correlation but a negative ß weight in the formula. This pattern is characteristic of a moderator effect, i.e. the entire formula's predictive characteristics are different at different values of the moderating variable. However, without statistically significant ß weights this cannot be confidently inferred.

The Psychomotor Retardation subscale shows two sources of variance, RT Avg and errors on the third modulation of the sorting Task (Sorting 3rd mod err). The latter measure reflects a distinctively moderate level of *impairment* on the sorting task; that is, patients who are severely impaired or not impaired at all score low on this measure. A high score indicates that the patient is in a mid-range of impairment, possibly due to a different type of impairment in the cognitive processes which support task performance (this is discussed in more detail later in this chapter). The solutions for the other two subscales are very similar to those for Social Competence and Total Assets, except that RT trials > 1 sec captures the preponderance of predictive variance, instead of RT Avg. Given the similarity between these measures, the differences between the Stepwise solutions is probably due to chance fluctuations in the bivariate correlations.

To summarize these parts of the analyses, there is a single attentional factor which affects several COGLAB performance measures, which is measured best by simple reaction time measures, and which is related in turn to overall social functioning in the rehabilitation milieu. In addition, the cognitive functions associated with high false alarms in a vigilance task may contribute a separate component to

Table 3. Cross-sectional relationships of NOSIE scores with COGLAB measures at Time 2.

Full Model				Stepwise			
1. NOSIE Social Competence (COM)							
$R = .66$		$R^2 = .43$	$AdjR^2 = .36$	$R = .63$		$R^2 = .40$	$AdjR^2 = .37$
$F = 6.04$		$p < .0001$		$F = 15.09$		$p < .0001$	
var	r	beta	F of Beta	var	r	beta	F of Beta
Sorting Random err	.25	.080	.48	RT trials > 1 sec	.53	.372	10.41***
RT Crossover	.26	.282	8.50***	RT Crossover	.26	.274	8.51***
Masking funct	.28	.125	1.25	RT Avg	.48	.272	5.60**
RT trials > 1 sec	.53	.433	11.25***				
Masking Tot	.19	.100	.81				
Vig Fls Alarms	.30	.121	1.28				
Vig Hits	.25	.102	.73				
RT Avg	.48	.173	1.48				
2. NOSIE Social Interest (INT)							
$R = .24$		$R^2 = .06$	$AdjR^2 = .04$	$R = .24$		$R^2 = .06$	$AdjR^2 = .04$
$F = 4.59$		$p < .035$		$F = 4.59$		$p < .035$	
var	r	beta	F of Beta	var	r	beta	F of Beta
Size estimation	.24	.236	4.59*	Size estimation	.24	.236	4.59*
3. NOSIE Neatness (NEA)							
$R = .58$		$R^2 = .34$	$AdjR^2 = .28$	$R = .48$		$R^2 = .23$	$AdjR^2 = .21$
$F = 5.97$		$p < .0001$		$F = 12.56$		$p < .0001$	
var	r	beta	F of Beta	var	r	beta	F of Beta
Sorting Random err	.37	.302	6.65**	RT trials > 1 sec	.44	.38	13.74***
Sorting 3rd mod	-.20	-.108	1.05	Sorting Tot err	.37	.29	8.13***
RT trials > 1 sec	.44	.376	8.32***				
Vig Fls Alarms	.37	.208	3.67				
Vig Hits	.20	.140	1.19				
RT Avg	.38	.014	.01				
4. NOSIE Irritability (IRR)							
$R = .34$		$R^2 = .10$	$AdjR^2 = .08$	$R = .24$		$R^2 = .06$	$AdjR^2 = .05$
$F = 4.24$		$p < .018$		$F = 6.67$		$p < .034$	
var	r	beta	F of Beta	var	r	beta	F of Beta
RT Crossover	.21	.212	3.64	RT trials > 1 sec	.24	.244	6.67*
RT trials > 1 sec	.24	.247	4.95*				
5. NOSIE Psychoticism (PSY)							
$R = .58$		$R^2 = .34$	$AdjR^2 = .30$	$R = .56$		$R^2 = .31$	$AdjR^2 = .29$
$F = 9.20$		$p < .0001$		$F = 16.51$		$p < .0001$	
var	r	beta	F of Beta	var	r	beta	F of Beta
Sorting Random err	.34	.263	6.11**	RT trials > 1 sec	.50	.452	20.74***
Mueller Lyer	.19	.167	3.00	Sorting Random err	.34	.247	6.22**
RT trials > 1 sec	.50	.469	15.63***				
RT Avg	.33	-.048	.14				
6. NOSIE Motor Retardation (RET)							
$R = .38$		$R^2 = .14$	$AdjR^2 = .10$	$R = .28$		$R^2 = .08$	$AdjR^2 = .07$
$F = 3.00$		$p < .024$		$F = 6.72$		$p < .012$	
var	r	beta	F of Beta	var	r	beta	F of Beta
Sorting Tot err	.22	.114	.98	Masking Tot	.29	.288	6.72**
Vig Hits	.25	.117	.93				
Masking Tot	.29	.177	2.14				
RT Avg	.27	.142	1.32				
7. NOSIE Total Assets (TOT)							
$R = .53$		$R^2 = .28$	$AdjR^2 = .22$	$R = .48$		$R^2 = .23$	$AdjR^2 = .21$
$F = 4.51$		$p < .0006$		$F = 10.76$		$p < .0001$	
var	r	beta	F of Beta	var	r	beta	F of Beta
Sorting Random err	.26	.126	1.08	RT trials > 1 sec	.42	.427	17.25***
RT Crossover	.22	.219	4.55*	RT Crossover	.22	.217	4.49*
RT trials > 1 sec	.42	.329	5.92**				
Vig Fls Alarms	.21	.120	1.14				
RT Avg	.38	.132	.92				

prediction of dishevelment and poor grooming, and factors associated with a moderate level of concept manipulation impairment may be associated with lethargy and withdrawal. The strength of these relationships is weak to moderate, with variance in cognitive functioning accounting for 7% to 24% of the variance in social behavior.

2.3.1   Do the relationships change over time?

Table 3 summarizes the results of multiple regression analyses identical to those in Table 2, except that the predictor and target variables are measures collected at Time 2 instead of Time 1 (i.e. after 6 months of treatment and rehabilitation). The most evident difference between the Time 1 and Time 2 analyses is the larger adjusted R^2 values at Time 2 for COGLAB prediction of 3 NOSIE-30 scales. The R^2 for Total Assets increases from 16% to 21%, for Social Competence it increases from 14% to 36%, and for Psychoticism it increases from 24% to 29%. A weak relationship appears between Social Interest and COGLAB Size Estimation where there was none at Time 1. Prediction of Neatness and Psychomotor Retardation remains the same, and prediction of Irritability decreases from 10% to 5%. These remarkable changes strongly suggest that at least some of the relationships between cognitive and social-behavioral functioning are stronger after six months of treatment and rehabilitation. There could be several factors responsible for this phenomenon. One possibility is that despite lengthy periods of restabilization before patients come to the ECU, some nevertheless arrive in a lingering acute psychotic state which dissipates over the next six months. If it can be assumed that a psychotic process generally obfuscates the relationships between cognitive functioning and behavior, this could suppress measured correlations at Time 1. However, previous findings about COGLAB changes over the course of psychotic recompensation are inconsistent with this hypothesis (Penn et al, 1993). The COGLAB measures mostassociated with recompensation are those derived from the concept manipulation task. Measures associated with molecular attentional functioning in general and reaction time in particular show little or no change as patients recover from acute relapse. This is the opposite of the overall picture produced by the present analyses.

Another possibility concerns the interaction of cognitive functioning with the social expectations patients experience in a rehabilitation milieu. When patients first enter the milieu they encounter expectations to follow a daily personal schedule (however simple it may be initially), attend various skill training sessions and participate in structured activities. Most patients find this difficult at first, especially if they have experience with more conventional institutional care programs which place minimal demands on patients. Over time, some patients adjust to the structure of rehabilitation better than others. It may be that this variance is expressed in the NOSIE-30 at Time 2, especially in the Social Competence subscale. The fact that Social Competence shows the most increase in R^2 from Time 1 to Time 2 would corroborate this view.

It is also noteworthy that the Stepwise analyses at Time 2 show a more differentiated predictive set, with RT Avg, RT trials > 1 sec and RT Crossover each contributing unique components to the prediction of Social Competence. This is reminiscent of the finding that normals have a more differentiated COGLAB factor structure than schizophrenic subjects. It is possible that at Time 2, when Social Competence is generally more reflective of cognitive functioning, subtle differences between discrete attentional impairments can be detected which are obscured at Time 1.

The effects of time in the milieu may also explain the COGLAB prediction of NOSIE-30 Neatness. The Stepwise solution reveals that part of the prediction is contributed by RT trials > 1 sec, presumably for the same reason that measure predicts Social Competence. Expectations in a rehabilitation milieu include appropriate hygiene, grooming and dress. However, sorting task performance also contributes significantly to this prediction. Inasmuch as concept manipulation is thought to be associated with acute psychosis, this may mean that personal dishevelment is an indication of subtle persisting psychosis, less evident in a patient's ability to conform to a daily schedule and meet related expectations. This is further corroborated by the finding that at Time 2 the sorting task also contributes significantly to prediction of NOSIE-30 Psychoticism.

To summarize these parts of the analyses, the relationships between cognitive and social-behavioral functioning are more evident after six months in a rehabilitation milieu. This is partly due to the effects of residual psychosis, expressed in the relationships between conceptual manipulation impairment, personal dishevelment and observable psychotic behavior. A stronger effect is attributable to the relationship between lingering attentional impairments and patients' ability to respond to the structure and expectations of the psychiatric rehabilitation approach. It would thus appear that molecular attentional impairments, which tend not to come and go with psychotic episodes, represent obstacles to achieving the purposes of rehabilitation. This conclusion is corroborated by other studies which more specifically address the effects of molecular attentional impairments on performance in social skills training (Kern & Green, 1994; Bowen, 1988).

2.3.2 What changes in cognition reflect changes in social functioning?

Analysis of changes introduces a new statistical complication. For many biological and psychological measures, the significance of any change over time is powerfully mediated by the overall elevation of the initial measurement. For example, a change of temperature in a system from 20° to 25° may not mean the same as a change of 100° to 105°, even though the change is 5° in both cases. Similarly, the meaning of a given absolute change in a NOSIE-30 or COGLAB score may be dependent on the initial value of that score. In a multiple regression approach this can be taken into account by strategically partialling variance associated with initial values effects. First, a change score is computed, the simple arithmetic difference between a Time 1 and Time 2 score. The change score is designated the target variable. Then the initial (Time 1) value of the target variable can be forced into the predictive solution, as the first step of a Stepwise analysis. Predictor variables which subsequently enter the solution then are predicting the change score after the initial values effect has been taken into account. An alternative method is to create a residualized change of score, by computing a separate regression formula wherein the change score is predicted by the initial value. The residual, or variance remaining after prediction, is the amount of the change score not attributable to the initial value effect, and this is used to adjust the change score to the residualized change score. The results produced by the residualized change score method are somewhat easier to describe, because the resulting formula does not include the extra variable of the target's initial value. Therefore, that method will be reported hereafter. All the analyses using change scores presented here were performed with both methods, and the results proved substantially the same.

Table 4 summarizes the results of predicting residualized NOSIE-30 change scores with residualized COGLAB change scores. The solutions show what changes

Table 4. Relationship of residualized NOSIE subscale change scores with residualized COGLAB change scores (all initial values effects removed).

	Full Model				Stepwise		
1. NOSIE Social Competence (COM)							
$R = .44$		$R^2 = .19$	$AdjR^2 = .13$	$R = .40$		$R^2 = .16$	$AdjR^2 = .13$
$F = 2.93$			$p < .020$	$F = 6.14$			$p < .004$
var	r	beta	F of Beta	var	r	beta	F of Beta
RT trials > 1 sec	.24	.123	.94	Masking Tot	.29	.280	6.06***
Masking Tot	.29	.230	3.58	Vig Fls Alarms	.28	.276	5.88**
Vig Hits	.22	.079	.30				
Vig Fls Alarms	.28	.231	3.59				
SAT	.22	.060	.16				
2. NOSIE Social Interest (INT)							
$R = .42$		$R^2 = .17$	$AdjR^2 = .12$	$R = .28$		$R^2 = .08$	$AdjR^2 = .06$
$F = 2.95$			$p < .028$	$F = 4.83$			$p < .032$
var	r	beta	F of Beta	var	r	beta	F of Beta
Vig Fls Alarms	.25	.188	2.22	Masking Tot	.28	.275	4.83*
Masking Tot	.28	.227	2.76				
RT Avg	.27	.189	2.24				
Masking funct	.23	.067	.24				
3. NOSIE Neatness (NEA)							
$R = .42$		$R^2 = .17$	$AdjR^2 = .15$	$R = .42$		$R^2 = .17$	$AdjR^2 = 15$
$F = 4.19$			$p < .0013$	$F = 7.30$			$p < .0013$
var	r	beta	F of Beta	var	r	beta	F of Beta
Sorting rndm err	.28	.232	4.45*	Vig Fls Alarms	.35	.307	7.76**
Vig Fls Alarms	.35	.307	7.76**	Sorting rndm err	.28	.232	4.45**
4. NOSIE Irritability (IRR)							
$R = .42$		$R^2 = .17$	$AdjR^2 = .15$				
$F = 0.62$			NS		(no variables entered)		
5. NOSIE Psychoticism (PSY)							
$R = .25$		$R^2 = .06$	$AdjR^2 = .05$	$R = .25$		$R^2 = .06$	$AdjR^2 = .05$
$F = 4.84$			$p < .031$	$F = 4.84$			$p < .031$
var	r	beta	F of Beta	var	r	beta	F of Beta
Mueller Lyer	.25	.251	4.84*	Mueler Lyer	.25	.251	4.84*
6. NOSIE Motor Retardation (RET)							
$R = .44$		$R^2 = .20$	$AdjR^2 = .19$	$R = .28$		$R^2 = .08$	$AdjR^2 = .07$
$F = 5.44$			$p < .002$	$F = 5.96$			$p < .017$
var	r	beta	F of Beta	var	r	beta	F of Beta
RT distractn	-.24	-.276	5.88**	Masking Tot	.28	.282	5.97**
Masking Tot	.28	.243	4.86*				
RT trials > 1 sec	.24	.262	5.50*				
7. NOSIE Total Assets (TOT)							
$R = .42$		$R^2 = .18$	$AdjR^2 = .11$	$R = .32$		$R^2 = .10$	$AdjR^2 = .09$
$F = 2.65$			$p < .031$	$F = 7.27$			$p < .009$
var	r	beta	F of Beta	var	r	beta	F of Beta
RT trials > 1 sec	.22	.091	.50	Vig Fls Alarms	.32	.320	7.27***
Masking Tot	.22	.172	2.05				
Vig Hits	.21	.116	.92				
Vig Fls Alarms	.32	.254	4.28*				
RT Avg	.19	.066	.27				

in cognitive functioning accompany changes in social-behavioral functioning, after initial values effects of both NOSIE-30 and COGLAB scores have been removed.

The Full Model solutions are similar to the previous solutions for cross-sectional relationships, especially for predicting Social Competence, Psychomotor Retardation and Total Assets. However, the Stepwise solutions suggest that the central source of predictive variance has shifted away from the reaction time measures, to include backward masking and vigilance/span of apprehension performance. Backward masking measures cognitive processing at the pre-attentional level. There is some previous evidence that backward masking performance improves in response to antipsychotic medication (Braff & Saccuzzo, 1982). The present data corroborate that finding, but also suggest that the effect is associated with overall functional improvement in a longer time frame. Also inasmuch as there is no evident relationship between changes in masking and Psychoticism, the medication effect on masking would appear to be more associated with recovery of normal functioning than with suppression of psychotic symptoms.

The involvement of the vigilance false alarms score in several of the solutions is an especially interesting result. It suggests that changes in patients' response biasing characteristics are more closely associated with social-behavioral change than are changes in attentional functioning. Response biasing is a type of cognitive strategy whereby subjects adjust the probability of a missed detection vs. a false alarm, according to task demands and their own perceptual acuity, to achieve an optimal level of performance. It is not strictly an attentional process, but one which operates in conjunction with perceptual and attentional processes. When a subject's false alarm rate decreases without an attendant decrease in correct detection's, it may mean the subject is no longer attempting to compensate for suboptimal perceptual or attentional functioning. Thus, social-behavioral improvement appears to be associated with a decreased need to compensate for perceptual or attentional deficits, at least as perceived by the patient. Some attentional changes are occurring in association with social-behavioral improvement, as evidenced by inclusion of the vigilance, span of apprehension and reaction time measure in the Full Model solutions. However, it would appear that the subjects' biasing response to their own attentional improvements is a better measure than the attentional measures themselves.

Concept manipulation performance is again associated with changes in NOSIE-30 Neatness. If, as previously discussed, Neatness is the best measure of lingering psychosis, this further corroborates the previous finding that concept manipulation performance is especially sensitive to changes in psychotic status. It is unclear why Psychoticism is not also associated with concept manipulation, as it is in the cross-sectional analyses. It is possible that in this population Psychoticism is more reflective of a stable, socialized behavior pattern, while Neatness is more associated with fluctuating mental status. Patients with chronically impaired concept manipulation may be more likely to develop socialized psychotic behavior, or more likely to express psychotic symptoms in their social behavior (hence the cross-sectional relationship), and less likely to show changes in either concept manipulation or symptomatic behavior over time (hence the lack of a longitudinal relationship).

The appearance of the Meuller-Lyer illusion measure in predicting changes in Psychoticism is somewhat puzzling. It appeared in the cross-sectional Full Model prediction of Psychoticism at Time 2. Possibly there is some aspect of Meuller-Lyer performance which is associated with a fluctuating proclivity to express psychotic symptoms. However, the R^2 is rather small, and may be a statistical artefact.

To summarize these parts of the analyses, improvement in social-behavioral functioning is associated with improvements in cognitive functioning. The cognitive improvements involve a number of preattentional, attentional, response biasing and concept manipulation processes. Improvements in following a daily routine, sociability, personal hygiene and grooming, and behavioral activation are most closely associated with improvements in preattentional functioning and reduced compensation for attentional impairments. In addition, improvements in concept manipulation are associated with improved grooming and hygiene, probably indicative of improvement in a lingering psychotic state.

2.3.3 Do cognitive measures predict changes in social-behavioral functioning?

Despite the smaller relationships between cognitive and social-behavioral functioning at Time 1, it is possible that cognitive functioning at Time 1 has important prognostic implications for patients' subsequent response to the rehabilitation milieu. This is especially true if, as previously discussed measures of social-behavioral functioning at Time 2 are more meaningful than at Time 1. Table 5 summarizes the results of analyses in which NOSIE-30 changes are prognostically predicted by COGLAB scores at Time 1. To control for NOSIE-30 initial values effects, the target variables are residualized change scores. The most evident result is that the R^2 values are all rather small, and in most cases the direction of prediction is counterintuitive. Improvement in Social Competence, Psychomotor Retardation and Total Assets is predicted by a poorer score on the third modulation of the concept manipulation task (Sorting 3rd mod), and improvement in Psychomotor Retardation is also predicted by more false alarms on the vigilance/span of apprehension task. While superficially counterintuitive, these relationships are quite interpretable, but this requires more extensive description of the concept manipulation task.

The subject is presented with four sorting bins, each labeled by figures representing a combination of three sorting criteria, one red square, two green triangles, three yellow circles and four blue diamonds. The subject is dealt one card at a time, which must be sorted according to one of the criteria. Feedback is given for every trial according to whether the sort is correct or incorrect. The subject must determine through trial and error the correct criterion and sort accordingly. For example, if the criterion is color and the dealt card is two blue circles, the correct sort is to the bin labeled with four blue diamonds. After five correct sorts the criterion 'modulates', or changes to a new criterion. The subject must apprehend that the criterion has changed, and once again use trial and error to determine the new correct one. There are five modulations in the entire task.

The sorting task measures which figured in the previous analyses, total errors and random errors, reflect the subject's conceptual understanding of the task and ability to learn and remember the correct concept. The Sorting 3rd mod score is the number of errors made on the third criterion modulation of the task, compared to the other four modulations. More errors are typically made on this modulation, in patients and normal subjects, because it requires apprehension of the third concept, color, relatively late in the task. Some patients who otherwise perform within normal limits on the task have such difficulty on the third modulation that it

Table 5. Prediction of residualized NOSIE change scores at Time 2 by COGLAB scores at Time 1 (NOSIE initial values effects removed).

Full Model				Stepwise			
1. NOSIE Social Competence (COM)							
R = .27	R² = .07		AdjR² = .05	R = .21	R² = .05		AdjR² = .04
F = 3.84			p < .025	F = 4.57			p < .035
var	r	beta	F of Beta	var	r	beta	F of Beta
Sorting 3rd mod	-.21	-.178	3.18	Sorting 3rd mod	-.21	-.212	4.57*
RT Avg	.21	.174	3.01				
2. NOSIE Social Interest (INT)							
R = .38	R² = .15		AdjR² = .12	R = .34	R² = .12		AdjR² = .10
F = 5.49			p < .002	F = 6.34			p < .0003
var	r	beta	F of Beta	var	r	beta	F of Beta
Sorting 3rd mod	-.19	-.206	4.70*	Size estimation	-.27	-.288	8.93***
RT Crossover	-.19	-.176	3.47	Sorting 3rd mod	-.19	-.214	4.93*
Size estimation	-.27	-.287	9.10***				
3. NOSIE Neatness (NEA)							
R = .29	R² = .08		AdjR² = 0				
F = .41			NS	(no variables entered)			
4. NOSIE Irritability (IRR							
R = .30	R² = .09		AdjR² = 0				
F = .46			NS	(no variables entered)			
5. NOSIE Psychoticism (PSY)							
R = .26	R² = .07		AdjR² = .05				
F = 3.41			p < .037	(no variables entered)			
var	r	beta	F of Beta				
RT Crossover	.18	.179	3.32				
RT Anticip err	.18	.187	3.60				
6. NOSIE Motor Retardation (RET)							
R = .29	R² = .08		AdjR² = .06	R = .29	R² = .08		AdjR² = .06
F = 4.33			p < .016	F = 4.32			p < .016
var	r	beta	F of Beta	var	r	beta	F of Beta
Sorting 3rd mod	-.20	-.203	4.32*	Vig Fls Alarms	-.20	-.211	4.64*
Vig Fls Alarms	-.20	-.211	4.64*	Sorting 3rd mod	-.20	-.203	4.31*
7. NOSIE Total Assets (TOT)							
R = .22	R² = .05		AdjR² = .04	R = .22	R² = .05		AdjR² = .04
F = 4.93			p < .029	F = 4.93			p < .029
var	r	beta	F of Beta	var	r	beta	F of Beta
Sorting 3rd mod	-.22	-.219	4.93*	Sorting 3rd mod	-.22	-.219	4.93*

distinguishes their performance from normal. Patients who perform normally on the task show only a slight elevation in 3rd mod errors. Patients who are grossly impaired show no elevation in 3rd mod errors, because their error rate on the other modulations is so high. A high 3rd mod score, thus, reflects a moderate degree of impairment on the task, and this is what predicts improvement on the NOSIE-30 scales. Patients with no impairment at Time 1 are less likely to show NOSIE-30 improvement, and patients with severe impairment at Time 1 are less likely to show NOSIE-30 improvement.

The sorting task appears to be predicting something different in this analysis, compared to what it was predicting in the previous analyses. The evidence in the previous analyses converged on a relationship between total or random errors, NOSIE-30 Neatness and a lingering psychotic state. The 3rd mod score predicts changes in other aspects of social behavior, mostly engagement in rehabilitation activities and management of a personal daily routine. This may mean that patients who have severe impairments in concept manipulation at Time 1 are expressing either a temporary psychosis-linked deficit, or a chronic, stable cognitive impairment. Patients whose impairment is psychosis-linked show an improvement in sorting task performance as the psychosis remits, and when they do, it is correlated with improvement in Neatness. However, because of the heterogeneity of the patients severely impaired at Time 1, severe impairment at Time 1 does not have overall prognostic value. Moderate impairment does have prognostic value, but not for measures associated with lingering psychosis. Patients with moderate impairment at Time 1 show more improvement in the other NOSIE-30 scales by Time 2 than patients with severe impairment at Time 1, because a moderate impairment is less of an obstacle than either a psychosis-linked or chronic severe impairment. It remains unclear, however, why patients with moderate concept manipulation impairment would improve more than patients with little or no impairment.

An additional clue is provided by the superficially counterintuitive relationship between vigilance false alarms and NOSIE-30 Psychomotor Retardation. If a high false alarm rate indicates an attempt to compensate for other cognitive impairments, it may be that this measure, together with the 3rd mod score, is identifying patients who have a psychosis-linked concept manipulation deficit which has nearly returned to baseline. Having become aware of their lingering impairments, they are showing evidence of compensatory efforts. This would be less likely to be observed in patients with more chronic severe concept manipulation deficits, because those patients would be less aware of their deficits, and/or have given up compensatory efforts.

These last interpretations become somewhat speculative, given their complexity compared to the size of the R^2 values in the prognostic regression analyses. However, the converging evidence of heterogeneity of the patients at Time 1 suggests that the prognostic significance of COGLAB measures may be greater for some patients than for others. To explore this hypothesis, the multiple regression analyses predicting NOSIE-30 Total Assets at Time 2 with COGLAB at Time 1 were repeated after dividing the patients into two subgroups. Subgroup 1 consists of patients whose Time 1 Total Assets score falls in the poorer half of the distribution; Group 2 scores fall in the upper half. Because of the exploratory nature of this analysis, all 13 COGLAB measures were included in the Full Model solutions regardless of bivariate correlations. The results are shown in Table 6. Remarkably, there is no prognostic value of COGLAB measures for the patients with poor Time 1 Total Assets, but COGLAB predicts Total Assets improvement in the initially high group with an R^2 value of 29%. Clearly, the prognostic significance of cognitive functioning is heavily moderated by the patient's level of social-behavioral functioning at that time. This probably means that at Time 1 a patient's social-behavioral functioning can be poor for a number of reasons, including but not limited to the cognitive impairments measured by COGLAB. For patients with better initial social-behavioral functioning, cognitive function may have an important impact on changes in functioning.

Table 6. Prediction of residualized NOSIE change scores in two subgroups, showing high versus low initial NOSIE TOTAL ASSETS scores (NOSIE initial values effects removed).

1. Subgroup 1: Lower 50%tile initial NOSIE TOTAL ASSETS scores (N=56).

Full Model			Stepwise		
$R = .39$	$R^2 = .15$	$AdjR^2 = 0$			
$F = 0.27$		NS	(no variables entered)		

2. Subgroup 2: Higher 50%tile initial NOSIE TOTAL ASSETS scores (N=56).

Full Model				Stepwise			
$R = .69$		$R^2 = .48$	$AdjR^2 = .27$	$R = .58$		$R^2 = .34$	$AdjR^2 = .29$
$F = 2.32$			$p < .025$	$F = 7.27$			$p < .0005$
var	r	beta	F of Beta	var	r	beta	F of Beta
Sorting Tot err	-.05	-.226	.73	Sorting 3rd mod	-.36	-.341	7.45***
RT Crossover	-.11	-.053	.14	RT trials > 1 sec	.33	.281	4.97*
Mueler Lyer	.05	.012	.01	Size estimation	.30	.280	4.89*
RT Avg	.16	.337	3.10				
RT Anticip err	.01	.022	.02				
Sorting 3rd mod	-.36	-.275	4.08				
Size estimation	.30	-.277	3.80				
RT distraction	-.20	-.333	4.58*				
Masking Tot	.13	.289	3.84				
Vig Hits	.26	.097	.41				
Vig Fls Alarms	-.14	-.097	.34				
RT trials > 1 sec	.33	.072	.14				
Sorting rndm err	.02	.370	1.21				

2.4 Conclusions

These analyses reveal some important relationships between cognitive functioning and social-behavioral functioning in a rehabilitation milieu, in both cross-sectional and longitudinal perspectives. Neither the relationships themselves, nor their changes over time are simple and monotonic. Different cognitive factors are related to different social-behavioral characteristics. Some cognitive impairments appear to respond therapeutically to the rehabilitation milieu while others do not. The prognostic significance of cognitive functioning near the beginning of rehabilitation is heavily mediated by social-behavioral functioning at that time.

The present results may have important implications for treatment which endeavors directly to modify or remediate cognitive impairments. The processes associated with concept manipulation appear to have an especially important role as the patient emerges from psychosis and engages in rehabilitation. Previous studies suggest that these processes are amenable to psychosocial treatment (Bellak et al, 1989). The present study suggests that improvement in this domain is associated with better progress in other aspects of rehabilitation. Concept manipulation should thus be a high priority as cognitively-focused treatment approaches are developed.

The finding regarding vigilance false alarms and response biasing is also noteworthy in this regard. Although it has long been known that schizophrenic subjects show various abnormalities in response bias, it has never been proposed that this could be a suitable target for treatment. Most interestingly, the nature of response biasing suggests that changes in schizophrenic patients reflects self-initiated compensatory attempts. In general, treatment approaches for schizophrenia have neglected the possibility that patients engage in compensatory strategies or self-treatment in the cognitive domain (Brenner *et al*, 1987b; Böker & Brenner, 1983). An approach which takes better advantage of natural self-help inclinations on the part of the patient, should be expected to more successfully engage the patient in treatment as well as potentiate the specific effects of the self-help strategies.

By continuing to pursue these kinds of analyses, we will gradually build a comprehensive understanding of the role of cognitive impairments in the rehabilitation process. This will lead to better clinical decision making based on data from both laboratory and treatment milieu, and to design of increasingly effective treatment strategies for remediating cognitive impairments or reducing their impact on patients' personal and social functioning and *quality of life*.

Chapter C.3

A Training Program for Coping with Maladaptive Emotions: Further Development to the Integrated Psychological Therapy for Schizophrenic Patients

Bettina Hodel and Hans D. Brenner

3.1 Cognitive and Emotional Processing in Schizophrenia

Information processing disorders, which are considered to be a 'core psychological deficit' in schizophrenia (cf. Lang & Buss, 1965; Gjerde, 1983; Nuechterlein & Dawson, 1984b; Braff, 1991; Corrigan et al, 1992a; Cornblatt et al, 1992), are increasingly being analyzed in interaction with emotional processing (cf. Hemsley, 1994; Berenbaum & Oltmanns, 1992; Dworkin, 1992), which, in turn, is also considered to be a prominent feature of schizophrenia (cf. Morrison & Bellack, 1984; Jackson et al, 1989; Bellack et al, 1990; Heimberg et al, 1992; Bellack, 1997).

Several assumptions have been made about the underlying mechanisms of the relationships between cognitive impairment and emotional processing: Gjerde (1983) postulated that emotion can aggravate information processing disorders, while Brenner (1987) specified that *emotions* may increase the pervasive effects of cognitive impairments on behavioral functioning. Hemsley (1994) suggested that the cognitive impairment in schizophrenia is due to structural deficits, i.e. an impaired neural substrate of the cognitive capacity, and that they can be reinforced by emotional stress, which overtaxes the individual's available coping skills and leaves him/her incapable of dealing with situations in a well-adjusted manner.

Brenner (1989) has recently developed a heuristic model which outlines the interactions between the neural, cognitive, and emotional processes involved in behavioral control. It is based on the distinction, elaborated by Pribram (1981), between episodic and participatory processes, linking the latter ones to positive *emotions* and the former ones to negative *emotions*. Participatory processes tolerate incongruities between one's own expectations and a current situation for the purpose of perceiving new external stimuli which are considered to be relevant. Therefore, they are linked to perceptual information processing, which, in turn corresponds both to the arousal system and to external control, since the neurochemical substrate of the arousal system consists of reciprocal norepinephrinergic and serontonergic pathways which, coming from the brain stem, reach widespread brain areas and thus support responsiveness to external stimuli (Brenner, 1989). By comparing new external stimuli to previous experiences, the current situation may seem to be more controllable so optimistic feelings, e.g. interest and hope, may well arise.

On the other hand, Brenner's heuristic model postulates that episodic processes tend to block external stimuli which are incongruent with one's own expectations. The stimuli that are not blocked are transformed by conceptual information processing which corresponds to the activation system and to internal control. This is due to the fact that the activation system is regulated through nigrostriatal and mesolimbic-mesocortical dopamine pathways, partly in combination with cholinergic neuronal systems, where internal control is predominant. The failure to compare new external stimuli to previous experiences results in an inability to react adequately to current situations and in pessimistic feelings, such as fear and social alienation. Due to the activation system's inherent bias towards a predominance of internal control, connected with the rigid planning of behavior, schizophrenic patients are easily 'frozen' into a state of negative outcome expectancy. Negative emotions corresponding to episodic processes increase rigid information processing. Thus, the schizophrenic patient withdraws more and more from reality and his relationship to the environment becomes fragmentary and irregular.

In addition to the elaboration of theoretical concepts, several experimental studies have also explored the mechanisms of the relationship between cognitive and emotional processing in schizophrenia: earlier investigations focused on emotional perception and appraisal. There is evidence that schizophrenic patients are less capable of perceiving emotions adequately than depressive patients, and that both groups perform more poorly than normals (Cutting, 1981; Walker *et al*, 1984; Feinberg *et al*, 1986; Gessler *et al*, 1989). Under emotional stress schizophrenics react rigidly with perceptual withdrawal (Käsermann, 1986; Berenbaum *et al*, 1987; Mandal & Gewali, 1989). Additionally, they perform more poorly in emotional perception tasks than other groups of psychiatric patients, but show relatively adequate performance in emotional appraisal under structured laboratory conditions (Dougherty *et al*, 1974; Walker *et al*, 1984; Feinberg *et al*, 1986). However, both the reproduction and appraisal of stressful and adverse situations may be impaired in schizophrenia (Russel & Fehr, 1987) and negative emotions in particular may be misconceived or even ignored (Muzekari & Bates, 1977; Novic *et al*, 1984). The overall appraisal of other people's emotions - which can be estimated by skills of miming - has been found to be impaired in non-paranoid schizophrenics, suggesting that they have weak cognitive *schemata* for emotional information. However, paranoid patients were found to be more accurate at appraising negative facial emotions, suggesting better developed negative emotional aspects in their cognitive schema (Kline *et al*, 1992).

Current investigations focus on the differentiation between and within emotions, as well as on the skills of emotional miming in schizophrenic patients: impaired emotional discrimination does not seem to depend on the nature of the emotions depicted. Instead, *impairment* can be significantly associated with the severity of negative symptoms like social withdrawal or mental retardation (Heimberg *et al*,

1992). On the other hand, impairment can result from an incapacity to discriminate cues representing different qualities of an emotion (Bellack, 1997). Pitman *et al* (1987) rated facial expression in non-paranoid and paranoid schizophrenic patients, as well as in a control group. While non-paranoid subjects were found to have significantly less eye contact compared to the other subjects, paranoid patients displayed significantly fewer facial movements. Schneider *et al* (1990) showed that both emotional information processing and emotional responsiveness might be impaired in schizophrenia: schizophrenic patients were found to exhibit reduced facial activity in social interaction more often than depressive patients. Berenbaum & Oltmanns (1992) showed that schizophrenics differed significantly from both depressive and normal subjects in their facial expressions of emotion, but not in any self-reported emotional experiences, except for positive ones.

3.2 Interventions for Reducing Disturbed Emotional Processing in Schizophrenia

One of the earliest procedures for reducing disturbed emotional processing in schizophrenia was Meichenbaum & Cameron's (1973) self-instruction training, which involves four steps for the management of emotional stress in schizophrenia. First, self-instructions are used to reduce emotional arousal (e.g. "Don't worry. Worrying won't help"). Second, self-instructions are used in the form of task self-guidance (e.g. "One step at a time. You can handle the situation"). Third, self-instructions are initiated to handle failure and frustration (e.g. "It will soon be over"). In the last step, self-reinforcement is practiced (e.g. "It worked. You did it"). Liberman *et al* (1975) demonstrated within the framework of personal-effectiveness training how schizophrenic patients can learn adequate behavior for expressing emotions, if modeling, shaping, and prompting are used in short role-plays devised by the patients themselves. Learning to identify and express emotions is particularly emphasized in training for friendship and dating skills (Liberman *et al*, 1989). Falloon (1987) developed a method of thought-stopping which involved instructions for the patients to shout 'stop' to reduce arousal, when overwhelmed by emotions. Kraemer *et al* (1991, 1994) devised a four-step training intervention to introduce patients to emotionally-loaded situations: first, the problematic situations are defined ("What is the problem?"). Second, alternative solutions are generated. Third, strategies for controlling heightened arousal are specified ("How can I reduce my panic?"). In a final step, the consequences of behavior are anticipated (cf. Kraemer *et al*, 1991).

Brenner *et al* (1987a, 1990, 1992, 1994) have developed a special training program to improve both cognitive and behavioral functioning in schizophrenic patients: *Integrated Psychological Therapy for Schizophrenic Patients* (IPT) consists of five sub-programs which focus on the remediation of cognitive and behavioral dysfunctions, and at the same time also introduce the patients to emotionally-loaded stimuli. IPT is described in more detail in Chapter 2.

3.3 Emotional Management Training

Both research and practical experience have showed that the cognitive improvements made in therapy might not be lasting (Hodel, 1993a). Analyses of therapy outcomes revealed, on the one hand, that cognitive deficits might re-emerge if emotions overwhelm the patients' ability to cope with them, and on the other, that emotional influences could block or reduce cognitive improvement acquired in IPT training (Brenner et al, 1990, 1992; Hodel, 1993a). These results recently prompted the development of an additional IPT sub-program for reducing the disruptive influence of maladaptive emotions on cognitive functioning in schizophrenia. The aim of 'Emotional Management Training' is to improve the ability to cope with emotions by means of both cognitive and behavioral interventions (Sandner et al, 1991; Konen et al, 1993; Hodel, 1993b). It involves a sequence of eight steps (see Figure 1), which starts with a visual presentation. A main therapist and a co-therapist accompany a group of five - seven schizophrenic patients.

---

1. Description and Analysis of Depicted Emotions
2. Description of the Patients' Emotions
3. Description of Patients' Coping Strategies
4. Elaboration of Alternative Coping Strategies
5. Analysis of Adequacy of Coping Strategies
6. Individualization of Coping Strategies
7. Role-Plays
8. Habituation to Individual Coping Strategies

Figure 1. Therapeutic Steps of Emotional Management Training.

In a **first step**, both the emotions and the context stimuli depicted on slides are described in detail (e.g. quality, intensity, duration, and cause of the emotions). In a **second step**, patients describe their own experiences with similar emotions to encourage them to reflect about their own emotions. In a **third step**, patients tell about their own experiences and the consequences of their ways of perceiving and responding to these emotions (e.g. "How was the emotion - cognitively and/or behaviorally - reduced or prolonged"?). This step should enable the patient to understand the relationship between emotion, behavior and cognition. In a **fourth step**, alternative strategies are generated using 'brain-storming'; this should help patients to elaborate new methods of coping. In **a fifth step**, coping strategies are analyzed in terms of their 'constructiveness' and 'practicability'; this should encourage reflection about the adequacy of possible emotional coping strategies. In a **sixth step**, appropriate strategies are noted and each patient decides which one is possible but not frightening for him, and which would be in line with his individual interests and behavior patterns. This step should result in the creation of highly individualized emotional coping strategies for specific emotionally-loaded situations. In a **seventh step**, individualized strategies are role-played and are subsequently evaluated both by patients and therapists; this can be considered a 'warming-up' process with new coping strategies. In an **eighth** and **final step**, each patient practices his individual coping strategy in additional role-plays to ensure habituation. To promote the generalization of the acquired strategies, patients are advised to write down the individual coping strategies and the situations enacted. At follow-up, they are asked if and how they actually used the strategies acquired in therapy in everyday life, and what the outcomes were. In case of failure, alternative coping strategies are chosen, which are then tested and rehearsed in role-plays.

Emotional Management Training was evaluated in two steps. In a first step, an effect comparison was carried out between Emotional Management Training and an Anti-Stress Training, (e.g. muscle relaxation, co-ordination of breathing and motor behavior, cf. Andres *et al*, 1992). The second step was an effect comparison between Emotional Management Training and the IPT sub-program for Cognitive Differentiation. The visual presentations used in Emotional Management Training were initially rated according to their emotional content and stress by 64 normal subjects, and were then incorporated into the IPT sub-program 'Social Perception' (cf. Roder *et al*, 1988, 1992).

3.3.1 Evaluative studies on Emotional Management Training

The present report involves 31 DSM-III-R schizophrenic patients who were recruited in our clinic. They had a mean age of 31 years (m = 31.2, s.d. = 6.8) and average intelligence (IQ of m = 104.2, s.d. = 12.6). Their mean length of hospitalization was about two years (m = 2.5, s.d. = 3.9) and their mean length of illness about six years (m = 5.9, s.d. = 2.2). Subjects were assigned to one of four groups matched according to the criteria of age, sex, hospitalization and illness duration. Two groups (one with seven and one with nine patients) participated in the comparison between Emotional Management Training and Anti-Stress Training, and two other groups (one with eight and one with seven patients) underwent the comparison between Emotional Management Training and Cognitive Differentiation. All groups received two weekly sessions of 45 minutes each, over a seven-week study period. Training was conducted in both groups by a main therapist and a co-therapist, while a psychologist was responsible for the measurements.

3.3.1.1 Measures

For rating and assessing treatment effects, the following measures were administered prior to and after each of the training procedures: (1) PE[1] (Pictures with Emotions, Hodel, 1992) and the FCS (Frankfurt Subjective Condition Scale, Süllwold & Herrlich, 1987) to assess emotional information processing; (2) three subtests of the RPM (Repeated Psychological Measurement, Fahrenberg *et al*, 1977) Syllable Memorizing, Word Recognition and Crossing-out Numbers, as well as the FCQ (Frankfurt Complaint Questionnaire, Süllwold, 1986a) to assess cognitive

---

[1] PE was developed in our clinic. It consists of two series of 15 photographs for repeated measurement, each of which should be rated as either 'agreeable', 'disagreeable' or 'don't know'. Before being used in this study, this task had undergone preliminary tests for validity and reliability with 15 normal subjects (Zehnder, 1992).

information processing; (3) the NOSIE (Honigfeld et al, 1966) to assess social adjustment.

3.3.1.2 Results

Before examining the effects of each comparison, the prior measurements of the groups were compared by means of the Mann Whitney U-Test. There were no sig-

Table 1. Comparison of pre- and post-scores in the Emotional Management Training and the Anti-Stress Training group using Wilcoxon Tests.

(a) Emotional Management Training group (n=7)

Measures/Groups	Mean		SD		Wilcoxon Tests	
	pre	post	pre	post	z	p
Pictures with Emotions	6.75	14.63	7.94	10.34	-2.52	0.01
FCS	31.88	18.13	19.98	12.28	-2.52	0.01
Syllable M.	4.00	8.75	2.67	2.05	-2.52	0.01
Word R.	18.00	17.36	6.74	6.52	-1.60	n.s.
Crossing N.	4.88	5.38	1.36	1.30	-1.83	n.s.
FCQ	27.50	19.00	4.24	4.57	-2.52	0.01
NOSIE	6.13	10.75	1.89	3.69	-2.52	0.01

(b) Anti-Stress Training group (n=9)

Measures /Groups	Mean		SD		Wilcoxon Tests	
	pre	post	pre	post	z	p
Pictures with Emotions	7.89	10.67	7.34	8.22	-1.19	n.s.
FCS	32.11	20.33	16.65	11.48	-2.66	0.01
Syllable M.	3.44	4.00	2.24	2.59	-1.83	n.s.
Word R.	17.56	16.56	7.21	5.70	-1.26	n.s.
Crossing N.	6.11	7.56	1.17	1.74	-2.20	0.05
FCQ	27.00	25.78	4.21	4.30	-1.47	n.s.
NOSIE	4.22	4.78	1.86	1.56	-1.48	n.s.

nificant differences in the initial measurements. Table 1 shows the results of the Wilcoxon Test. This test analyzed the within-group changes of the comparison between Emotional Management Training and Anti-Stress Training. Emotional Management Training resulted in significant improvements in the following measures: Pictures with Emotions, FCS, Syllable Memorizing, FCQ and NOSIE. In contrast, the group receiving Anti-Stress Training only showed significant improvements in FCS and in Crossing-out Numbers. Additionally, the efficiency-increases of both groups were compared for each measure by means of the Mann Whitney U-Test as shown in Table 2.
Syllable Memorizing, FCQ and NOSIE significantly differentiated both groups. The

Syllable Memorizing, FCQ and NOSIE significantly differentiated both groups. The Emotional Management Training group showed superior results in these three measures (cf. averages in Table 2). In addition to this, the pre-post differences in both groups were adjusted according to the variance of the pre-therapy scores of all 16 patients (cf. Smith *et al*, 1980), yielding the 'effect size' (cf. Grawe *et al*, 1990) as shown in Figure 2. Emotional Management Training yielded greater effect sizes than Anti-Stress Training.

Table 2. Comparison of the efficiency-increases of the groups "Emotional Management Training" and "Anti-Stress Training" by Mann Whitney U-Test.

Measures /Groups	Emotional Management Training (n=7)		Anti-Stress Training (n = 9)		Mann Whitney U-Test	
	Mean pre-post	SD pre-post	Mean pre-post	SD pre-post	z	p
Pictures with Emotions	7.88	6.18	2.78	5.69	-1.12	n.s.
FCS	-13.75	13.92	-11.78	7.53	-1.30	n.s.
Syllable M.	4.75	2.37	0.56	0.72	-3.42	0.01
Word R.	-0.64	0.92	-1.00	2.08	-1.76	n.s.
Crossing N.	0.50	0.54	1.45	1.41	-1.39	n.s.
FCQ	-8.50	5.50	-1.22	2.28	-2.95	0.01
NOSIE	4.63	2.56	0.56	1.01	-3.12	0.01

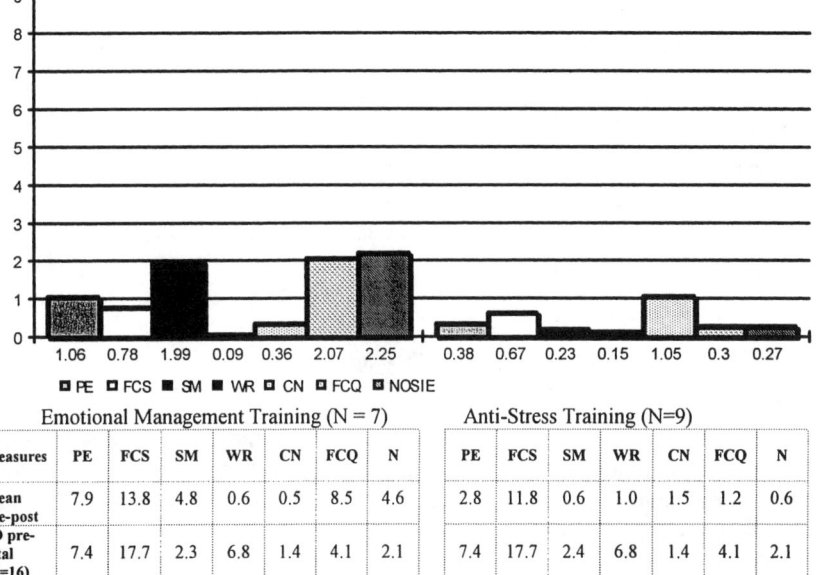

	Emotional Management Training (N = 7)						Anti-Stress Training (N=9)					
Measures	PE	FCS	SM	WR	CN	FCQ	N	PE	FCS	SM	WR	CN	FCQ	N
Mean pre-post	7.9	13.8	4.8	0.6	0.5	8.5	4.6	2.8	11.8	0.6	1.0	1.5	1.2	0.6
SD pre-total (N=16)	7.4	17.7	2.3	6.8	1.4	4.1	2.1	7.4	17.7	2.4	6.8	1.4	4.1	2.1

PE = Pictures with Emotions; SM = Syllable Memorizing; WR = Word Recognition; CN = Crossing Numbers;

Figure 2. Effect Sizes of Emotional Management Training and Anti-Stress Training.

The next table shows the results of other Wilcoxon Tests analyzing the comparison between Emotional Management Training and Cognitive Differentiation (Table 3). Different courses of the within-group changes were found: Significant improvement was found in the Emotional Management Training group in all measures except NOSIE. In contrast to this, the group receiving Cognitive Differentiation improved significantly only in Crossing out Numbers and in FCQ. Results of the subsequent comparison of the groups' efficiency-increases by means of the Mann Whitney U-Test are given in Table 4.

Table 3. Comparison of pre-post scores in the Emotional Management Training and the Cognitive Differentiation group by Wilcoxon Tests.

"Emotional Management Training" group (n=8)

Measures/Groups	Mean		SD		Wilcoxon Tests	
	pre	post	pre	post	z	p
Pictures with Emotions	12.63	19.00	6.78	7.31	-2.52	0.05
FCS	27.25	19.00	19.49	14.51	-2.31	0.05
Syllable M.	6.63	10.38	0.52	3.07	-2.38	0.05
Word R.	20.25	13.13	6.52	1.96	-2.20	0.05
Crossing N.	5.00	9.25	1.51	1.17	-2.52	0.05
FCQ	31.25	18.00	3.88	4.54	-2.52	0.05
NOSIE	8.50	9.13	1.20	1.13	-1.83	n.s.

(Table 3. continued)

Cognitive Differentiation group (n=7)

Measures/Groups	Mean		SD		Wilcoxon Tests	
	pre	post	pre	post	z	p
Pictures with Emotions	11.57	12.71	6.43	1.99	-1.47	n.s.
FCS	29.00	28.43	17.66	17.31	-1.83	n.s.
Syllable M.	6.86	7.14	0.38	0.69	-0.91	n.s.
Word R.	19.14	17.71	7.38	5.90	-1.83	n.s.
Crossing N.	5.71	7.57	2.49	1.51	-2.20	0.05
FCQ	31.00	19.00	4.58	4.44	-2.37	0.05
NOSIE	8.43	8.57	1.39	1.27	-1.00	n.s.

Pictures with Emotions, FCS, Syllable Memorizing, and Crossing out Numbers significantly differentiated both groups. The Emotional Management Training group performed significantly better in these four measures (cf. averages in Table 3).

Table 4. Comparison of scores after Emotional Management Training and Cognitive Differentiation by Mann Whitney U-Test.

Measures/Groups	Emotional Management Training (n = 8)		Cognitive Differentiation (n = 7)		Mann Whitney U-Test	
	Mean pre-post	SD pre-post	Mean pre-post	SD pre-post	z	p
Pictures with Emotions	6.37	4.53	1.14	1.67	-3.11	0.01
FCS	-8.25	7.72	-0.57	0.54	-2.25	0.05
Syllable M.	3.75	2.71	0.28	0.76	-2.51	0.05
Word R.	-7.12	5.61	-1.43	1.61	-1.54	n.s.
Crossing N.	4.25	1.58	1.87	1.34	-2.51	0.05
FCQ	-13.25	1.98	-12.00	4.40	-1.57	n.s.
NOSIE	0.63	0.74	0.14	0.37	-0.77	n.s.

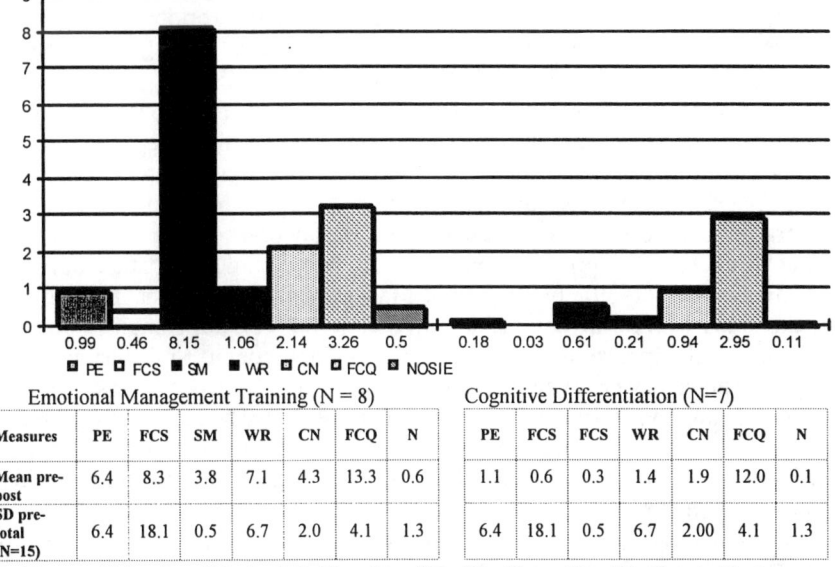

PE = Pictures with Emotions; SM = Syyllable Memorizing; WR = Word Recognition; CN = Crossing Numbers;

Figure 3. Effect-Sizes of Emotional Management Training and Cognitive Differentiation.

The results of the analysis of the effect sizes is shown in Figure 3. The results in Figure 3 show that Emotional Management Training led in all measures to greater effect sizes than Cognitive Differentiation.

3.4 Discussion

Although disorders of emotional processing have been considered a hallmark of schizophrenia since Bleuler's (1950) pioneering work, there has been a paucity of experimental research on techniques for modifying them. This might be due to the problem of operationalizing both the emotions **per se** and an individual's style of coping with emotions. For instance, Nuechterlein et al (1992) showed that the concept of Expressed Emotion (EE) is based on critical or benign comments, or on hostile or overprotective behavior shown by significant others towards the patient. Nevertheless, the patient's manner of coping with EE has not been assessed at all, or if so, it has been based on measures that are global, e.g. number of relapses, or on excessively isolated behavioral patterns, e.g. number of eye movements.

As long as the individual manner of coping with emotions cannot be adequately assessed, neither can the effects of emotion training. However, several procedures for modifying emotional coping have been developed over the past two decades. They can be divided into two groups: direct training procedures which help patients to deal with and control emotions by means of behavior therapy techniques (Meichenbaum & Cameron, 1973; Kraemer et al, 1991, 1994; Falloon, 1987), and indirect training procedures which rely on modeling or on working with emotionally-loaded therapy material for habituation effects and for raising the emotional threshold (Liberman et al, 1975, 1989; Brenner et al, 1992, 1994).

The mechanisms of Emotional Management Training that we devised attempt to incorporate both direct and indirect procedures: in the first steps, visual aids depicting emotions foster habituation to emotional stressors (indirect procedure), whereas in subsequent steps, alternative ways of appraising emotions and their behavioral consequences are generated and behavioral coping strategies are rehearsed (direct procedure). This combination is based on the heuristic model conceived by Brenner (1989). In Emotional Management Training, habituation may lower the arousal level, thereby making it possible for stressful stimuli to be processed. Emotional appraisal and rehearsal of behavioral coping strategies may activate both participatory processes and relevant perceptual information processing, so that stressful situations may seem to be more controllable. The results of our studies are in line with these assumptions: 'combined' Emotional Management Training yielded greater therapy effects than either anti-stress therapy or a focused cognitive remediation procedure.

Two methodological aspects of the results obtained especially confirm the efficacy of Emotional Management Training: Only the effect sizes of Emotional Management Training are comparable with those of the overall evaluations of IPT (Brenner et al, 1994), and effect sizes of Syllable Memorizing are strikingly evident after Emotional Management Training. Results such as these deserve attention. First, comparable effect sizes of IPT and Emotional Management Training are evidence of equivocal efficacy. Second, effect sizes of Syllable Memorizing should be highlighted, since verbal memory can be directly linked with the acquirement of new social skills (Kern et al, 1992; Corrigan et al, 1992a).

When questioned as to their subjective experiences with Emotional Management

Training, nearly all patients reported actually having used the coping skills acquired in therapy in real-life situations, and experienced them as having a particularly stabilizing effect emotionally (Hodel *et al*, 1995). Therefore, Emotional Management Training might serve as protection against emotionally-loaded situations (Holzman & Bivens, 1988), since the capacity to deal with one's social environment seemed to improve (cf. Brenner, 1989; Verres, 1990). Such in vivo transfer could be facilitated by the intervention techniques of Emotional Management Training: (1) new coping strategies are acquired in cognitive and behavioral processes; (2) new coping strategies are acquired which are tailored to the patients' individual interests and behavioral patterns; (3) new coping strategies are acquired until habituation has occurred.

However, the results of these studies should be considered to be preliminary, due to the limited sample sizes and to measures used which could be criticized as lacking specificity to emotional functioning in general, and to individual ways of coping in particular. Nevertheless, the samples show no significant differences between their socio-demographic variables. In addition, fewer significant improvements might emerge if validity or reliability analyses were carried out (e.g. α-Adjustment by Kaehler, 1990) to test for any overlap between the dependent variables which might bias the results.

Even though the results are preliminary, our Emotional Management Training might be a promising new aspect in the rehabilitation of schizophrenic patients.

Chapter C.4

Cognitive Behavior Therapy and its Differential Effects in the Treatment of Chronic Schizophrenic Patients

Sibylle Kraemer[1]

4.1 Introduction

Schizophrenia is probably the most serious, and the most complex, but also the most fascinating disorder among all mental illnesses. It is manifested in a great many ways, ranging from creative fantasy worlds, linguistic inventions, emotional storms, or extremely fine sensitivity and perception, to extreme lack of drive, and at least apparent emptiness. The illness is a burden to all those who are affected by it, in the first place the patients themselves, but also their relatives and the professional staff caring for them; yet at the same time it is a great challenge. In the case of schizophrenic disorders dialectic principles could be applied, as has been done by Linehan (1993) for borderline disorders. For this it is necessary to assume and accept the thesis of vulnerability or abnormal sensitivity to stress. The antithesis is that changes are possible just as with any other severe psychiatric illness. Good therapy will be aimed at achieving a synthesis.

In the western world therapeutic measures consist essentially of medication and sociopsychiatric or rehabilitative treatment. Carefully planned medication is the most important component of relapse prophylaxis, while various possible rehabilitation measures often prevent long periods of hospitalization and help to achieve integration in the community. But several large-scale catamnesis studies (Häfner, 1988; Müller et al, 1998) have shown that even with these measures and without any exacerbation of symptoms, about two thirds of the patients still suffer from serious psychosocial difficulties, such as lack of contacts, anhedonia, inactivity, etc. Additional psychotherapeutic interventions are required, related to the specific problems of these difficult patients.

It is not only a question of relapse prophylaxis - this can also be achieved on long-stay wards where no demands are made - but of extending the behavior range and improving the quality of life. An effective cognitive behavior therapy should

---

[1] For discussion remarks I would like to thank E. Palme, Dipl. Psych.

take into account the overlapping goals shown in Table 1. These therapy goals in

Table 1: Overlapping therapy goals

Acceptance	Change
Vulnerability; Reduced degree of freedom	Insight Self-control
Sensitive to stress	Coping with stress
Emotional imbalance	Trusting emotions
Communication problems	Communication
Restricted radius of activity	Activities; quality of life

their turn follow a dialectic principle: on the one hand, both patients and therapists need to accept certain conditions, but at the same time they should aim at changing these conditions. This means, for example, that there may be restrictions due to a certain vulnerability or sensitivity. However, it is possible to respond to these restrictions by setting goals such as gaining insight into the processes of the illness and practicing self-control and self-efficacy. Many of the patients have cognitive disorders which they experience subjectively. These can be improved either directly or through compensation strategies. Special sensitivity to stress, emotional imbalance (i.e. fluctuation between blocking and inhibition of feelings), specific communication difficulties with special sensitivity to negative and positive feelings (see HEE) and restricted behavior possibilities must also be accepted at first. Yet not only will certain situations be avoided as a result of these restrictions, but specific individual strategies can be developed for coping with stress, for trusting emotions, for relief and more clarity in communication, and for quality of life in general.

A disturbance-related indication for the following types of cognitive behavior therapy can be derived from these considerations (Table 2). These interventions should

Table 2: Interventions

1. Information and discussion on subjective understanding of illness
2. Cognitive behavior therapy
   2.1 Cognitive training (cognitive differentiation, social perception, computeraided cognitive training)
   2.2 Psychoeducation
   2.3 More complex cognitive processes (problem solving, coping with stress, cognitive restructuring, selfregulation strategies, imagination)
3. Behavior exercises (role plays, relaxation training, in-vivo-exercises)
4. Work with relatives

form a series of stages which build on each other. According to clinical experience and empirical investigations (Brenner *et al*, 1990) it has proved useful to apply cognitive methods before behavioral ones. Cognitive training and cognitive behavior therapy take into account the fact that the patients are very likely to have cognitive disorders. If cognitive performance is improved through specific cognitive training methods, the patients will profit more from subsequent more complex therapy and rehabilitation measures, even if the cognitive skills deteriorate again (cf. Liberman *et al*, 1995). Theoretical considerations suggest that an improvement of discrimination capabilities and contextual utilization of earlier experiences can be achieved through cognitive interventions. These capabilities would then be represented in a kind of "cognitive map" (Tolman in Fröhlich, 1993), which can be used to plan and organize subsequent activities effectively. Only then would it be possible to adequately classify and assess the effects of subsequent behavioral methods and produce realistic expectations, which according to Tolman is the most important learning effect.

Within the framework of a therapy plan, a flexible, individual manner of proceeding is desirable. Prochaska *et al* (1992) developed an individual phase model for patients with dependence disorders. The choice of method will depend on the readiness or the condition of the patients ("join the client where he is", Kanfer, 1989). We have modified this model for schizophrenic patients (Table 3). The

Table 3: Therapy process model for schizophrenic patients (after: Prochaska *et al*, 1992)

Phases	1. Clarification/ motivation	2. Intention to change	3. Therapy preparation	4. Therapy	5. Maintenance
Interventions	-Relationship -Diagnosis -Medication -Available choices -Structure of day -Planning of nursing care (acute) -Recognizing resources -Information -Art therapy -Social counselling (acute)	-Discussion about nature of illness -Behavior analysis -Cognitive training if required -Work with patient's family -Psycho-education -Occupational therapy	-Biographical nalysis -Formulation of goals -Relaxation training -Social perception training if required -Work therapy -Social counselling (rehabilitation)	-Cognitive behavior therapy -Later:Social competence training -Preparation for discharge	-Out-patient sessions if required, with the same therapist, until transfer to further therapy

phases are related here to in-patient therapy and restricted on the whole to cases where certain cognitive behavior therapy measures are indicated. These need to be embedded in an overall rehabilitative treatment plan, as we have tried to show. In the clarification/motivation phase, the patients can still be relatively acute. In addition to essential standard measures such as medication, a transparent, calming structure to the day, and informative feed-back, other indicated measures may be started, mostly relatively free, unconditional activities such as art therapy. Self-control processes and self-efficacy could be encouraged here through a small amount of freedom of decision, participating in decisions and possible choices. Attention should also be paid to the strong points and skills of the patients. In the final analysis it is essentially a question of promoting a good therapeutic relationship with the goal of creating motivation for change. When the patients are ready and able (i.e. largely remitted) to take further measures (intention to change), discussions can begin on the nature of the illness, the analysis of the most important problem areas, and cognitive training where applicable. These methods will help to promote processes of insight (David, 1990) and processes of self-regulation (Kanfer, 1994) and self-efficacy (Bandura, 1977).

Therapy preparation includes measures such as deciding on settings, carrying out biographical analysis (conditions of development of disorders and strengths), joint definition of goals, and continuation of cognitive training with training of social perception (Roder et al, 1992). Psychoeducative interventions and interventions involving the patient's family are indispensable (Bäuml et al, 1998). These interventions help to provide structure and transparency, as well as skill in discrimination and observation. By involving the relatives, communication becomes easier and they are helped to understand the patient.

Within the framework of actual psychotherapy, in our case cognitive behavior therapy, methods of problem solving, cognitive restructuring, differentiation of feelings, and stress management (e.g., Meichenbaum, 1991) are used. As mentioned above in the theoretic discussion, these components must come before behavioral methods such as social competence training with role plays or in vivo exercises for promoting social skills or coping with fear (cf. Kraemer, 1998). In this way, self-regulation processes are made usable and overlap with the components self-observation, self-evaluation and self-strengthening (Kanfer, 1994). In the interest of continuity of treatment, it is important that further out-patient sessions be held with the same therapist in order to sustain the effects obtained, before the patient progresses to other therapeutic measures.

The central feature of the treatment is the fourth phase (actual therapy), and in most cases this needs to be well integrated into the individually-determined preceding and following units. Such a stepped procedure is most successful, although time-consuming, when carried out in the in-patient setting. As yet there is still no empirical confirmation of the single phases. Clinically this kind of forward-looking and flexible planning strategy has proved effective with schizophrenic patients.

In the following sections we describe two investigations carried out by ourselves for the purpose of determining the effects of various measures. We refer to the phase of intention to change (phase 2) and to the phase of actual therapy (phase 4). The effects on cognitive deficits and psychopathological symptoms of a computer-aided cognitive training course were examined, related to a module in the second phase. In connection with the fourth phase an investigation was carried out to compare cognitive behavior therapy with a behavioral method, namely social competence training with role plays.

4.2 Computer-aided Cognitive Training with Schizophrenic Patients: Effects on Cognitive Deficits and Psychopathology[2]

4.2.1 Pilot Study

Cognitive training methods are today a fixed component of integrative psychological therapy programs for schizophrenic patients. In the context of the vulnerability-stress model, cognitive training methods are related to at least two factors. In connection with Brenner's modified pervasiveness model (Brenner et al, 1994) and the model of transaction of cognitive basic disturbances in psychopathological phenomena by Hemsley (1987), cognitive training methods were theoretically aimed not only at cognitive deficits, but also at psychopathological symptoms, since these, to put it simply, are assumed to be systematically related. However there has been no empirical confirmation as yet of these complex ideas. Cognitive training (not to be confused with cognitive behavior therapy which has more far-reaching effects, Kraemer et al, 1987) had no generalized connection with psychopathology nor with social behavior and vice versa. Moreover cognitive performance did not correlate with productive psychopathological phenomena, but only with negative symptoms of schizophrenia (Zinner et al, 1990, Hain et al, 1993) and social behavior (Goldberg & Gold, 1995). Apparently specific interventions are needed for specific areas.

However, with the group cognitive training materials from the Integrated Psychological Therapy program (IPT) (Roder et al, 1992), subjective effects were more positive than objective results, in other words less good than was hoped, although patient acceptance was generally high and the patients perceived a definite link with their subjectively experienced cognitive limitations (Gansert & Olbrich 1992; Brenner et al, 1990; Olbrich & Mussgay, 1990; Mussgay, 1993). Due to contradictory findings, it is unclear whether the low improvement rate reflects vulnerability, or traits, as is frequently claimed. It was therefore decided to use computer-aided training, which would be free of any effects due to group dynamics, i.e. confusion with social interactions and thus affective participation, to achieve results which would be objectively more positive.

A preliminary pilot study with an A-B-A design and 21 patients gave only weak, if any, support to the hypothesis that cognitive performance is improved by such training courses (Kraemer et al, 1999a) (Table 4). The results for the cognitive parameters at the four measuring times (baseline observation, after three weeks of training, and in catamnesis) showed improvements in cognitive performance, in some cases already in the baseline observation (d2), but which were hard to assess, and not in all parameters: Hit rate and reaction time in the Continous Performance Test (CPT) and the Span of Apprehension test (SAT) were only measured before and after the course and without a control group.

---

[2] In cooperation with R.Waerum, J.Rothbauer and N. Sobizack

Table 4. Pilot study: data of cognitive variables

Span of Apprehension Test	TIME 1		TIME 2	
HITS	Mean value	SD	Mean value	SD
Experimental group	29.67	4.27	30.25	2.86
Control group	29.45	4.95	28.40	4.53
Group x time	n.s.			

Span of Apprehension Test	TIME 1		TIME 2	
REACTION TIME	Mean value	SD	Mean value	SD
Experimental group	1263	396.47	1153	270.52
Control group	1454.45	337.56	1530.40	702.50
Group x time	n.s.			

d-2	TIME 1		TIME 2	
GZ-F	Mean value	SD	Mean value	SD
Experimental group	346.33	118.96	332.92	109.96
Control group	309.18	155.34	329.27	154.34
Group x time	n.s.			

Word Recognition Test	TIME 1		TIME 2	
HITS	Mean value	SD	Mean value	SD
Experimental group	17.75	7.47	20.73	6.93
Control group	22.20	10.54	20.80	11.52
Group x time	n.s.			

Word Recognition Test	TIME 1		TIME 2	
ERRORS	Mean value	SD	Mean value	SD
Experimental group	18.17	11.98	18.64	10.30
Control group	8.90	6.26	13.40	11.40
Group x time	n.s.			

Word Recognition Test	TIME 1		TIME 2	
ERRORS:HITS	Mean value	SD	Mean value	SD
Experimental group	1.20	1.01	0.99	0.69
Control group	0.45	0.27	1.14	1.60
Group x time	n.s.			

Although psychopathology was only touched on marginally and no improvement was expected in this area, since the course was specifically aimed at cognitive disturbances, a small but interesting effect was noticed (Table 5): There was a significant reduction in self-assessed paranoid symptoms during the training period. However, since there was no control group, this result had to be regarded critically. Therefore a further study was carried out, which is described below.

Table 5: Psychopathology and Social Anxiety

		X	(SD)	p
Paranoid Symptoms	t1	9,95	(7,9)	
	t2	9,52	(8,0)	
	t3	8,32	(9,2)	<.03
	t4	7,90	(8,8)	
Depressive Symptoms	t1	12,80	(9,8)	
	t2	12,80	(6,9)	n. s.
	t3	14,00	(8,6)	
	t4	15,00	(9,2)	
Social Anxiety	t1	44,80	(20,8)	
	t2	46,40	(22,2)	n.s.
	t3	44,30	(20,4)	
	t4	43,61	(23,1)	

4.2.2 Main Study: Methods

The aim of this study was to investigate more closely the effects of computer-aided training programs on psychopathology. The following hypotheses were formulated on the basis of the preliminary study:

1. The cognitive performance of the experimental group is improved.
2. The psychopathological symptoms of the experimental group are improved.

The study was carried out as a control-group study with random assignment of in-patients at a district hospital near Munich/Germany[3]. A total of 22 patients took part, of whom 12 were in the experimental group and 11 in the control group (one patient was in both groups). Before and after the three-week period (training program versus usual treatment such as work or occupational therapy) the following parameters were recorded for all patients:

The following instruments were used to measure **cognitive performance**:
1. Span of Apprehension Test (SAT)
2. d2 concentration test (Brickenkamp, 1981)
3. Word recognition test (WET) Repeated Psychological Measurements (RPM) (Fahrenberg *et al*, 1977)

Psychopathology was assessed with:
1. Brief Psychiatric Rating Scale (BPRS) (productive symptoms) (Overall & Gorham, 1962)
2. Scale for Assessment of Negative Symptoms (SANS) (Andreasen, 1981)
3. AMDP (plus and minus symptoms) (AMDP, 1981)
4. Paranoid-Depressivity Scale (PD-S) (self-assessed paranoid and depressive symptoms) (von Zerssen, 1981)

Qualitative interview: At the end of the training course ten standard questions were asked about the subjective experience of the patients in the experimental group with regard to the course. Six of these questions are shown descriptively.

Statistics: The statistical methods used consisted of a MANOVA and additional t-tests in the case of significant group x time interactions.

---

[3] Our grateful thaanks for their cooperation go to Prof. Dr.Dr. M. Albus, Dr. C. Arviv, Dr. U. Franz, Dr. M. Hanke, Dr. W. Hubmann and the nursing staff on wards 9/I,18,26 and 27.

Procedure: Two patients worked at the same time in one room. The therapist (RW) was present in order to give initial instruction in the use of the PC and to help with other technical questions. All patients in the experimental group (N:12) had 15 one-hour sessions. The training sessions took place during normal work therapy or occupational therapy times, while the control group (N:11) continued these programs as usual.

Content of the training course: In the first five sessions the patients worked with the computer program Cognition I, subprograms Attention and Concentration, containing 9 and 8 tasks respectively (Marker, 1989). These exercises were selected in order to focus on signal detection processes. In the following ten sessions the patients worked with the program Planning and Deciding (von Cramon & Zihl, 1988). Originally this program was developed for patients who have suffered damage to the frontal lobe of the brain. However, it is also suitable for schizophrenic patients, since it practices complex cognitive processes such as problem-solving (executive functions). This program therefore contains more difficult tasks which really fall into the realm of information processing. It has three menus, each of which contains four exercises. **Description of the patients**: see Tab.6.

Table 6: Patient data

	EXP. GROUP (N: 12)		CON. GROUP (N: 11)		TOTAL	
	Mean	SD	Mean	SD	Mean	SD
AGE	33.17	8.46	34.00	6.34	33.57	7.37
FIRST MANIFESTATION	5.92	2.74	7.81	6.27	6.83	4.75
LENGTH OF HOSPITALIZATION	0.49	0.26	0.77	0.36	0.62	0.34
CLOZAPIN	268.18	103.13	253.50	96.03	261.19	97.59
DIAGNOSIS WITH ICD-10						
F 20.0: Paranoid schizophrenia	F 20.0: 8		F 20.0: 8			
F 20.1: Hebephrenic schizophrenia	F 20.1: 2		F 20.1: 3			
F 20.2: Catatonic schizophrenia	F 20.2: 1					
F 20.3: Undifferent. schizophrenia	F 20.3: 1					

All the test persons were classified as chronic schizophrenics in accordance with ICD-10. On average they were about 30 years old, had been ill for well over five years, had been in hospital for about six months, and almost all were taking Clozapine (one patient was taking Haloperidol).

4.2.3 Second Study: Results

All patients in the experimental group attended all fifteen sessions. Drop-outs were recorded only for the following instruments, measuring times and groups:

BPRS, SANS, AMDP: Time 2:   1 test person in the control group
PD-S: Time 1:   dto
                           2 test persons in the experimental group
                Time 2:   dto
SAT: dto   1 test person in the control group
WET: dto   1 test person in the experimental group

Although it may sometimes seem so from the following charts, there were no significant differences in the prevalues between the two groups. The tables 7 and 8 (see below) show the results of the MANOVA and of the additional t-tests for significant group x time interactions.

Cognitive performance:
d2 concentration test (Figure 1).

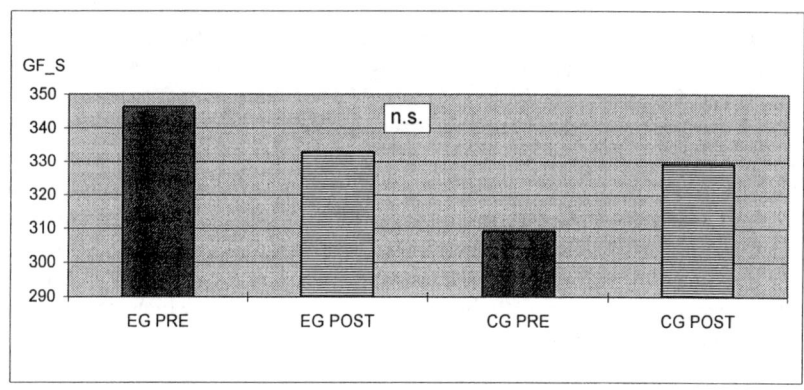

Figure 1. Mean values in Concentration test-d2
(The higher the value, the better the performance)

There were no significant changes in both groups. Optically it even looks as if the experimental group deteriorated and the control group improved. If the rate of improvement/deterioration is calculated in percent, the experimental group showed a 4% deterioration, and the control group a 6% improvement.

Span of Apprehension Test (SAT) (Figure 2)

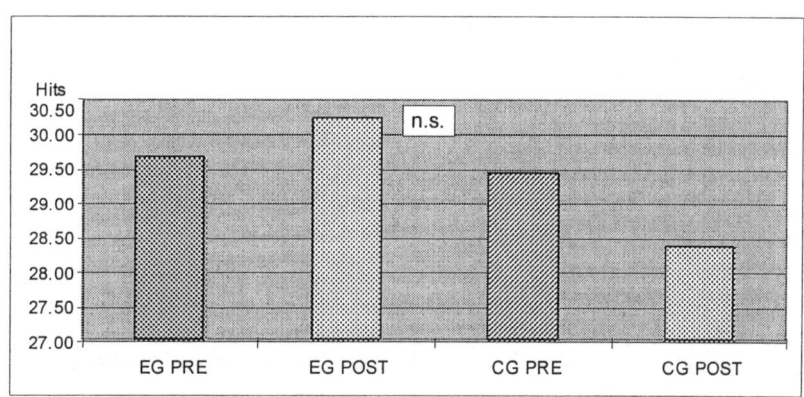

Figure 2. Mean values in Span of Apprehension Test (SAT) : Number of hits
(The higher the value, the better the performance)

There was no significant improvement in the number of hits in the Span of Apprehension test in either group. The experimental group showed only 2% more hits, and the control group 4% less.

Span of Apprehension Test (SAT) (reaction time RT) (Figure 3)

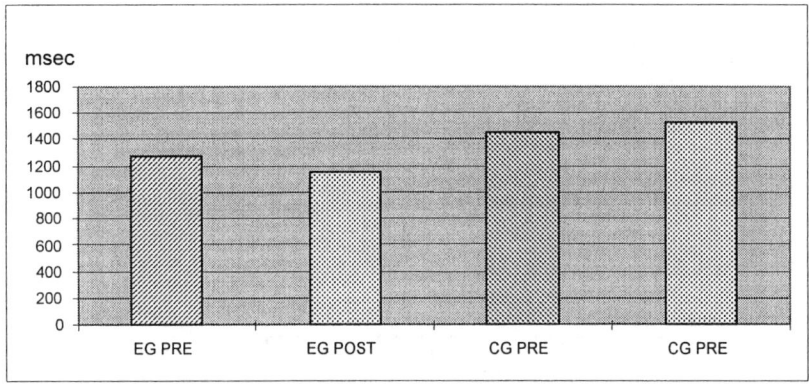

Figure 3. Mean values in Span of Apprehension Test (SAT) Reaction time
(The lower the value, the better the performance)

Statistically there was no great change in the reaction time (in msec), probably a measure of drive, in either group. The speed of the experimental group increased by 9%, while that of the control group decreased by 5%.

Word recognition Test (WET)   (Figure 4)

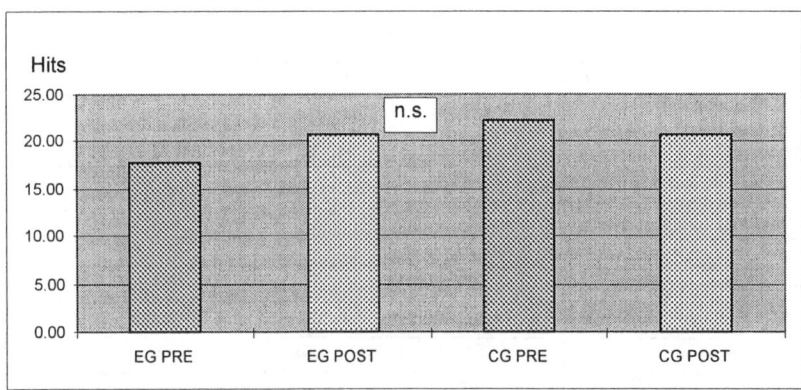

Figure 4. Mean values in Word Recognition test from RPM Hits
(The higher the value, the better the performance)

The number of recognized, meaningful words also showed no statistical significance in the group x time interaction. Expressed in percent, the experimental group improved by 14% (hits) and 17% (errors) respectively, while the control group deteriorated by 7% (hits) and 153% (errors).

The results of the MANOVA with mean values and standard deviations are shown in Table 7.

Table 7. Cognitive variables

Span of Apprehension Test	TIME 1		TIME 2	
HITS	Mean value	SD	Mean value	SD
Experimental group	29.67	4.27	30.25	2.86
Control group	29.45	4.95	28.40	4.53
Group x time	n.s.			

Span of Apprehension Test	TIME 1		TIME 2	
REACTION TIME	Mean value	SD	Mean value	SD
Experimental group	1263	396.47	1153	270.52
Control group	1454.45	337.56	1530.40	702.50
Group x time	n.s.			

d-2	TIME 1		TIME 2	
GZ-F	Mean value	SD	Mean value	SD
Experimental group	346.33	118.96	332.92	109.96
Control group	309.18	155.34	329.27	154.34
Group x time	n.s.			

Word Recognition Test	TIME 1		TIME 2	
HITS	Mean value	SD	Mean value	SD
Experimental group	17.75	7.47	20.73	6.93
Control group	22.20	10.54	20.80	11.52
Group x time	n.s.			

Word Recognition Test	TIME 1		TIME 2	
ERRORS	Mean value	SD	Mean value	SD
Experimental group	18.17	11.98	18.64	10.30
Control group	8.90	6.26	13.40	11.40
Group x time	n.s.			

Word Recognition Test	TIME 1		TIME 2	
ERRORS:HITS	Mean value	SD	Mean value	SD
Experimental group	1.20	1.01	0.99	0.69
Control group	0.45	0.27	1.14	1.60
Group x time	n.s.			

Overall it was found that all patients had a very low initial level in the cognitive performance tests, and showed no great improvement after 15 one-hour sessions of computer-aided training.

Psychopathology:
We shall first look at the total values for the various scales:

Brief Psychiatric Rating Scale (BPRS) (Figure 5)

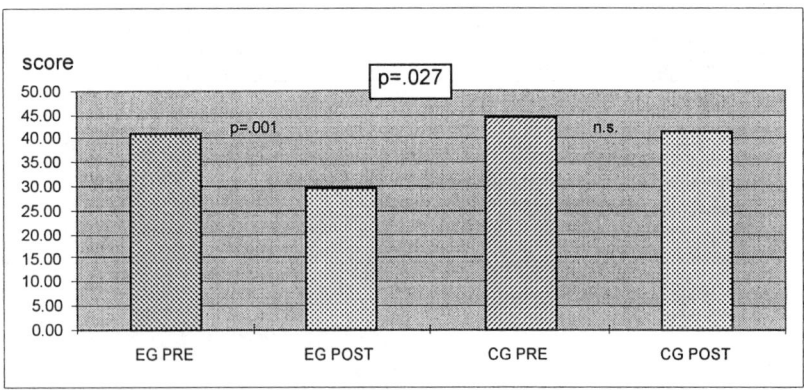

Figure 5. Mean Values in Brief Psychiatric Rating Scale (BPRS): Sum Score

The total value for the experimental group shows significant improvement. In percent, the experimental group improved by 28%, and the control group by 7%.

Scale for the Assessment of Negative Symptoms (SANS) (Figure 6)

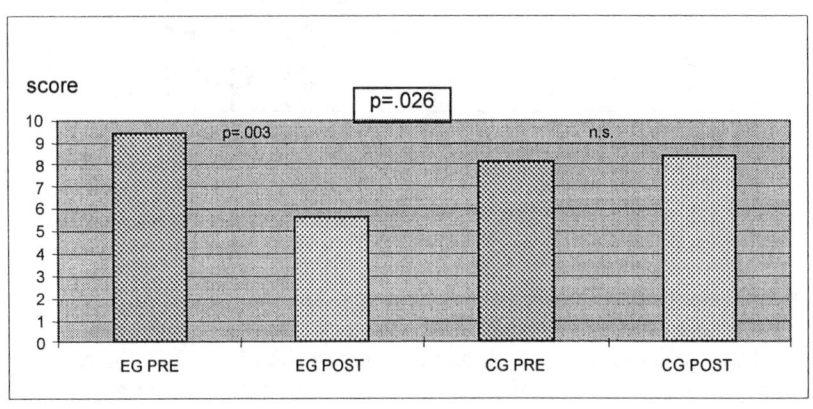

Figure 6. Scale for the Assessment of Negative Symptoms (SANS): Total value without global Items

Here too there is considerable improvement of minus symptoms. The experimental group shows a 42% improvement, while the control group has deteriorated by 3%.

AMDP (Figure 7)

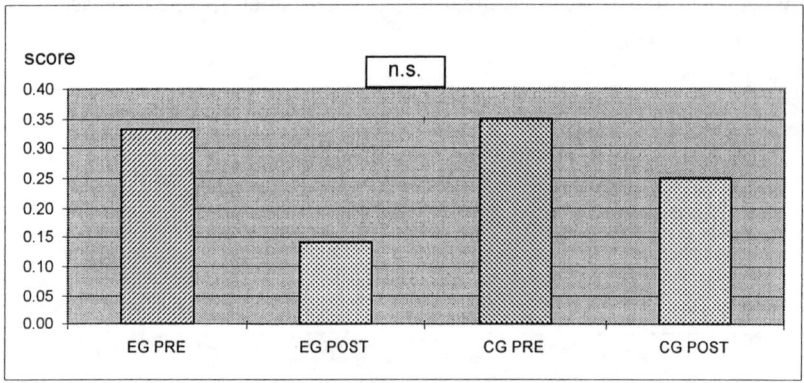

Figure 7. Mean values in psychopathological findings (AMDP)
(The lower the value, the less the psychopathology)

In the AMDP there were no significant changes, but the experimental group has improved by 58%, and the control group only by 29%.

PD-S (Figure 8)

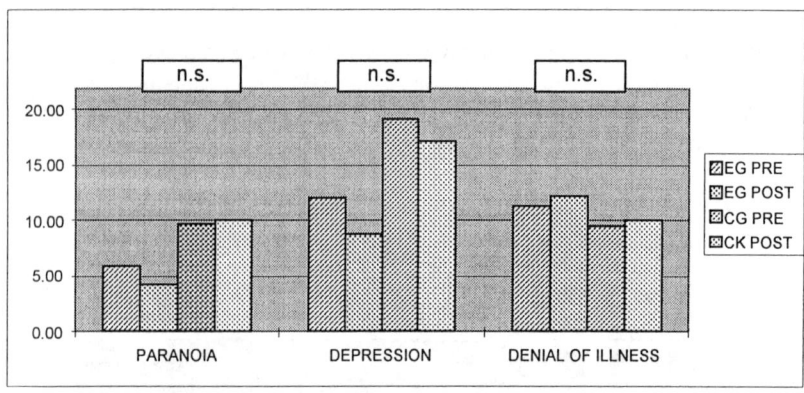

Figure 8. Mean values in Paranoid-Depressivity-Scale (PD-S)
(The lower the value the less the psychopathology)

The results of the first study were not reproduced. Self-assessment of psychopathological symptoms showed no significant changes. But the experimental group improved by 29% in respect of paranoid symptoms, and by 26% in respect of depressive symptoms. The control group deteriorated by 5% in the case of paranoid symptoms, and improved by 11% in respect of depressive symptoms. It might be supposed that in the BPRS the anergy scale has affected the total value in such a way that psychopathological improvements could be chiefly attributed to reduction of minus symptoms. We will therefore look at the results of the individual scales. In the

BPRS it is true that there was significant reduction in the anergy scale, but also in the hostility scale and optically also in the other positive symptom scales (Figure 9).

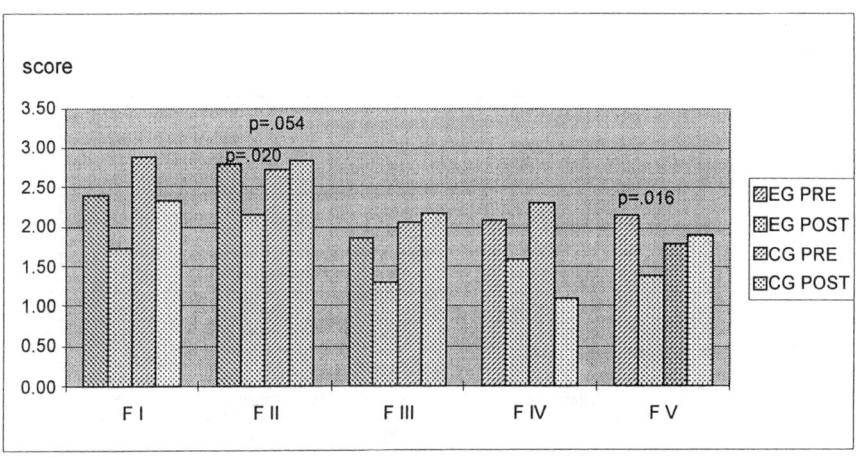

Figure 9. Mean values in Brief Psychiatric Rating Scale (BPRS):
   Factor I: Anxiety & Depression   Factor II: Anergia
   Factor III: Thought Disorders   Factor IV: Activation
   Factor V: Malevolence
   (The lower the value the less Psychopathology)

Emotion and drive in the SANS showed significant improvement, but not anhedonia and attention (Figure 10). The alogia factor was only significant in the interaction due to opposite effects.

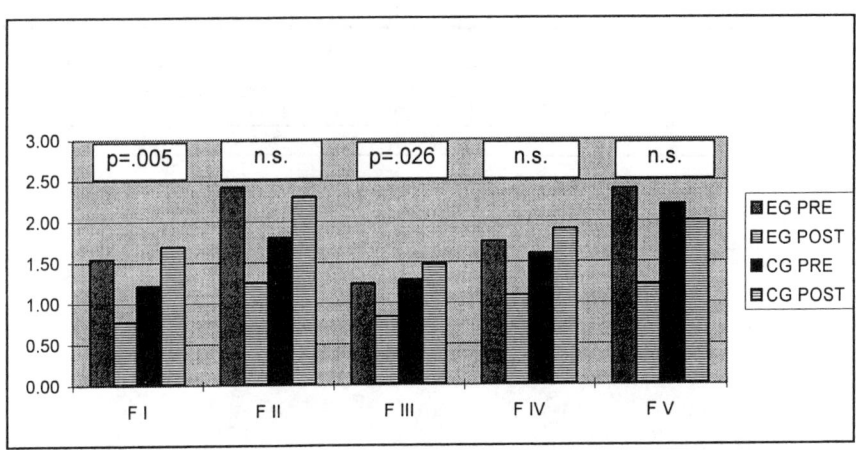

Figure 10. Mean values in Scale for the Assessment of Negative Symptoms (SANS)
   Factor I: Flattening or fixedness of affect Factor II: Alogia
   Factor III: Abulia-apathy   Factor IV: Anhedonia - social retirement
   Factor V: Attention
   (The lower the value, the less the psychopathology)

The results of the MANOVA with mean values and standard deviations are shown in table 8.

Table 8. Psychopathology
BPRS

	TIME 1		TIME 2		T-Test
FACTOR I	Mean value	SD	Mean value	SD	
Experimental group	2.40	1.09	1.73	0.68	
Control group	2.89	0.94	2.33	1.21	
Group x time			n.s.		
FACTOR II	Mean value	SD	Mean value	SD	
Experimental group	2.79	1.15	2.15	0.68	p=.020
Control group	2.73	1.13	2.85	1.09	n.s.
Group x time			F(1)=4.24 p=.054		
FACTOR III	Mean value	SD	Mean value	SD	
Experimental group	1.85	0.90	1.29	0.37	
Control group	2.05	0.94	2.18	1.22	
Group x time			n.s.		
FACTOR IV	Mean value	SD	Mean value	SD	
Experimental group	2.08	0.89	1.58	0.67	
Control group	2.30	1.10	2.07	0.86	
Group x time			n.s.		
FACTOR V	Mean value	SD	Mean value	SD	
Experimental group	2.14	1.37	1.39	0.55	p=.016
Control group	1.80	1.02	1.90	0.69	n.s.
Group x time			F(1)=4.43 p=.050		
FACTOR VI	Mean value	SD	Mean value	SD	
Experimental group	40.83	8.94	29.58	4.52	p<.001
Control group	44.30	9.79	41.30	13.28	n.s.
Group x time			F(1)=5.84 p=.027		

(Table 8. continued)
SANS

	TIME 1		TIME 2		T-Test
	Mean value	SD	Mean value	SD	
FACTOR I					
Experimental group	1.54	1.33	0.77	0.71	p=.015
Control group	1.21	1.05	1.69	1.30	n.s.
Group x time	F(1)=10.52 p=.005				
FACTOR I Global	Mean value	SD	Mean value	SD	
Experimental group	2.42	1.51	1.25	1.06	p=.002
Control group	1.80	1.40	2.30	1.49	n.s.
Group x time	F(1)=15.55 p=.001				
FACTOR II	Mean value	SD	Mean value	SD	
Experimental group	1.23	1.07	0.83	0.59	n.s.
Control group	1.28	1.34	1.48	1.26	n.s.
Group x time	F(1)=5.13 p=.036				
FACTOR II Global	Mean value	SD	Mean value	SD	
Experimental group	1.75	1.49	1.08	0.79	n.s.
Control group	1.60	1.51	1.90	1.45	n.s.
Group x time	F(1)=4.65 p=.045				
FACTOR III	Mean value	SD	Mean value	SD	
Experimental group	2.39	1.25	1.22	0.80	p=.003
Control group	2.20	1.68	2.00	1.65	n.s.
Group x time	F(1)=5.90 p=.026				
FACTOR III Global	Mean value	SD	Mean value	SD	
Experimental group	2.83	1.34	1.75	1.06	p=.004
Control group	2.80	1.87	2.50	1.84	n.s.
Group x time	F(1)=3.61 p=.074				
FACTOR IV	Mean value	SD	Mean value	SD	
Experimental group	3.10	1.41	2.35	0.96	
Control group	2.83	1.09	2.92	1.47	
Group x time	n.s.				
FACTOR IV Global	Mean value	SD	Mean value	SD	
Experimental group	3.17	1.47	1.92	0.90	p=.002
Control group	3.10	1.37	3.10	1.29	n.s.
Group x time	F(1)=4.58 p=.046				
FACTOR V	Mean value	SD	Mean value	SD	
Experimental group	1.13	1.17	0.46	0.66	
Control group	1.40	1.39	1.20	1.80	
Group x time	n.s.				
FACTOR V Global	Mean value	SD	Mean value	SD	
Experimental group	1.42	1.56	0.58	0.79	
Control group	1.27	1.35	1.10	1.60	
Group x time	n.s.				
SUM	Mean value	SD	Mean value	SD	
Experimental group	20.97	11.24	12.22	5.97	p=.002
Control group	19.61	11.56	20.14	12.53	n.s.
Group x time	F(1)=7.61 p=.013				
SUM - Global	Mean value	SD	Mean value	SD	
Experimental group	9.38	5.08	5.64	2.62	p=.003
Control group	8.17	4.97	8.39	5.86	n.s.
Group x time	F(1)=5.95 p=.026				

Overall the results show that psychopathological symptoms underwent interesting changes.

Qualitative feedback from the patients:

At the end of the training course the patients (N: 11, since one patient had been discharged and therefore declined to answer) were asked about their impressions and their opinion of the course. It turned out that nearly all of them rated the course very positively and felt it had positive effects. But it was also interesting that almost all patients felt subjectively that it had no effect on concentration (Figure 11).

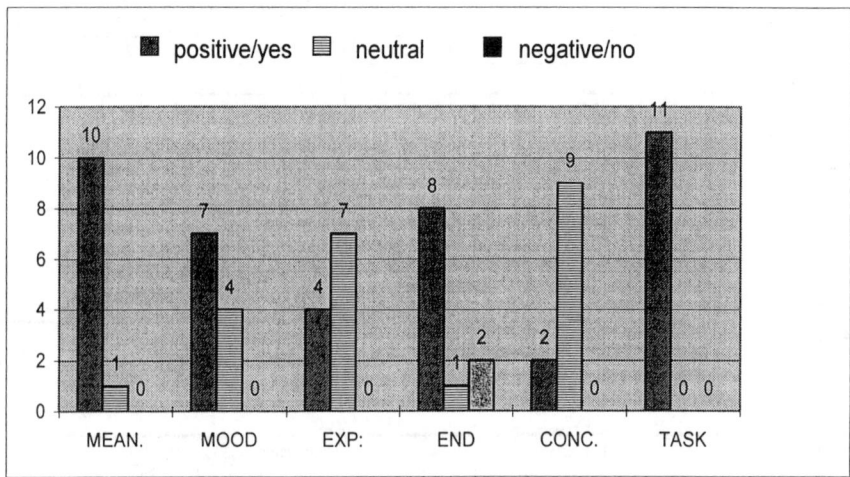

Figure 11. Qualitative interview (N=11)
MEAN.: Meaning oft the training course
MOOD: Influence on mood
EXP.: Expectations at the beginning of the course
END: Did the end of the course arouse regret
CONC.: Any effects noticed on concentration?
TASK: Improvement noticed with tasks?

4.2.4 Second Study: Discussion

Field studies of this kind are especially vulnerable to criticism in respect of method. We shall consider the most important aspects: The number of patients involved was of course small. And yet this makes the significant psychopathology results all the more astonishing. An important factor could be the weakness of the empty control group. It is likely that the feeling of receiving extra attention played a role here. It had been planned to let the control patients form waiting groups and to transfer them into the experimental group. Since the second phase of the investigation had to be postponed for quite a long time for organizational reasons, all the patients except one had been discharged. But why should extra attention not cause improvement of cognitive performance, as it did with psychopathology? Medication definitely played no important role, since it was only changed marginally and then in both groups.

Why was there no improvement or only slight improvement in cognitive performance? And yet there was possibly a discrete difference between basic and complex parameters. The variables rated as basic show no improvement, while the more complex area covered by "Word recognition" shows improvement in the mean values, even if these are not significant, to the advantage of the experimental group. If this is interpretable at all, could it be a reflection of what Olbrich and Mussgay (1990) supposed? Namely that such cognitive training is more likely to improve complex performance by way of compensation. Should we further conclude that the basic parameters are vulnerability indicators?

This is a far-reaching hypothesis. For it is still unclear whether the parameters used are sufficiently specific or valid. It is also still an open question whether these particular programs, Cognition and Planning, are sufficiently specific. Cognition was partly developed in relation to schizophrenic cognitive abilities. However, Planning is a more complex program and was originally developed for deficits in planning behavior of people with frontal lobe brain damage. Since this program is theoretically aimed at information processing rather than information reception, as in the case of Cognition, two thirds of the available time were devoted to it. Is it possible that Planning is too complex and that it might hide possible effects from Cognition? In respect of the specificity of the training programs used, Mussgay (1993) concluded in his overview of computer-aided training methods that improvements can also occur on the basic level if the content of the program is specifically aimed at this level. In connection with the great variety of cognitive disturbances in schizophrenic patients, he proposed, in accordance with Spaulding *et al* (1986), to create individual performance profiles to which the program content could be adapted. It is thus possible that in our studies the selected variables were too specific and that the methods used were too unspecific.

Why did the psychopathological parameters improve? The negative symptoms were most affected. This can be explained fairly plausibly by an increase in drive due to the highly structured demands and the instructions to work quickly. In more general terms it is possible that something occurred such as self-efficacy or an improvement in self-confidence. The subjective experience of the patients supports this. Although the hostility factor only offers an indirect indication of the effect of cognitive training on positive symptoms, qualitative tendencies should also be included in the interpretation. Even then the data would substantiate neither Brenner's pervasivity model, nor Hemsley's transaction model, since for this the cognitive performance would have to improve.

Until further studies have got to the bottom of this phenomenon, whereby a specific computer-aided cognitive training program is more likely to improve psychopathological symptoms than cognitive performance, we can only make a pragmatic assumption for the time being: It seems that neutral reality testing, continually forced by the PC (together with carefully considered medication), may help to reduce irrational fantasies. This might be more difficult to achieve in the social context. Therefore the claim we made at the beginning, i.e. that it is better to carry out cognitive training first in order to improve the chances of success of subsequent more complex programs, could prove to be valid for different reasons. Not the improvement of cognitive skills, but the improvement of irrational cognition (as a synonym for productive psychopathology) would then be the essential aspect. Further research projects should investigate these interesting questions.

In conclusion here is one of the many positive comments made by the patients. On his way to a training session, a patient met two others who were leaving after a session and he saw them talking and laughing. He said: "You know, I have been on the same ward as them for five months, I see them day in, day out. I have never even seen them smile. That is what the computer training does for us." Putting cognitive training before more complex treatment elements therefore has not only the advantage of strengthening the receptivity by improving cognitive deficits, but possibly even causes a reduction in respect of psychopathology. This observed improvement in psychopathological symptoms probably results in improved receptivity for subsequent interventions of a more far-reaching nature. And perhaps the most important factor for further therapeutic measures is strengthened motivation and intention to change (see phase 2 of the therapy process model). The second investigation, described below, relates to phase 4 (actual therapy), and is concerned with the specific effectiveness of more complex cognitive-behavior therapeutic methods in comparison to behavioral interventions such as social skills training.

4.3 A comparison between cognitive therapy and social skills therapy with chronic schizophrenic patients. Do these interventions have specific effects? [4]

4.3.1 Introduction

Investigation into the specific effects of different program components in schizophrenia therapy seems necessary in the first place for practical and economic reasons. Why should patients be offered a global broad-spectrum program, if in their case only certain components are required? This question is also valid in view of the risks of overstimulation in treating schizophrenics. Secondly, the question of specific effects is interesting for theoretical reasons. It ought to be possible to demonstrate empirically the effect of any therapeutic methods specially developed to treat basic schizophrenic disturbances that are known to exist. The fundamental problem here is surely that up to now we only have an approximate idea as to what basic disturbances are. We also do not know whether the basic disturbances shown in experimental investigations are specific to schizophrenia. The knowledge gained about possible relationships between basic disturbances and therapeutic methods will inevitably be limited, if the programs used are made up of a variety of methods, with different theoretical and practical bases. The specific effects of any particular method, thought to be effective in treating basic disturbances, can only be investigated, if it is used alone and compared for control purposes with other methods directed at different behaviors, for example social behavior. In the vulnerability-stress model, therapy that is meant to treat basic disturbances is oriented toward the vulnerability of the patients, while therapy meant to improve social skills tends to be related to stress factors in their social environment. Psychophysiological activation is taken to be the modulatory target variable. It plays a role in both cases and is treated

---

[4] In collaboration with H.-J. Zinner and H.J. Möller

with relaxation training. Figure 12 shows the general scheme for such an investigation.

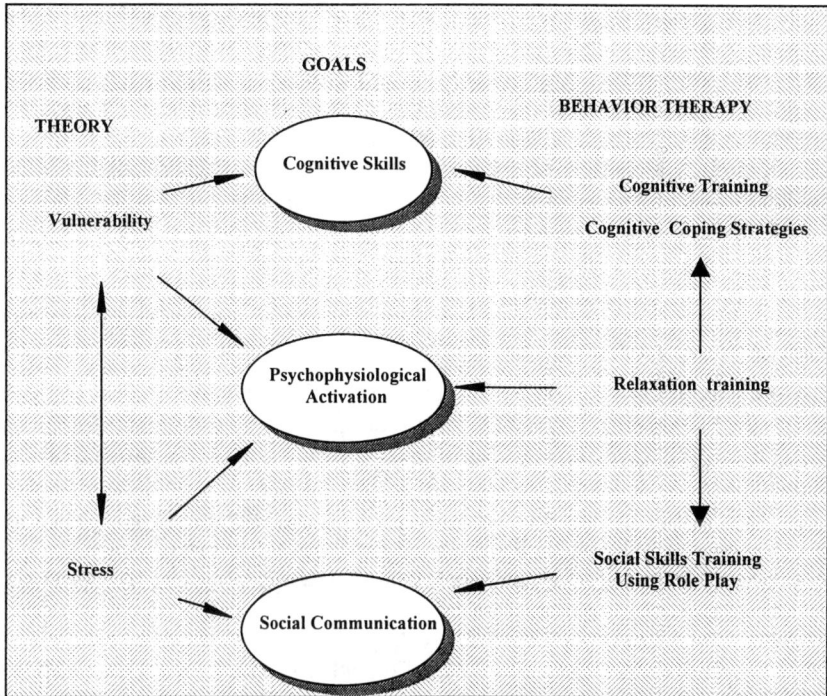

Figure 12. Scheme for comparing cognitive therapy and social skills training in chronic schizophrenic patients.

The investigation was based on the following hypotheses:
1. The main effect of cognitive therapy is to improve cognitive skills.
2. The main effect of social skills training is to improve social behavior.
3. A supplementary open question was asked: What is the effect of the therapy on the patient's state of well-being (feeling of discomfort versus feeling of well-being)? This question was included in order to monitor overstimulation caused by the therapy as a possible intervening variable.

4.3.2 Method of investigation

In a rehabilitation center for schizophrenic patients[5], two groups were conducted for approximately the same duration of time, (3-4 months), number of hours (79), intervals between sessions (up to 4 times a week), basic therapeutic methods used, therapists and number of clients, with random distribution of the patients. One group

---

[5] Sociopsychiatric Center of the DPWV Munich. Director: Hans Kiefer (Dipl.-Päd.). We thank all staff whose whole-hearted cooperation contributed to the success of this project, with special thanks to the deputy director, Dr. Monika Wetzel.

was treated with methods based on cognitive therapy, while the other group was given social therapy. The cognitive therapy program contained the components cognitive differentiation, social perception (Roder *et al*, 1988, 1992), and training in self-instruction problem-solving devised by Meichenbaum (1977a). The social therapy methods included role-plays with video feedback to promote social skills devised by Liberman *et al* (1989). In both groups, general therapy included information about the vulnerability-stress model or discussion of the patients' subjective model of their illness and relaxation training.

Hypothetical basic disturbances, basic symptoms, psychopathology and social behavior were taken account of by extensive documentation on several levels: Under **basic disturbances**, we understand relatively elementary functions, which have been thoroughly tested in the field of experimental psychology, and which can perhaps be described as typical or close to the substrate. These functions were measured using the following cognitive tests and activation-methods: three subtests from Repeated Psychological Measurements (RPM; Fahrenberg *et al*, 1977); d2 test (Concentration; Brickenkamp, 1981); Continuous Performance Test (CPT)[6]; Span of Apprehension Test (SAT)[6]; reaction time (RT)[6]; electrodermal activity (orienting reaction).

The second level (**basic symptoms**) is in our opinion more complex and phenomenological, and could possibly reflect the subjective and objective impression of the basic disturbance. We used the FCQ Questionnaire (Frankfurt Complaints Questionnaire; Süllwold, 1986a); the Scale for Assessment of Negative Symptoms (SANS, Andreasen, 1981); and the Scale of Intentionality (InSka) by Mundt *et al*, (1985).

As a third level, we recorded **psychopathology** using the following scales: the Brief Psychiatric Rating Scale (BPRS; Overall & Gorham, 1962); the AMDP system (AMDP, 1981); the Paranoid-Depressivity Scale (PD-S) and the Disturbance-List (D-L); (the latter scales taken from von Zerssen, 1981).

Finally, variables of **social behavior** were recorded using the Uncertainty (U) Questionnaire (Ullrich & Ullrich de Muynck, 1976b), together with an assessment by the therapeutic staff, and the Social Interview Schedule (Social Maladjustment Schedule) (SIS; Hecht *et al*, 1987). The effect of therapy on the patient's subjective condition was checked before and after each session using a visual analogue scale (extreme feeling of discomfort versus extreme feeling of well-being).

Of the 56 patients recruited, 43 remained for the evaluation. Eleven patients were not included, either as a result of other diagnoses or because they stopped coming for therapy (of which two declined to continue and six were prematurely discharged from the Center). The cognitive remediation group consisted of 23 participants, and the social training group had 20.

---

[6] In grateful cooperation with Prof. Dr. K. Hahlweg, Dr. G. Hank, and Dr. M. Römer, formerly Max Planck Institute for Psychiatry. CPT and SAT: Nuechterlein version.

The patients were characterized by the following variables (mean value and range):

DSM-IV diagnosis (295.30; 295.10):	Chronic schizophrenic disturbance
Age:	34 (22 - 49)
Intelligence:	106 (88 - 136)
Duration of illness:	11 years (3 - 26)
Hospitalization:	16 months (0 -26)
Duration of rehabilitation in this center:	20 months (3 - 76)
Medication/patient:	On average 12'000 or 380 chlorpromazine equivalence units per month or day respectively

Statistics: After checking the distributions, single-factor analysis of variance was possible for most variables. Where this was not the case, the testing method is given in the text[7].

4.3.3 Results concerning the effects of the therapy

First we shall answer the supplementary question concerning the unspecific effects of the therapy on the patient's sense of well-being. To determine this, a visual analogue scale with the poles 'Extreme feeling of discomfort' versus 'Extreme feeling of well-being' was given to the patients before and after every session.

In both groups, the patients felt significantly better after the sessions than they did immediately before (Wilcoxon test: $p \leq 0.5$). Now it might be thought that the patients were happy when the session was over. However, we are inclined to think that the therapeutic methods themselves had a positive effect, because during the whole course of therapy, the way the patients felt before the sessions also improved progressively: 15 out of 20 patients (75%) in the social training program felt increasingly better (binomial test $p \leq .01$). In the cognitive therapy program, 13 out of 23 patients (57%) felt better (n.s.). Fluency, Number Cancellation, Letter Symbolization and Concentration (d2) improved significantly. The reaction time in the Span of Apprehension Test also sank significantly. Electrodermal activity decreased significantly (stimuli till habituation). Spontaneous fluctuations at rest and in the test were also reduced, but not significantly (Table 9).

To come now to the real effects of the therapy, these can be described as follows:

Basic disturbances: The results of the two-factor ANOVA (Analysis of Variance) with one group factor (cognitive vs. social skills training) and one repeated-measurements factor, showed significant improvements on the time factor in various parameters. Basic vigilance skills (Continuous Performance Test) and span of apprehension showed almost no improvement. On the other hand, some rather more complex parameters in the Repeated Psychological Measurements such as Word Fluency, Number Cancellation, Letter Symbolization and Concentration (d2) improved significantly. The reaction time in the Span of Apprehension Test also sank significantly. Electrodermal activity decreased significantly (stimuli till habituation). Spontaneous fluctuations at rest and in the test were also reduced, but not significantly.

Basic symptoms: There were improvements in the total scores for all parameters. Symptoms such as loss of drive, disorders of thought and perception, anhedonia and loss of automatism were significantly reduced in both groups. The differences in the

---

[7] Statistics program: BMDP 3 D on Siemens BS 2000. Our thanks to Mr. H. Mayr for the statistical evaluation.

mean values show that patients receiving cognitive therapy had more high values (Table 10).

Table 9. Hypothetical basic disturbances: Results of cognitive therapy in comparison to social skills therapy.

Variables	Cognitive Therapy		Social skill training		Source	df	F	p
	pre M (SD)	post M (SD)	pre M (SD)	post M (SD)				
SAT hits	49 (6)	50 (5)	49 (8)	50 (8)	G	1	.03	-
					T	1	0.37	-
					GxT	1	0.28	-
CPT Sens. Index	83 (10)	85 (11)	82 (12)	84 (11)	G	1	.06	-
					T	1	3.01	*
					GxT	1	.03	-
RPM^1	19 (10)	28 (11)	19 (8)	26 (11)	G	1	.08	-
					T	1	60.4	***
					GxT	1	.22	-
RPM^2	132 (45)	150 (48)	121 (51)	136 (50)	G	1	1.12	-
					T	1	11.29	***
					GxT	1	.16	-
RPM^3	56 (20)	55 (20)	59 (21)	61 (22)	G	1	.59	-
					T	1	.20	-
					GxT	1	.96	-
d2	39 (37)	41 (37)	37 (36)	44 (36)	G	1	.00	-
					T	1	3.7	**
					GxT	1	.96	-
Reaction time (SAT)	1118 (325)	936 (260)	975 (235)	868 (209)	G	1	1.85	-
					T	1	28.14	**
					GxT	1	1.87	-
EDA (N stimuli to habituation)	4 (4)	3 (4)	7 (7)	5 (6)	G	1	3.11	-
					T	1	4.47	**
					GxT	1	.33	-
EDA Spont.fluct. Rest	30 (76)	20 (24)	24 (27)	21 (30)	G	1	.06	-
					T	1	.48	-
					GxT	1	.12	-
EDA Spont.fluct. Test	20 (39)	15 (17)	23 (23)	19 (26)	G	1	.21	-
					T	1	.61	-
					GxT	1	.02	-

Mean values, standard deviations, and results of analysis of variance; * $p \leq .09$; ** $p \leq .05$; *** $p \leq .01$
G = group, T = time; SAT = Span of Apprehension; CPT = Continuous Performance Test; RPM = Repeated Psychological Measurements; RPM1 = RPM Recognizing words; RPM2 = RPM Crossing out numbers, RPM3 = RPM Number symbol; EDA = Electrodermal Activity.

Psychopathology: Table 11 shows self-rating and ratings by others for various psychopathological symptoms. On the level of self-assessment (Paranoid-Depressivity Scale, Disturbance List), there were no significant changes, and the same was true of such a generalized scale as the Clinical Global Impressions. With rating by others, however, the total score on the Brief Psychiatric Rating Scale (BPRS) was reduced, and depressive and psycho-organic symptoms in the AMDP were significantly reduced on the time factor (Table 11).

Table 10. Basic symptoms or negative symptoms. Results of cognitive therapy compared with social training.

Basic Symptoms	Cognitive Therapy		Social skill training		Source	df	F	p
	pre M (SD)	post M (SD)	pre M (SD)	post M (SD)				
FBF (□)	25 (23)	18 (20)	22 (20)	15 (21)	G	1	.37	-
					T	1	13.30	***
					GxT	1	.02	-
SANS 6	44 (36)	36 (21)	43 (20)	40 (20)	G	1	.04	-
					T	1	17.07	***
					GxT	1	3.27	*
SANS 7	10 (4)	9 (5)	10 (5)	9 (4)	G	1	.01	-
					T	1	13.14	***
					GxT	1	3.20	*
INSKA 7	24 (10)	21 (9)	24 (10)	23 (10)	G	1	.24	-
					T	1	10.88	***
					GxT	1	1.56	-

Mean values, standard deviations, and results of analysis of variance; * $p \leq .09$; ** $p \leq .05$; *** $p \leq .01$
SANS = Scale for Assessment of Negative Symptoms; FBQ = Frankfurt Complaint Questionnaire (Symptoms questionnaire); INSKA = Intentionality Scale

Table 11. Psychopathology. Results of cognitive therapy compared with social skills training.

Psycho-pathology	Cognitive Therapy		Social skill training		Source	df	F	p
	pre M (SD)	post M (SD)	pre M (SD)	post M (SD)				
BPRS (□)	35 (8)	32 (9)	35 (8)	33 (9)	G	1	0.8	-
					T	1	8.39	***
					GxT	1	0.9	-
AMDP 10 (paran., hall.)	4 (4)	3 (4)	4 (4)	4 (4)	G	1	.01	-
					T	1	1.35	-
					GxT	1	.37	-
AMDP 11	9 (6)	7 (5)	9 (5)	7 (4)	G	1	.09	-
					T	1	16.14	***
					GxT	1	.10	-
AMDP 12=3 (psychoorg.)	2 (2)	1 (1)	2 (2)	2 (2)	G	1	.05	-
					T	1	6.05	**
					GxT	1	2.07	-
CGI (1) Degree of severity of illness	5 (1)	5 (1)	5 (1)	5 (1)	G	1	.03	-
					T	1	1.13	-
					GxT	1	.01	-
PD-S (paranoid)	9 (7)	7 (9)	9 (16)	6 (6)	G	1	.03	-
					T	1	2.19	-
					GxT	1	.45	-
PD-S (depress.)	12 (8)	11 (10)	12 (9)	12 (9)	G	1	.04	-
					T	1	.68	-
					GxT	1	.01	-
B-L (psycho-veget.)	21 (14)	19 (16)	21 (15)	19 (15)	G	1	.00	-
					T	1	2.23	-
					GxT	1	.00	-

Mean values, standard deviations, and results of analysis of variance; * $p \leq .09$; ** $p \leq .05$; *** $p \leq .01$
G = group, T = time; BPRS = Brief Psychiatric Rating Scale; AMDP = Psychopathological findings; CGI = Clinical Global Impression; PD-S = Paranoid-Depressivity Scale

Social skills: In self-assessment (Uncertainty Questionnaire) there were significant improvements in both groups in five out of six factors. Here again the differ ences in the mean values are more clearly marked in the cognitive therapy group. Assessment by others using more global scales, i.e. the Social Interview Schedule, and ratings by ergotherapeutic staff, showed no changes (Table 12).

Table 12. Social skills. Results of cognitive therapy compared with social skills training.

Social skills	Cognitive Therapy pre M (SD)	Cognitive Therapy post M (SD)	Social skill training pre M (SD)	Social skill training post M (SD)	Source	df	F	p
U1 (Fear of failure)	33 (16)	23 (16)	33 (16)	33 (181)	G	1	1.77	-
					T	1	5.35	**
					GxT	1	5.87	**
U2 (Fear of criticism)	31 (15)	23 (15)	31 (12)	26 (16)	G	1	.16	-
					T	1	16.26	***
					GxT	1	.83	-
U3 (Making demands)	41 (11)	48 (14)	43 (13)	45 (13)	G	1	.00	-
					T	1	7.27	***
					GxT	1	.05	-
U4 (Fear of rejection)	25 (11)	22 (10)	26 (12)	24 (11)	G	1	.39	-
					T	1	6.15	**
					GxT	1	.05	-
U5 (Guilt feelings)	7 (5)	6 (6)	6 (5)	6 (6)	G	1	.48	-
					T	1	.37	-
					GxT	1	1.12	-
U6 (Respect-ability)	12 (5)	10 (6)	13 (7)	11 (6)	G	1	.48	-
					T	1	4.75	**
					GxT	1	.23	-
Ergotherapy assessment (EBP)	18 (6)	20 (6)	20 (6)	21 (5)	G	1	1.61	-
					T	1	2.76	-
					GxT	1	.15	-
SIS Objective conditions	25 (2)	25 (3)	24 (4)	24 (4)	G	1	1.61	-
					T	1	.15	-
					GxT	1	.15	-
SIS Management Problems	22 (5)	22 (5)	23 (4)	22 (4)	G	1	.25	-
					T	1	.56	-
					GxT	1	.00	-
SIS Satisfaction	37 (6)	38 (6)	39 (6)	40 (5)	G	1	1.59	-
					T	1	2.60	-
					GxT	1	.05	-
SIS Social Support	12 (2)	12 (2)	13 (3)	13 (3)	G	1	.17	-
					T	1	.07	-
					GxT	1	.12	-

Mean values, standard deviations, and results of analysis of variance; * $p \leq .09$; ** $p \leq .05$; *** $p \leq .01$
G = group, T = time; U = Uncertainty Questionnaire; SIS = Social Interview Schedule

4.3.4 Summary of results and discussion

First it is important to stress the need for great care in interpretation, as the methods used in the investigation were not sufficiently stringent on some important points. Despite the high number of variables, no α-adjustment was carried out; this seemed legitimate in a pilot study. Trends were also interpreted, and for organizational reasons (duration of project) no control group was recruited. In view of these methodological weaknesses, the results can be used qualitatively and for the generation of hypotheses.

Having said this, we can now summarize the results of the investigation: Both types of treatment - cognitive therapy and social skills training - clearly produced a positive effect on the way schizophrenic patients felt. In both cases, the patients felt better after the sessions than they had before, and the way they felt before the sessions showed progressive improvement during the course of therapy. It seems that the patients liked coming to therapy sessions. Confirmation of this can be seen in statements made by the patients themselves, in the relatively low absence rate, and in the small number of drop-outs. The main question being investigated, however, was if the two interventions would have specific effects on cognitive deficits, coping strategies and social skills respectively.

1. To sum up, it must be said that, contrary to the hypotheses, both therapeutic methods produced some effects in all behavior areas. As only the effects over a certain time were significant, the results do not say anything about whether cognitive therapy specifically modified cognitive impairments, in the sense of basic disturbances and basic symptoms, or whether social skills training specifically modified social deficits. As it was not possible to recruit a control group, it is legitimate to ask whether the patients might have improved anyway, even without this special treatment. This seems unlikely if one considers that all the patients had already been in rehabilitation for a long time, and also considering the fact that significant effects were achieved at all. The patients in the group showed no special motivation. It was planned to carry out these programs in addition to existing rehabilitation programs, but this turned out to be impossible; at the most 5% of the participants were recruited. Another objection is that there might have been influences such as the novelty effect, or that this was a special form of attention from persons in another institution. However, this seems unlikely in view of the clinical impression, the relatively high frequency of the sessions, the duration of therapy, and the statements made by the patients themselves, who always related back to their special problems. There were also no relevant changes in medication, and no correlation in any sense between medication and the variables measured. If one considers the absolute differences in the mean values, the cognitive therapy group generally did better. Within the variables which became significant at all (17 out of 22), there were clearer differences in the case of patients receiving cognitive therapy in eleven variables, and in only two variables in the case of patients receiving social skills training. This was also confirmed in pre-post comparisons within the groups using t-tests and non-parametric methods (Kraemer *et al*, 1991). Although we must not let ourselves be deceived by illusions, these clues do appear to suggest that cognitive therapy with chronic schizophrenic patients, even if not very specific, is a suitable instrument for improving some cognitive skills, and reducing negative symptoms (see SANS, InSka, FCQ, BPRS, AMDP) and social uncertainty.

2. Independent of the specificity of the therapeutic methods used, these results lead to further interesting questions. Among those variables which were defined as basic disturbances, neither vigilance (CPT) nor span of apprehension (SAT) nor the phasic measure of activation based on spontaneous fluctuations showed any significant change, while reaction time, a tonic measure of activation (reactions up to habituation), and three other cognitive parameters did. It would probably be too speculative, in view of the methods used in this not very stringent field study to assume that the unchanged parameters represent traits in the sense of

vulnerability indicators or basic disturbances. However, Spring et al (1990) attribute these features to vigilance and span of apprehension. Is it possible therefore that 'only' compensating strategies are improved, which are then reflected in the other variables? Or is there, perhaps, improvement of an unspecific, general variable, such as drive (see reaction time), which has certain variables as concomitants but not others? To answer these questions, more finely differentiated studies would be required, for it is certainly possible to find simpler explanations with less risk of circular reasoning.

4.4 Outlook

These investigations show that specific therapeutic inventions can help schizophrenic patients. Important aspects of their psychopathology are improved and the therapy probably gives them something like self-efficacy and quality of life. In the light of the therapy process model of Prochaska et al (1992), these selected studies seem to indicate that before entering more complex therapy programs patients should first be offered specific help in addressing cognitive problems which they experience subjectively. This has been discussed in the context of improving information processing through cognitive training with a view to more far-reaching interventions (Brenner et al, 1994; Liberman et al, 1995). But preliminary cognitive therapy would also seem to play a useful role in reducing demoralization and encouraging the patient in his or her intention to change.

The actual, more complex psychotherapy methods, whether cognitive or behavioral, are effective in important areas. The patients feel comfortable, i.e. the therapy has no intrusive effect, to which they would react with negative feelings. We can therefore assume that the degree of well-being reflects aspects of the therapeutic relationship and positive social interactions with other group members. A reduction in psychopathology was obtained, especially with regard to negative symptoms (including the psycho-organic syndrome in the AMDP system). This probably means that an important contributing factor in the chronicity of the illness can be modified by cognitive behavior therapy. The effects of computer-aided cognitive training suggest that it is possible to influence negative symptoms quite early on. The present study was carried out with chronic schizophrenic patients, but Hermautz and Gestrich (1991) have used this kind of cognitive training with acute patients and have observed an effect on psychopathology.

There was also a positive change in the patients' subjective impression with regard to social insecurity. It is possible that processes of self-efficacy contributed to this effect. Apart from these two limited studies there seems to be general agreement that the effects observed justify the amount of work involved. Behavior therapy measures tailored to suit the patient's individual problems seem to be useful for these patients. Of course financial resources should continue to be made available for research into the effects of psychotherapy. But it is equally important that investigations should be carried out into the therapy process (Clarkin, 1998), which has been taken into account only marginally in our studies. Thus, for example, attention could be directed towards therapy motivation in schizophrenic patients. For it is not possible to reach all of these patients nor to reach them at all times. Psychoeducative methods (Bäuml et al, 1998) and especially computer-aided cognitive training methods appear to be one way of addressing this problem. However, no investigations have yet been carried out on motivation processes. One aspect of therapy motivation is medication compliance, which can clearly be improved through participation in psychoeducative groups. It has also been possible to raise the acceptance rate for subsequent psychotherapy in the case of depressive patients in psychoeducative groups, in relation to motivation for more far-reaching psychotherapy (Jacob et al, 1987). In a controlled investigation on the effects of psychoeducation in schizophrenic patients (N:163), the number of patients who afterwards accepted psychotherapy was higher in the experimental group (34.6%) than in the control group (23.2%); statistically however the difference was not significant (Pitschel-Walz, 1999). This raises questions relating for example to how to communicate what is meant by psychoeducation, or to the processes used by doctors in deciding indications, and will certainly spur further research into the problem of motivation.

The therapeutic relationship, which has only very rarely been empirically investigated in schizophrenic patients, is considered as another variable in the therapy process. First results of case studies or *a posteriori* inquiry have yielded the following facts: the therapeutic relationship is important for these patients, just as with other types of disorder, and the patients are able to make discriminating assessments of it (Stark et al, 1992). What is known as the cooperation sequence, a possibility of operationalizing therapeutic relationships, defined by the emotional support given by the therapist and the initiative/cooperation of the patient (see coding system for interaction (CIP) in psychotherapy, Schindler, 1989), also occurs in schizophrenic patients (Kraemer et al, 1999c). However, there is no connection between this and the success of the therapy, as is the case with other disorders (Kraemer et al, 1999c). These results should be further investigated, since existing studies on this topic are unsatisfactory from a methodical point of view.

Another very interesting attempt to throw light on therapy processes in these patients is the analysis of emotion/abstraction patterns in verbatim records of interviews (Mergenthaler, 1998). These patterns can be used to identify key sessions or good phases during the course of psychotherapy. Mergenthaler's text analysis method showing emotion/abstraction patterns has already proved useful for identifying key sessions in the case of other disorders and analytic therapy. For schizophrenic patients and for cognitive behavior therapy it was used by us in a case study for the first time (Kraemer et al, 1999a,b). It includes both computer-aided frequency calculation and the relative level of intensity of emotionally colored terms and abstractions in transscribed therapeutic interviews. When intense emotional coloring is combined with a high level of abstraction in the recorded speech of the patient, this is called "connecting". This pattern ought to be related to a successful outcome of the therapy, since it represents insight backed by feeling. The questions in our study were related to pattern frequencies, links with success of the therapy, and connections between emotion/abstraction patterns and other process-oriented measurement scales such as well-being (emotion) and session assessment (reflection).

First results suggest that the distribution of patterns for our patients is similar to that for other disorders, that the "connecting" pattern is related to success of the therapy, and that there are plausible correlations with other relevant variables. As far as we know, these methods for investigating the therapy process are relatively theory-free and well operationalized, in comparison for example to the SASB (Benjamin, 1982). They can thus be usefully applied to various diagnosis groups and therapy methods. These suggestions represent only a few possibilities for research in the wide field of psychotherapy for schizophrenic patients. The further development of research and practice in this field is and remains a challenge. The primary goal must always be to help the patients.

Appendix

Appendix A:
Important Concepts in Cognitive Therapy

Attribution

Attribution theory is concerned with the study of perceived causation. With the process of attribution, an event that is a consequence of one's own or another person's behavior is ascribed cause and/or motive (Heider, 1958; Jones & Davis, 1965; Kelley, 1973). In general, three dimensions of attribution can be distinguished (Heider, 1958): 1. Causal attribution to one's self (internal) or to another person (external), 2. time dimension: the reason/cause for the event is stable or unstable over time, and 3. control attribution relates to the subjective experience of ability/disability to have an influence on certain events. The nature of, thus, always has an effect on emotions and behavior. On the one hand, the act of attribution has the function of giving an explanation for the past. On the other, it makes future events predictable (Forsyth, 1980).

Automatic Thoughts

Automatic thoughts develop from a person's system of attitudes and are at the same time the key to identify it (Beck *et al*, 1979). In the first place, it is a question of interpreting events and not so much an acting guide. In a wider sense, automatic thoughts are a non-reflective response to information input, and can include a broad array of subjects (e.g. appraising one's own abilities, judgments about the future, etc.). Automatic thoughts arise spontaneously, their course is very fast and stereotypical, and they seem very plausible. They influence both emotions and behavior.

Basic Cognitive (Dys)functions, Disturbances, Impairments

Research, diagnosis and therapy of basic cognitive functions has become the domain of neuropsychological and information processing approaches (Goldberg *et al*, 1991; Straube & Oades, 1992; Brenner *et al*, 1983; David & Cutting, 1994). Neuropsychological testing focuses on intelligence, memory, attention, language, perception and motor functions. Sophisticated tests, which are often administered with the assistance of computers, are now available to measure attentional and perceptual dysfunctions. This computerized diagnosis is a means of collecting 'micropsychopathological' data (Merlo & Studer, 1993). In combination with methods of neuroimaging and psychophysiology, a large body of data has emerged in the last years showing attentional and mnestic dysfunctions as well as impairments in abstraction and concept formation in schizophrenic patients. Data on attentional deficits were mainly collected with the Reaction Time Test (RT), the Continuous Performance Test (CPT), the Span of Apprehension Test (SAT) and the Backward Masking Test. Depending on the version of these tests employed, the capacity of the working memory has also been considered (Nuechterlein, 1991). The Wisconsin Card Sorting Test (WCST) is one of the most widely applied tests for measuring concept formation and abstraction (Grant & Berg, 1948; Milner, 1963).

Cognition

The term 'cognition' is a hypothetical construct, a generic term for the kind of information that we have stored in our memory. Cognition is the product of cognitive processes that are responsible for information processing (i.e. perception, appraisal, judgment, conclusions, attribution, etc.). **Negative cognitions**, a term used in Beck's theory, are specific thought patterns that are based on unrealistic schemata and on systematic mistake in thinking. Those schemata which include idiosyncratic negative knowledge about the self, the world and the future (the so-called 'cognitive triad'; Beck et al, 1979) support selective attention to schema-congruent subjects which are processed in a distorted way due to systematically distorted way of thinking. These schemata and negative cognitions are supported and stabilized by selective reception and distorted information processing. With time, negative cognitions can appear as automatic thoughts.

Cognitive Remediation

Disturbances in information processing are widely accepted to be a basic disorder in psychosis and a result of an overall poor information processing. This working model is based on the underlying assumption that cognitive dysfunction remains relatively stable over the course of time and that it is a trait marker for vulnerability to schizophrenia (Nuechterlein & Dawson, 1984a; Green et al, 1993; Perry & Braff, 1994).

There exists a category of subtle cognitive impairments beyond florid thought disorders, which persists even after the acute phase. These subtle cognitive impairments influence the ability to derive benefit from therapy and also have an effect on social functioning and on rehabilitation.

The goal of the cognitive remediation, which has as yet not gained widespread dissemination either in the treatment and research of schizophrenia, is to improve cognitive functioning. So far, the focus has been on rating cognitive impairments and not so much on producing a profile of the competencies and deficits, which should then be used for a rehabilitation program. In general, the prevailing opinion is that cognitive impairments are irremediable. On the other hand, cognitive remediation programs have been used for brain-injured persons for many years, and with great success.

With regard to possibilities for therapy, Erickson & Binder (1986) remark that just those procedures that are used for neuropsychological assessment potentially offer the basis for a well-grounded cognitive remediation program. Extensive approaches for the remediation of cognitive impairments as for example the IPT-program developed by Brenner *et al* (1994) or the method proposed by Spaulding *et al* (1991) are still an exception.

Cognitive Therapy

The basic assumption of cognitive therapy is that cognition is responsible for behavior and emotions. The individual reacts and behaves according to his cognitive way of thinking and less according to the actual environmental conditions. Schemata not in line with reality and negative cognitions have a central meaning in the development and the maintenance of psychological problems. A paradigm for cognitive therapy is that the requested changes in behavior can only be achieved by altering basic cognitions. To recognize and change negative and unrealistic ways of thinking is therefore a basic goal of this therapy.

Within cognitive therapy, several directions with different priorities have developed. These include: coping therapies (Meichenbaum, 1977b), cognitive restructuring therapies (Ellis, 1979; Beck, 1976; Beck *et al*, 1979), and problem-solving therapies (D'Zurilla & Goldfried, 1971). The various approaches recognize the important functional meaning of cognitions, but all sides emphasize the importance of the relation between cognitions, emotions and behavior, being interactive and depending on each other (Neimeyer & Mahoney, 1996). Cognitive restructuring methods are of central importance within those different approaches, indeed, but methods basing on behavior-learning theories are applied as well, so that it is more adequate to talk about cognitive-behavioral-therapies.

Emotions

This term has proven utterly refractory to definitional efforts. There are very narrow definitions and very broad ones (e.g. Kleinginna & Kleinginna, 1981). Plutchik (1962), whose theory has had a great impact on emotional research, supports a multidimensional approach. According to that, emotions could be reflected on the dimensions intensity, similarity and polarity. Following this approach, we can distinguish between eight primary emotions (rage, grief, acceptance, etc.), while other emotions must be regarded as a mixture of the primary emotions.

In general, emotion is a complex reaction-process caused by a stimulus in which different components take part (e.g. cognitive, neurophysiological, motivational, emotional and expressive components) (Wundt, 1910; McDougall, 1908; Schachter & Singer, 1962). Emotions have an action-directing function and a behavior-adjusting effect. Our motivational tendencies can be seen as well in emotional reactions. Recent approaches emphasize that emotions have a strong effect on cognitions, but they are determined by them as well. (for review: Strongman, 1987)

Expressed Emotion

The construct 'expressed emotion' (EE) has been one of the strongest predictors for the development of further psychotic episodes, and it was defined by Brown *et al* (1962) and Vaughn & Leff (1976) who showed in their analysis that the emotional atmosphere of a family is of central importance for the further development of the disease. The risk of relapse is much higher, if the patient lives in a family with high expressed emotion (high-EE) and additionally evidences poor medication compliance.

The assessment of the emotional climate of a family is based on statements made about the patient by a member of the family in a 90-minute interview. According to the stated emotions, it is either a highly emotional family-atmosphere (high-EE) or a low emotional atmosphere (low-EE). EE is assessed on the basis of the number of critical statements, hostility and emotionally-overinvolved behavior. EE is not necessarily a specific measure for schizophrenia, as it proved to be a reliable predictor of the course of other disorders (e.g. depression) as well. (see also: Leff & Vaughn, 1985; Kavanagh, 1992; Bebbington & Kuipers, 1994; Butzlaff & Hooley, 1998)

Impairment, Disability, Handicap

These terms have been proposed by World Health Organization (1980) to differentiate three levels of dysfunction connected to illness. **Impairment** is defined as the loss or abnormality of a psychological, physiological or anatomical structure or function. Psychological impairments in schizophrenia are e.g. cognitive impairments, the cause for physiological impairments are dysregulations of sleep. Impairments can cause reductions in social functioning, called **disability**. A patient may have reduced vigilance and therefore is not able to complete his work in due time. Impairment and disability may hinder the patient from fulfilling his social and/or vocational roles. Typical **handicaps** of schizophrenic patients are unemployment and the lack or loss of contacts to a peer group.

Integrated Psychological Therapy for Schizophrenic Patients, IPT

Integrated Psychological Therapy for Schizophrenic Patients (IPT) was developed over the last 15 years (Brenner et al, 1980; 1994; Roder et al, 1988, 1992). IPT is a multimodal therapy concept for a group-format to improve cognitive and social skills in schizophrenic patients. The therapeutic concept is based on the assumption that there is an interactional relationship between cognitive impairments and their effect on social functioning (Brenner et al, 1994). The aim of this therapy program is to reduce attentional, perceptive, cognitive and social dysfunctions as they were described in the pervasivity hypothesis by Brenner (1987).

IPT consists of five hierarchical sub-programs for 5 - 8 patients. Each program consists of a variety of therapeutic methods. The first sub-programs are very structured and task-oriented and concentrate on improving basic cognitive functions. The more advanced sub-programs proceed to more spontaneous group-interaction and require advanced conceptual abilities to increase social competence. Emotionally charged material and issues are introduced more and more in the course of the program. (also see Figure 1)

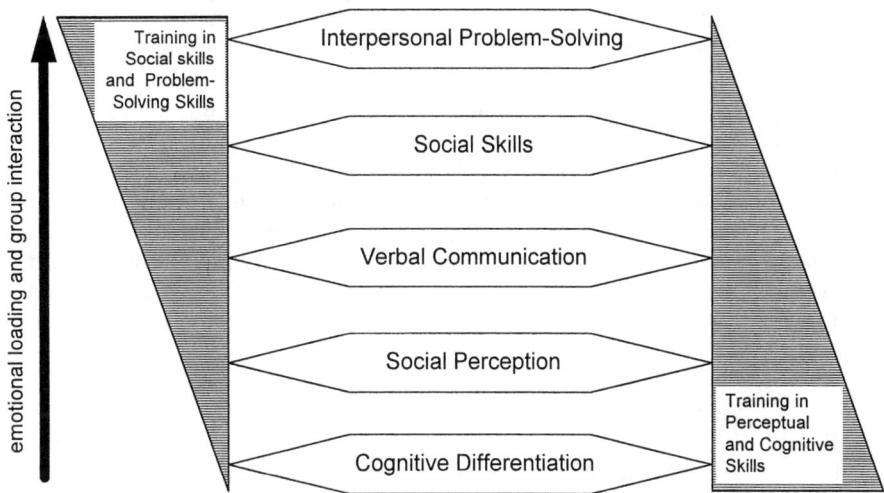

Figure 1. Integrated Psychological Therapy for Schizophrenic Patients (IPT).

1) The first sub-program **'Cognitive Differentiation'** aims at improving basic cognitive abilities (e.g. concentration, attention, concept formation).
2) The sub-program **'Social Perception'** aims at improving the apprehension and interpretation of social situations. The purpose of this sub-program is to improve the patient's visual perception and interpretation of social situations..
3) The third sub-program **'Verbal Communication'** focuses on improving conversational skills, i.e. listening, understanding and responding.
4) The sub-program **'Social Skills'** aims at enlarging the patients' repertoire of social skills to equip them to cope with specific social situations effectively.
5) **'Interpersonal Problem Solving'** strives at changing the way schizophrenic patients perceive emotional stress and social failure. The aim of this sub-program is to acquire realistic interpretations of a problem and its solutions.

Life Events

According to the vulnerability-stress-model, schizophrenic patients have a higher susceptibility to stress. Brown & Birley (1968) were the first to study the relation of life events to schizophrenia and they found an increase in events three weeks before onset. Although several studies have confirmed these findings, subsequent studies have not. The methodology for assessing life events is complicated because of the differentiation between dependent and independent events. Another problem is to consider the subjective interpretation of a life event. Parallel to the expansion of the vulnerability-stress-model, recent life-event research considers the individual impact of these events, i.e. the way the patient copes with them (for review: Bebbington & Kuipers, 1992; Norman & Malla, 1993)

Phases of Schizophrenic Disorders

In the treatment of schizophrenic disorders, a phase-oriented approach is necessary for psychosocial and for pharmacological interventions. Therefore, it is important to use the same definitions for describing these phases. In this book the definitions proposed by Keshavan & Schooler (1992) have been applied. These authors define the onset of illness with the first appearance of prodromal symptoms. The episode onset is characterized by psychotic, i.e. positive symptoms. The end of an episode is reached when no psychotic symptoms are present, whereas at the end of illness there are no more residual symptoms. The non-remitting illness has either continuous productive symptoms or continuous residual symptoms. Similar to bipolar disorders, the course of illness can show a pattern with intermitting exacerbation of psychotic symptoms without residual symptomatology outside these acute episodes.

Quality of Life

Especially for severely mentally ill patients, an assessment of their psychopathology is not sufficient to appraise their disability and the magnitude of their suffering. 'Quality of life' is a subjective view of well being and satisfaction. Different instruments have been developed to assess basic daily needs (i.e. health care, safety and security, food, housing, knowledge/education, key interpersonal relationships, finance and activities) (United Nations, 1990). Quality of life should be differentiated from standard of life: the latter reflects the objective dimensions of how well the basic needs of life are met (Skantze *et al*, 1992).

Psychophysiology

Psychophysiological methods are intensively applied to explore vulnerability-stress-models. Although psychophysiology has not been implemented in clinical practice, it has yielded important data in schizophrenia research on the processes interrelated between biological and psychological functions (Turpin & Clements, 1992). Usually, physiological correlates of psychological constructs (e.g. attention, arousal) are studied with the non-invasive peripheral and central nervous system. The following measures are usually employed: electroencephalogram (EEG), evoked potentials (EP), brain-mapping (BM), electromyographic activity (EMG), smooth eye movements (SPEM), electrodermal activity (EDA) and skin conductance level (SCL). Recently, functional brain-imaging has gained importance, e.g. positron-emission-tomography (PET) has been combined to cognitive tasks, (for review: Venables 1991).

Schema

Schemata are abstract, organizational units of condensed knowledge that developed through experiences. There are different kinds of schemata (e.g. event-schemata and scripts, self-schemata, etc.). They help to recognize and integrate every phenomenon of the environment and everything the organism experiences (Neisser, 1976). Schemata have an influence on how incoming information is selected and organized, but they are changed through it as well. Piaget (1976) described these two processes: with the process of **assimilation** the new information is integrated into the already existing schema. If the information cannot be assimilated into the existing schema, **accommodation** takes place. The schema changes according to the environmental information. These two processes are dialectically related to each other. They are an important motivational element and the basis for the development of schemata within the individual-environment-interaction. Every schema is integrated in the highest organization unit, the self-schema. In contrast to the *self-concept*, the **self-schema** is not object of the contents of consciousness, but can become a part of the self-concept by the process of reflecting abstraction (Grawe et al, 1994). This process of reflecting abstraction can be interpreted as the dialogue between the 'I' and the 'me' (Mead, 1934).

Unrealistic schemata, which contribute to the development and maintenance of mental disorders, are of therapeutic importance. If an individual does not succeed in reacting adequately to environmental information, the information will be faded out of perception or will be perceived in a distorted way. This results in schemata that are either not in line with reality or are inconsistent.

Secure Base

Attachment theory was developed by Bowlby in the 1960s (Bowlby, 1980, 1982) and has hitherto had a strong influence in developmental psychology. Providing a secure base for the child so that it is helped to feel protected enough to explore the 'world', is the characteristic of a positive attachment. For psychotherapy, attachment theory provides a basis for biological and psychological aspects of interpersonal relations (Holmes, 1993). Cognitive therapists use this concept to describe the therapeutic alliance which encourages the patient to find his way out of psychosis and back to everyday life (Perris et al, 1988).

Self-Concept

The self-concept is a construct for the image that an individual has of him in the form of lasting self-related cognitive representations, which is based on the human capacity for reflexivity. It is the sum total of the individual's thoughts and feelings about himself or herself. These self-related cognitive representations are internal self-models which consist among other things of cognitive components (self-perception, concept of ability) and affective components (self-esteem, self-confidence). Higgins et al (1985) differentiated three types of concept structures (real, ideal and expected self-concept). A discrepancy between these types of self-concept has various consequences (e.g. on emotion, cognition).

Social Cognition

Social cognition is an extensive term that relates to the functions of information processing as well as to its contents. The basic assumptions of social cognition research is that information processing and cognitions develop from social interactions, that they refer to social circumstances, and that they are socially accepted. This can be seen in the form of 'social representations' (Moscovici, 1981) which reflect the system of beliefs, the 'common sense' of a certain social group. Social cognitions are composed of different sectors, such as forming impressions, interpersonal perceptions, perceptions of self, stereotypes, attribution, etc.

Vulnerability-Stress-Model

In 1977, Zubin & Spring published their pivotal paper, which expanded the concept of diathesis into the modern interactive vulnerability-stress-model. These authors also emphasized the episodic nature of schizophrenia. The vulnerability-stress-model helps to integrate biological and psychosocial factors (Kaplan et al, 1994) and is therefore the best model for integrative pharmaco-psychotherapeutical treatment. Recently, it has been expanded to encompass adaptive mechanisms on biological as well as on psychological levels of functioning. The latter is studied within the coping paradigm as an interaction between the person and his environment (Folkman et al, 1986).

Appendix B: Rating Instruments

Association for Methodology and Documentation in Psychiatry, AMDP

AMDP (1971) is a comprehensive system for documentation in clinical work and research. The 140-item scales cover psychiatric symptomatology, including sociodemographic data, life events, psychiatric anamneses, psychopathological symptoms and somatic complaints. The goal of this multi-axial system is to standardize diagnoses and findings. Computer systems are available for handling the data collected.

Brief Psychiatric Rating Scale, BPRS

The clinical interview BPRS, developed by Overall and Gorham (1962), is a rapid evaluation procedure for assessing symptom changes in psychiatric patients. The original scale consisted of 16 items. The standard version, used since 1967, is an 18-item scale. The BPRS is the most frequently used psychiatric rating scale. Though it was not developed for schizophrenia only, it is widely used for this disorder. The advantage of the BPRS is that it covers both florid and deficit symptoms of schizophrenia. An expanded version of BPRS, worked out by Lukoff, Nuechterlein and Ventura (1986), contains an interview guide and operationalized anchor points, which guarantee standardized and reliable assessment.

Clinical Global Impressions, CGI

CGI, developed by the NIMH (NIMH, 1970), assesses the efficacy of psychopharmacological treatment. It is suitable for all types of psychiatric patients. An observer assesses three items: severity of illness, global improvement and efficacy index. There is no total score; each item is analyzed separately.

Disturbance-List, D-L

The Disturbance-List (von Zerssen, 1976) is a self-rating scale for psychiatric patients comprising 24 items. The score 'subjective impairment' consists of the patient's assessment of somatic and general disturbances. The D-L is not a diagnostic instrument in the usual sense, but a valuable screening instrument for the assessment of global impairment.

Frankfurt Complaint Questionnaire, FCQ

The FCQ (Süllwold, 1986) is a special self-report questionnaire for schizophrenic patients which assesses cognitive difficulties and the subjective experience of the psychotic dysfunction. In fact, most patients have differentiated self-perception, but talking about their dysfunction spontaneously is often more than they can handle. The FCQ comprises 98 complaint descriptions and, via the process of recognition, enables patients to make statements about their dysfunction. The FCQ is not a differential-diagnostic procedure in the usual sense, as it deals with assessing complaints rather than psychotic symptoms (Süllwold & Huber, 1986).

Frankfurt Subjective Condition Scale, FCS

The FCS (Süllwold & Herrlich, 1987) assesses the present subjective condition of schizophrenic patients on a 36-item scale. The condition can range between well being and discomfort. It takes only a short time for the patient to complete this scale. The FCS is not a diagnostic procedure in a narrower sense, but an instrument to register the current inner state and is therefore an appropriate method to describe schizophrenic subgroups.

Nurses' Observation Scale for Inpatient Evaluation, NOSIE

The NOSIE (Honigfeld & Klett, 1965; Honigfeld *et al*, 1966; Honigfeld, 1974) is the most commonly used rating scale for measuring symptoms and behavior in psychiatric patients. The staff, making daily observations of the patients, assesses the reported subjective symptoms and the observed behavior on a 30-item scale. This brief test is simple to use and is sensitive to changes in terms of time and treatment in psychiatric patients.

Paranoid-Depressivity Scale, PD-S

The Paranoid-Depressivity Scale (von Zerssen, 1981) helps to determine the severity of subjective impairment in anxious-depressive moods and the unrealistic, distorted or delusional thinking of psychiatric patients. This self-rating scale includes 16 items to measure paranoid tendencies, 16 items to diagnose depressivity, and 11 control items.

Scale for Assessment of Negative Symptoms, SANS

The SANS (Andreasen, 1981) is a semi-structured interview to measure changes in schizophrenic symptoms. An observer assesses negative symptoms on a 23-item scale. Andreasen (1982) established five categories, which describe negative symptoms of schizophrenic features. The individual items (e.g. poverty of speech) constitute a comprehensive assessment of negative symptoms.

Social Maladjustment Schedule, SMS

The SMS (Clare & Cairns, 1978; German-language version: Social Interview

Schedule, SIS; Hecht *et al*, 1987) is a semi-structured interview to assess the current social situation of patients with psychological problems. Nine categories (work, income, housing, etc.) are registered on three levels each (objective living conditions, social management, and subjective satisfaction with life). These categories provide the conceptual framework for the measures of 'social adjustment' or 'social maladjustment' that are determined by the actual social situation, and mental and physical illness.

Appendix C: Neuropsychological/ Experimental Psychological Tests

For many years, several testing devices from neuropsychology or experimental psychology have been used in schizophrenia research to measure basic cognitive impairments. These dysfunctions have been related to premorbid vulnerability in high-risk children studies (Watt *et al*, 1984) and to evaluation of impairments caused by psychosis or side effects of medication. Many aspects of information processing are studied with these instruments, e.g. memory, vigilance, concentration, abstraction.

Over the past few years the overall focus of research on neuropsychological test performance has undergone a radical change. Instead of attempting to identify "typical" patterns of cognitive impairement, today's research increasingly addresses the question of the relationship between the level of neurocognitive functioning and the outcome of illness (Goldberg & Gold, 1995; Green, 1998; Green & Nuechterlein, 1999).

Backward Masking

This task focuses on disturbances of early information processing and requires active rehearsal of the patient. Different versions have been developed to study incoming stimuli into the sensory register (e.g. forward and backward masking; acoustic or visual). In schizophrenia research, visual backward masking has mostly been applied. At the beginning, during a non-mask condition, target stimuli are presented in different exposure times, in order to find the individual threshold for perceiving the stimuli. During the task, a mask (crossed lines) are shown immediately after the stimuli. Then the interstimulus interval is shortened so that the patient is not able to identify the target. There is presumably not enough time for the information provided by the target to be transferred from sensory register to short-term store where the subject can recognize it. There is some evidence that backward masking is a vulnerability marker and that it is associated with negative symptoms but not with positive ones (for review: Braff, 1991).

Continuous Performance Test, CPT

First developed by Rosvold (1956), the goal of CPT is to measure vigilance (sustained attention). Several versions have been developed all of which have the following characteristics in common: 1) presentation of a random sequence of visual stimuli; 2) brief exposure time (40-200 ms); 3) response to target via button press. The stimuli are either projected by a tachistoscope or on a computer screen. The stimuli - digits, letters or figures - differ between the versions. In his original version, Rosvold (1956) showed an 'X' or an 'A' followed by an 'X'. Nuechterlein & Asarnow developed a special version, which displays blurred stimulus; the degraded version of the CPT has a low signal discriminability and is more sensitive for measuring premorbid vulnerability. (for review: Nuechterlein, 1991)

d2 Test (Concentration Endurance Test)

The d2 Test is a paper-and-pencil-test developed by Brickenkamp (1981). It assesses sustained attention, visual scanning ability and processing speed. In a given time, the patient should mark in several rows of d-letters those, which have two marks.

Reaction Time Test

The Reaction Time Test (RT) measures the response time and it is applicable for slight dysfunctions as it necessitates high processing loads (Jensen & Munro, 1979). Also, it measures processing speed and associated attentional deficits.

Span of Apprehension Test, SAT

This task is a selective test to examine cognitive functions of sensory storage. The original version was published by Estes & Taylor (1966) and used a 'wide visual angle'. There exist different versions with 0, 2, 4, 6, 8, 9 or 11 distracter targets and the additional test target. Asarnow & Nuechterlein (1983) developed a forced-choice computer-aided version. Three or twelve letters are shown on a computer monitor for the duration of about 50-70 ms. The patient has to decide whether he has seen a 'T' or an 'F' among two or eleven other letters. Schizophrenic patients have significantly more trouble to distinguish the target letters from the other letters when five or more letters are presented. It has been proposed that this task measures a 'mediating vulnerability factor' because it is sensitive to premorbid vulnerability (trait marker) and to acute psychoses (state marker). (for review: Asarnow *et al*, 1991).

Test Batteries

Different test batteries have been developed to study cognitive impairments. Here, Repeated Psychological Measurement (RPM) and COGLAB for cognitive laboratory will be described:
  a) RPM (Mefferd *et al*, 1966) is a battery specially devised for time row studies and it consists of the following paper-pencil-tests which are available in 20-30 parallel forms: 1) aiming, 2) flexibility closure, 3) number facility, 4) perceptual speed, 5) speed closure, 6) visualization, 7) word association, 8) memory for faces, 9) digit span.

b) The COGLAB (Spaulding *et al*, 1981, 1989a, 1989b) is a computer-aided test battery consisting of: 1) a 85-trial reaction time protocol, 2) perceptual task (Mueller-Lyer-Illusion), 3) size estimation task, 4) backward-masking task, 5) combined vigilance and span of apprehension task, 6) concept manipulation task (similar to WCST). (see also Chapter 7)

Wisconsin Card Sorting Test, WCST

The WCST was originally developed by Grant & Berg (1948) and later modified by Milner (1963). This test measures problem-solving behavior and conceptual flexibility. There are also several computerized versions. In this test, a response card should be matched with one of four reference cards, according to one of three criteria (color, number or shape). On the basis of positive or negative feedback, the patient has to find the rule, which governs the following sequence of response cards. After a certain amount of trials, the sequence rule is changed automatically. The patient has to recognize this change and to find the new organizing principle. Heaton, whose version is the most commonly used, proposed different criteria for evaluation (1981). Above all, this test is a sensitive indicator for frontal lobe damage and for schizophrenia.

References

Abels, D. (1974) *Konzentrations-Verlaufs-Test (KVT)* Göttingen: Testzentrale Göttingen.
Adams, H., Brantley, P., Malatesta, V. & Turkat, I. (1981) Modification of cognitive process: A case study of schizophrenia. *Journal of Consulting and Clinical Psychology*, 49, 460-464.
American Psychiatric Association (1994) *Diagnostic and Statistical Manual of Mental Disorders, ed 4 (DSM-IV)*. Washington, DC: American Psychiatric Association.
Andreasen, N. C. (1981) *Scale for assessment of negative symptoms (SANS)*. Iowa City: University of Iowa.
Andreasen, N. C. (1982) Negative symptoms in schizophrenia: Definition and reliability. *Archives of General Psychiatry*, 39, 784-788.
Andres, K., Brenner, H. D. & Bellwald, L. (1992) Körperzentrierte Arbeit mit schizophrenen Patienten. *Swiss Medicine*, 1-S, 40-42.
Angermeyer, M. C., Kuhn, L. & Goldstein, J. M. (1990) Gender and the course of schizophrenia: Differences in treated outcomes. *Schizophrenia Bulletin*, 16, 293-308.
Angst, J. (1988) European long-term follow-up studies of schizophrenia. *Schizophrenia Bulletin*, 14, 501-513.
Anonymous (1986) "Can we talk?" The schizophrenic patient in psychotherapy. *American Journal of Psychiatry*, 143, 68-70.
Arbeitsgemeinschaft für Methodik und Dokumentation in der Psychiatrie (AMDP) (1981) *Das AMDP-System. Manual zur Dokumentation psychiatrischer Befunde.* Berlin: Springer.
Arieti, S. (1974) *Interpretation of schizophrenia* (2nd ed). New York: Basic Books.
Asarnow, R. F. & MacCrimmon, D. J. (1978) Residual performance deficit in clinically remitted schizophrenics: A marker of schizophrenia? *Journal of Abnormal Psychology*, 57, 597.
Asarnow, R. F. & MacCrimmon, D. J. (1982) Attention/information processing, neuropsychological functioning, and thought disorder during the acute and partial recovery phases of schizophrenia: A longitudinal study. *Psychiatry Research*, 7, 309-319.
Asarnow, R. F., Granholm, E. & Sherman, T. (1991) Span of apprehension in schizophrenia. In S. R. Steinhauer, J. H. Gruzelier & J. Zubin (eds) *Neuropsychology, psychophysiology and information processing*, (Vol. 5). Amsterdam: Elsevier.

Baker, L. A., Cheng, L. Y. & Amara, I. B. (1983) The withdrawal of benzotropine mesylate in chronic schizophrenic patients. *British Journal of Psychiatry*, 143, 584-590.

Bales, R. F. & Cohen, S. P. (1979) SYMLOG. *A manual for the case study of groups*. New York: Macmillan Publishing.

Balint, M. & Balint, E. (1963) *Psychotherapeutische Techniken in der Medizin*. Bern: Huber.

Ball, A., Moore, E. & Kuipers, L. (1992) Expressed emotion in community care staff. A comparison of patient outcome in a nine month follow-up of two hostels. *Social Psychiatry and Psychiatric Epidemiology*, 27, 35-39.

Bandura, A. (1977) Self-efficacy: Toward a unifying theory of behavioral change. *Psychological Review*, 84, 191-215.

Bandura, A. (1986) *Social foundations of thought and action: A social cognitive theory*. Englewood Cliffs: Prentice Hall.

Bäuml, J., Pitschel-Walz, G. & Kissling, W. (1998) Psychoedukative Gruppen bei schizophrenen Psychosen unter stationären Behandlungsbedingungen. In W. Binder & W. Bender (eds) *Angehörigenarbeit in der Psychiatrie*. Claus Richter Verlag.

Beatty, J. (1982) Task evoked pupillary responses, processing load, and the structure of processing resources. *Psychological Bulletin*, 91, 276-292.

Bebbington, P. & Kuipers, L. (1992) Life events and social factors. In D. J. Kavanagh (ed) *Schizophrenia. An overview and practical handbook*. London: Chapman & Hall.

Bebbington, P. & Kuipers, L. (1994) The clinical utility of expressed emotion in schizophrenia. *Acta Psychiatrica Scandinavica*, 89 (suppl. 382), 46-53.

Beck, A. T. (1976) *Cognitive therapy and the emotional disorders*. New York: International Universities Press.

Beck, A. T., Emery, G. & Greenberg, R. L. (1985) *Anxiety disorders and phobias: A cognitive perspective*. New York: Basic Books.

Beck, A. T., Rush, A. J., Shaw, B. F. & Emery, G. (1979) *Cognitive therapy of depression*. New York: Guilford Press.

Bellack, A. S. & Hersen, M. (1978) Chronic psychiatric patients: Social skills training. In M. Hersen & A. S. Bellack (eds) *Behavior therapy in the psychiatric setting*. Baltimore: Williams & Wilkins.

Bellack, A. S. & Morrison, R. L. (1982) Interpersonal dysfunction. In A. S. Bellack, M. Hersen & A. E. Kazdin (eds) *International handbook of behavior modification and therapy*. New York: Plenum Press.

Bellack, A. S. & Mueser, K. T. (1993) Psychosocial treatment for schizophrenia. *Schizophrenia Bulletin*, 19, 317-336.

Bellack, A. S. (1989) A comprehensive model for the treatment of schizophrenia. In A. S. Bellack (ed) *A clinical guide for the treatment of schizophrenia*. New York: Plenum Press.

Bellack, A. S. (1992) Cognitive rehabilitation for schizophrenia: Is it possible? Is it necessary? *Schizophrenia Bulletin*, 18, 43-50.

Bellack, A. S. (1997) Social skills deficits and social skills training: New developments and trends. In H.D. Brenner, W. Böker & R. Genner (eds) *Towards a comprehensive therapy for schizophrenia.* Seattle: Hogrefe & Huber.

Bellack, A. S., Morrison, R. L., Wixted, J. T. & Mueser, K. T. (1990) An analysis of social competence in schizophrenia. *British Journal of Psychiatry*, 156, 809-818.

Bellack, A. S., Mueser, K. T., Morrison, R. L., Tierney, A. & Podell, K. (1989) Remediation of cognitive deficits in schizophrenia: Training on the Wisconsin Card Sorting Test. *American Journal of Psychiatry*, 147, 1650-1655.

Bellack, A. S., Turner, S. M., Hersen, M. & Luber, R. F. (1984) An examination of the efficacy of social skills training for chronic schizophrenic patients. *Hospital and Community Psychiatry*, 35, 1023-1028.

Bellissimo, A. & Steffy, R. A. (1972) Redundancy-associated deficit in schizophrenic reaction time performance. *Journal of Abnormal Psychology*, 80, 299-307.

Benedict, R. H. & Harris, A. (1989) Remediation of attention deficits in chronic schizophrenic patients: A preliminary study. *British Journal of Clinical Psychology*, 28, 187-188.

Benjamin, L.S. (1982) Use of Structural Analysis of Social Behavior (SASB) to guide intervention in psychotherapy. In D. Kiesler & J. Anchin (eds). *Handbook of interpersonal psychotherapy.* New York, Pergamon Press.

Bennett, D. (1983) The historical development of rehabilitation services. In F. N. Watts & D. H. Bennett (eds) *Theory and practice of psychiatric rehabilitation.* Chichester: Wiley.

Berenbaum, H. & Oltmanns, T. F. (1992) Emotional experience in schizophrenia and depression. *Journal of Abnormal Psychology*, 101, 37-44.

Berenbaum, H., Snowhite, T. & Oltmanns, T. F. (1987) Anhedonia and emotional responses to affect evoking stimuli. *Psychological Medicine*, 17, 677-684.

Birchwood, M. & Iqbal, Z. (1998) Depression and suicidal thinking in psychosis: a cognitive approach. In T. Wykes, N. Tarrier & S. Lewis (eds) *Outcome and innovation in psychological treatment of schizophrenia.* Chichester, UK: John Wiley & Sons.

Birchwood, M. (1999) Early intervention in psychosis: the critical period. In P. D. McGorry & H. J. Jackson (eds) *The recognition and management of early psychosis. A preventive approach.* Cambridge, UK: Cambridge University Press.

Blanco, S., Demontis, D. & Reda, M. A. (1990) Problemi psicoterapeutici con pazienti psicotici: Una ricerca sperimentale. In V. Volterra (ed) *New trends in schizophrenia.* Napoli: N.P.S.

Blanco, S., Marchi, E. & Reda, M. A. (1984) Risposte paradossali dei pazienti agorafobici all EMG-BFB training. In P. Pancheri (ed) *Terapia in medicina comportamentale.* Roma: Il Pensiero Scientifico.

Blankenburg, W. (1991) Wahn und Perspektivität. Störungen im Realitätsbezug des Menschen und ihre Therapie. In J. Glatzel, H. Krüger & C. Scharfetter (eds) *Forum der Psychiatrie.* Stuttgart: Ferdinand Enke.

Bleuler, E. (1950) *Dementia praecox or the group of schizophrenias.* New York: International Universities Press.

Bleuler, M. (1978) *The schizophrenic disorders: Long-term patient and family studies.* New Haven: Yale Universities Press.
Bleuler, M. (1979) On schizophrenic psychoses. *American Journal of Psychiatry,* 136, 1403-1409.
Bliss, E. (1986) *Multiple personality, allied disorders and hypnosis.* New York: Oxford University Press.
Böker, W. & Brenner, H. D. (1983) Selbstheilungsversuche Schizophrener. *Nervenarzt,* 54, 578-589.
Böker, W. & Brenner, H. D. (eds) (1992) Onset and course of schizophrenic disorders. Dynamic interactions between relevant factors. *British Journal of Psychiatry,* 161 (suppl. 18).
Böker, W. (1992) A call for partnership between schizophrenic patients, relatives and professionals. *British Journal of Psychiatry,* 161 (suppl. 18), 10-12.
Bowen, L. (1988) *Prediction of schizophrenic patients' response to skill training with laboratory assessment of attentional deficits.* Los Angeles: Doctoral dissertation, California School of Professional Psychology.
Bowen, L., Wallace, C. J., Glynn, S. M., Nuechterlein, K. H., Lutzker, J. R. & Kuehnel, T. G. (1994) Relationships among schizophrenic patients on attentional deficits, social problem solving, and performance in psychoeducational rehabilitation tasks. *Journal of Psychiatric Research,* 28, 289-301.
Bowers, K. S. (1984) On being unconsciously influenced and informed. In K. S. Bowers & D. Meichenbaum (eds) *The unconscious reconsidered.* New York: Wiley.
Bowlby, J. (1973) Self-reliance and some conditions that promote it. In J. Bowlby, *The making and breaking of affectional bonds.* London: Tavistock Publications.
Bowlby, J. (1980) *Attachment and loss,* (Vol. 3: Loss). London: Hogarth Press.
Bowlby, J. (1982) *Attachment and loss,* (Vol.1: Attachment. 2nd ed). London: Hogarth Press.
Bowlby, J. (1985) The role of childhood experience in cognitive disturbance. In M. J. Mahoney & A. Freeman (eds) *Cognition and psychotherapy.* New York: Plenum.
Braff, D. & Saccuzzo, D. P. (1982) The effect of antipsychotic medication on speed of information processing in schizophrenia. *American Journal of Psychiatry,* 139, 1127.
Braff, D. L. (1991) Information processing and attentional abnormalities in the schizophrenic disorders. In P.A. Magaro (ed), *Cognitive bases of mental disorders.* Newbury Park, CA: Sage Publications.
Breier, A. & Strauss, J. S. (1983) Self-control in psychotic disorders. *Archives of General Psychiatry,* 40, 1141-1145.
Brenner, H. D. (1987) On the importance of cognitive disorders in treatment and rehabilitation. In J. S. Strauss, W. Böker & H. D. Brenner (eds) *Psychosocial treatment of schizophrenia.* Toronto: Huber.
Brenner, H. D. (1989) The treatment of basic psychological dysfunctions from a systemic point of view. *British Journal of Psychiatry,* 155 (suppl. 5), 74-83.
Brenner, H. D., Böker, W., Hodel, B. & Wyss, H. (1989) Cognitive treatment of basic pervasive dysfunctions in schizophrenia. In S. C. Schulz, S. C. & C.A.

Tamminga (eds) *Schizophrenia: Scientific progress.* New York: Oxford University Press.

Brenner, H. D., Hodel, B., Kube, G. & Roder, V. (1987a) Kognitive Therapie bei Schizophrenen: Problemanalyse und empirische Ergebnisse. *Nervenarzt*, 58, 72-83.

Brenner, H. D., Böker, W., Müller, J., Spichtig, L. & Würgler, S. (1987b) On autoprotective efforts of schizophrenics, neurotics and controls. *Acta Psychiatrica Scandinavica*, 75, 405-414.

Brenner, H. D., Böker, W. & Genner, R. (eds) (1997) *Towards a comprehensive therapy for schizophrenia.* Seattle: Hogrefe & Huber Publishers.

Brenner, H. D., Hodel, B. & Merlo, M. C. G. (1991) Nonpharmacological treatment concepts of negative symptomatology. In A. Marneros, N. C. Andreasen & M. T. Tsuang (eds) *Negative versus positive schizophrenia.* Berlin: Springer.

Brenner, H. D., Hodel, B., Roder, V. & Corrigan, P. W. (1992) Treatment of cognitive dysfunction and behavioral deficits in schizophrenia: Integrated psychological therapy. *Schizophrenia Bulletin*, 18, 21-26.

Brenner, H. D., Kraemer, S., Hermanutz, M. & Hodel, B. (1990) Cognitive treatment in schizophrenia. In E. R. Straube & K. Hahlweg (eds) *Schizophrenia: Concepts, vulnerability and intervention.* Berlin: Springer.

Brenner, H. D., Rey, E. R. & Stramke, W. G. (eds) (1983) *Empirische Schizophrenieforschung.* Bern: Huber.

Brenner, H. D., Roder, V., Hodel, B. & Kienzle, N. (1994*) The integrated psychological therapy program for schizophrenic patients (IPT).* Seattle: Hogrefe & Huber.

Brenner, H. D., Stramke, W. G., Mewes, J., Liese, F. & Seeger, G. (1980) Erfahrungen mit einem spezifischen Therapieprogramm zum Training kognitiver und kommunikativer Fähigkeiten in der Rehabilitation chronisch schizophrener Patienten. *Nervenarzt*, 51, 106-112.

Bretherton, I. (1985) Attachment theory: retrospect and prospect. In I. Bretherton & E. Waters (eds) Growing points of attachment theory and research. *Monographs of the Society for Research in Child Development*, 50, 3-35.

Brickenkamp, R. (1981) *Test d2: Aufmerksamkeits-Belastungs-Test.* Göttingen: Hogrefe.

Broen, W. & Storms, L. (1966) Lawful disorganization: The process underlying a schizophrenic syndrome. *Psychological Review*, 73, 265-279.

Broen, W. E. (1968) *Schizophrenia: Research and theory.* New York: Academic Press.

Brown, G. W. & Birley, J. L. T. (1968) Crises and life changes and the onset of schizophrenia. *Journal of Health Social Behavior*, 9, 203-214.

Brown, G. W., Monck, E. M., Carstairs, G. M. & Wing, J. K. (1962) Influence of family life on the course of schizophrenic illness. *British Journal of Prevention and Social Medicine*, 16, 55-68.

Buchkremer, G., Stricker, K., Holle, R. & Kuhs, H. (1991) The predictability of relapses in schizophrenic patients. *European Archives of Psychiatry and Clinical Neuroscience*, 240, 292-300.

Butzlaff, R. L., Hooley, J. M. (1998) Expressed emotion and psychiatric relapse: a

meta-analysis. *Archives of General Psychiatry*, 55, 547-52.
Calev, A., Venables, P. & Monk, A. (1983) Evidence for distinct verbal memory pathologies in severely and mildly disturbed schizophrenics. *Schizophrenia Bulletin*, 9, 247-264.
Callaway, E. & Naghdi, S. (1982) An information processing model for schizophrenia. *Archives of General Psychiatry*, 39, 339-347.
Carmin, C. N. & Dowd, E. T. (1988) Paradigms in cognitive psychotherapy. In W. Dryden & P. Trower (eds) *Developments in cognitive psychotherapy*. London: Sage.
Carpenter, W. T. Jr., Heinrichs, D. W. & Alphs, L. D. (1985) Treatment of negative symptoms. *Schizophrenia Bulletin*, 11, 440-452.
Carr, V. (1988) Patients' techniques for coping with schizophrenia: An exploratory study. *British Journal of Medical Psychology*, 61, 339-352.
Chadwick, P. & Birchwood, M. (1994) The omnipotence of voices: A cognitive approach to auditory hallucinations. *British Journal of Psychiatry*, 164, 190-201.
Childers, S. E. & Harding, C. M. (1990) Gender, premorbid social functioning, and long-term outcome in DSM-III schizophrenia. *Schizophrenia Bulletin*, 16, 309-318.
Ciompi, L. & Müller, C. (1976) *Lebensweg und Alter der Schizophrenen. Eine katamnestische Langzeitstudie bis ins Senium*. Berlin: Springer.
Ciompi, L. (1980) Ist die chronische Schizophrenie ein Artefakt? Argumente und Gegenargumente. *Fortschritte Neurologie und Psychiatrie*, 48, 237-248.
Ciompi, L. (1985) Aging and the schizophrenic psychosis. *Acta Psychiatrica Scandinavica*, 71 (suppl. 319), 93-105.
Ciompi, L. (1988) *The psyche and schizophrenia. The bond between affect and logic*. Cambridge, Mass: Harvard University Press.
Ciompi, L. (1991) Affects as central organizing and integrating factors. A new psychosocial/biological model of the psyche. *British Journal of Psychiatry*, 159, 79-83.
Ciompi, L., Dauwalder, H.P., Maier, C. & Aebi, E. (1991) Das Pilotprojekt 'Soteria Bern' zur Behandlung akut Schizophrener. I. Konzeptuelle Grundlagen, Praktische Realisierung, klinische Erfahrungen. *Nervenarzt*, 62, 428-35.
Ciompi, L., Kupper, Z., Aebi, E. et al (1993) Das Pilotprojekt 'Soteria Bern' zur Behandlung akut Schizophrener. II. Ergebnisse einer vergleichenden prospektiven Verlaufsstudie über 2 Jahre. *Nervenarzt*, 64, 440-50.
Clare, A. W. & Cairns, V. E. (1978) Design, development, and use of a standardized interview to assess social maladjustment and dysfunction in community studies. *Psychological Medicine*, 8, 589-604.
Clarkin, J. (1998) Research designs to answer clinical questions – an overwiew Lecture II. Psychotherapiekongreß der Deutschen Gesellschaft für Psychiatrie, Psychotherapie und Nervenheilkunde Freiburg 4.-7.März
Cohen, C. I. (1990) Outcome of schizophrenia into later life: an overview. *Gerontologist*, 30, 790-7.
Cohen, S. & Kahn, A. (1990) Antipsychotic effect of milieu in acute treatment of schizophrenia. *General Hospital Psychiatry*, 12, 248-251.

Collegium Internationale Psychiatriae Scalarum (CIPS) (1981) *Internationale Skalen für Psychiatrie.* Weinheim: Beltz.

Cornblatt, B. A., Lenzenwerger, M. F., Dworkin, R. H. & Erlenmeyer-Kimling, L. (1992) Childhood attentional dysfunctions predict social deficits in unaffected adults at risk for schizophrenia. *British Journal of Psychiatry*, 161 (suppl. 18), 59-64.

Corrigan, P. W., Schade, M. L. & Liberman, R. P. (1992b) Social skills training. In R. P. Liberman (ed) *Handbook of psychiatric rehabilitation.* New York: Macmillan.

Corrigan, P. W., Wallace, C. J. & Green, M. F. (1992a) Deficits in social schemata in schizophrenia. *Schizophrenia Research*, 8, 129-135.

Corrigan, P. W., Wallace, C. T., Schafe, M. L., Green, M. F. (1994) Learning medication self-management skills in schizophrenia: Relationships with cognitive deficits and psychiatric symptoms. *Behavior Therapy*, 25, 5-15.

Cortese, L., Malla, A. K., McLean, T. & Diaz, J. . (1999) Exploring the longitudinal course of psychotic illness: a case-study approach. *Canadian Journal of Psychiatry*, 44, 881-6.

Cramer, P., Weegmann, M. & O'Neil, M. (1989) Schizophrenia and the perception of emotions. *British Journal of Psychiatry*, 155, 225-228.

Cromwell, R. L. & Spaulding, W. (1978) How schizophrenics handle information. In W. E. Fan, A. D. Caravan, A. D. Pokorny & R. L. Williams (eds) *Phenomenology and treatment of schizophrenia.* New York: Spectrum.

Csernansky, J. G., Kaplan, J. & Hollister, L. E. (1985) Problems in classification of schizophrenics as neuroleptic responders and nonresponders. *Journal of Nervous and Mental Disease*, 173, 325-331.

Cutting, J. (1981) Judgment of emotional expression in schizophrenia. *British Journal of Psychiatry*, 139, 1-6.

D'Zurilla, T. J. & Goldfried, M. R. (1971) Problem solving and behavior modification. *Journal of Abnormal Psychology*, 78, 107-126.

Dahl, D. (1986) *Reduzierter Wechsler-Intelligenztest (WIP)* 2nd ed Bern: Huber Verlag.

David, A. S. & Cutting, J. C. (1994) *The neuropsychology of schizophrenia.* Hove,UK: Lawrence Erlbaum.

David, A. S. (1990) Insight and psychosis. *British Journal of Psychiatry*, 156, 798-808.

Davis, J. M. (1975) Overview: Maintenance therapy in psychiatry: I. Schizophrenia. *American Journal of Psychiatry*, 132, 1238-1245.

Dawson, M.E. & Nuechterlein, K.H. (1984) Physiological dysfunctions in the developmental course of schizophrenic disorders. *Schizophrenia Bulletin*, 10, 204-232.

Décarie, T. G. (1978) Affect development and cognition in a Piagetian context. In M. Lewis & L. A. Rosenblum (eds) *The development of affect.* New York: Plenum Press.

Deister, A. & Marneros A. (1994) Die Bedeutung von Plus- und Minussymptomatik für den Langzeitausgang schizophrener Psychosen. In H.-J. Möller & G. Laux (eds) *Fortschritte in der Diagnostik und Therapie schizophrener Minussymptomatik*. Wien New York: Springer.

Delahunty, A., Morice, R. & Frost, B. (1993) Specific cognitive flexibility rehabilitation in schizophrenia. *Psychological Medicine*, 23, 221-227.

Diaz, A. & Colon, F. (1985) Autocontrol: Una revision bibliografica/Self-control. A bibliographic review. *Analysys y Modificacion de Conducta*, 11, 441-458.

Dixon, L. B. & Lehman, A. F. (1995) Family interventions for schizophrenia. *Schizophrenia Bulletin*, 21, 631-43.

Dougherty, F. E., Bartlett, E. S. & Izard, C. E. (1974) Responses of schizophrenics to expressions of fundamental emotions. *Journal of Clinical Psychology*, 30, 243-246.

Dworkin, R. H. (1992) Affective deficits and social deficits in schizophrenia: What's what? *Schizophrenia Bulletin*, 18, 59-64.

Eckman, T. A., Wirshing, W. C., Marder, S. R. et al (1992) Technology for training schizophrenics in illness self-management: A controlled trial. *American Journal of Psychiatry*, 149, 1549-1555.

Eikelmann, B. & Reker, T. (1991) A modern therapeutic approach for chronically ill patients – results of a four-year prospective study. *Acta Psychiatrica Scandinavica*, 84, 357-363.

Ellis, A. (1962) *Reason and emotion in psychotherapy*. New York: Lyle Stuart.

Ellis, A. (1979) Rational-emotive therapy. In R. Corsini (ed) *Current psychotherapies* (2nd ed). Itasca: F. E. Peacock.

Ellis, E. S. (1986) The role of motivation and pedagogy on the generalization of cognitive strategy training. *Journal of Learning Disabilities*, 19, 667-670.

Engel, G. (1977) The need for a new medical model: A challenge for biomedicine. *Science*, 196, 129-136.

Erickson, R. C. & Binder, L. M. (1986) Cognitive deficits among functionally psychotic patients: A rehabilitative perspective. *Journal of Clinical and Experimental Neuropsychology*, 8, 257-274.

Erlenmeyer-Kimling, L. (1979) Advantages of a behavior-genetic approach to investigating stress in the depressive disorders. In R. A. Depue (ed) *The psychobiology of the depressive disorders*. New York: Academic Press.

Estes, W. K. & Taylor, H. A. (1966) Visual detection in relation to display size and redundancy of critical elements. *Perception & Psychophysics*, 1, 9.

Eysenck, H. J. (1986) Theories of parapsychological phenomena. *Encyclopaedia Britannica*, 13, 1002.

Fahrenberg, J., Kuhn, M. & Kulick, B. et al (1977) Repeated psychological measurement. *Diagnostica*, 23, 15-36.

Fahrenberg, J., Kuhn, M., Kulick, B. & Myrtek, M. (1977) Methodenentwicklung für psychologische Zeitreihenstudien. *Diagnostica*, 23, 15-36.

Falloon, I. R. H. & Liberman, R. P. (1983) Interactions between drug and psychosocial therapy in schizophrenia. *Schizophrenia Bulletin*, 9, 543-554.

Falloon, I. R. H. (1987) Cognitive and behavioral interventions in the self-control of schizophrenia. In J. S. Strauss, W. Böker & H. D. Brenner (eds) *Psychosocial treatment of schizophrenia*. Toronto: Huber.

Falloon, I. R. H., Boyd, J. L. & McGill, C. W. (1984) *Family care of schizophrenia. A problem-solving approach to the treatment of mental illness.* New York, London: Guilford Press.

Falloon, I. R. H., Boyd, J. L., McGill, C. W. et al (1982) Family management in the prevention of exacerbations of schizophrenia: A controlled study. *New England Journal of Medicine,* 306, 1437-1440.

Falloon, I. R., McGill, C. W., Boyd, J. L. & Pederson, J. (1987) Family management in the prevention of morbidity of schizophrenia: Social outcome of a two-year longitudinal study. *Psychological Medicine,* 17, 59-66.

Fecteau, G. W. & Duffy, M. (1986) Social and conversational skills training with long-term psychiatric inpatients. *Psychological Reports,* 59, 1327-1331.

Feinberg, T. E., Rifkin, A. & Schaffer, C. et al (1986) Facial discrimination and emotional recognition in schizophrenia and affective disorders. *Archives of General Psychiatry,* 43, 276-279.

Ferguson, B. (1990) Clinical audit - a proposal. *Psychiatric Bulletin,* 14, 275-277.

Fitts, P. M. & Posner, M. L. (1967) *Human performance.* Belmont, CA: Brooks/ Cole.

Folkman, S., Lazarus, R. S., Gruen, R. J. & DeLongis, A. (1986) Appraisal, coping, health status, and psychological symptoms. *Journal of Personality and Social Psychology,* 50, 571-579.

Forsyth, D. R. (1980) The function of attributions. *Social Psychology Quarterly,* 43, 184-189.

Foss, L. & Rothenberg, K. (1988) *The second medical revolution. From biomedicine to infomedicine.* Boston: New Science Library. Shambhala Publications.

Frank, A. F. & Gunderson, J. G. (1990) The role of the therapeutic alliance in the treatment of schizophrenia. *Archives of General Psychiatry,* 47, 228-236.

Friedrich, W. & Henning, W. (1988) *Der sozialwissenschaftliche Forschungsprozess.* Berlin: VEB.

Frith, C. D. (1992) *The cognitive neuropsychology of schizophrenia.* Hove, UK: Lawrence Erlbaum Associates.

Fröhlich, W.D. (ed) (1993) *Wörterbuch zur Psychologie.* München: Deutscher Taschenbuch Verlag.

Gansert, U. & Olbrich, R. (1992) Die Einführung eines computergestützten kognitiven Trainings für schizophrene Kranke in Gruppenform: Ein Erfahrungsbericht. *Schizophrenie,* 7, 26-31.

Gessler, S., Cutting, J. & Frith, C. D. et al (1989) Schizophrenic inability to judge facial emotion: A controlled study. *British Journal of Clinical Psychology,* 28, 19-29.

Gestrich, J. & Hermanutz, M. (1991) *Therapieverfahren bei schizophrenen Patienten.* München: Zuckschwerdt.

Gjerde, P. F. (1983) Attentional capacity dysfunction and arousal in schizophrenia. *Psychological Bulletin,* 93, 57-72.

Glick, I. D., Clarkin, J. F., Spencer, J. H., et al (1985) A controlled evaluation of inpatient family intervention. *Archives of General Psychiatry,* 42, 882-886.

Gmür, M. (1987) *Die Prognose der Schizophrenie unter sozialpsychiatrischer Behandlung.* Stuttgart: Enke.

Gmür, M. (1991) Die Rehabilitation von Schizophrenen – Der Rehabilitationsstern als Modell. In T. Platz, R. Schubert & R. Neumann (eds) *Fortschritte im Umgang mit schizophrenen Patienten*. Wien New York: Springer.

Goldberg, T. E., Gold, J. M. & Braff, D. L. (1991) Neuropsychological Functioning and time-linked information processing in schizophrenia. In A. Tassman & S. M. Goldfinger (eds) *Review of Psychiatry. Volume 10*. Washington, DC: American Psychiatric Press.

Goldberg, T. E., Weinberger, D. R., Berman, K. F., Pliskin, N. H. & Podd, M. H. (1987) Further evidence for dementia of the prefrontal type in schizophrenia? A controlled study of teaching the Wisconsin Card Sorting Test. *Archives of General Psychiatry*, 44, 1008-1014.

Goldberg, T. E. & Gold, J. M. (1995) Neurocognitive Deficits in Schizophrenie In S. R. Hirsch & D. R. Weinberger. *Schizophrenia*. London: Blackwell Sciences.

Goldman-Rakic, P. S. (1991) Prefrontal cortical dysfunction in schizophrenia: The relevance of working memory. In B. J. Carroll & J. E. Barrett (eds) *Psychopathology and the brain*. New York: Raven Press.

Goldstein, M. J. (1987) Psychosocial issues. *Schizophrenia Bulletin*, 13, 157-172.

Goldstein, M. J. (1994) Psychoeducational and family therapy in relapse prevention. *Acta Psychiatrica Scandinavica*, 89 (suppl. 382), 54-57.

Gottesman, I. I. & Shields, J. (1971) Schizophrenia. Geneticism and environmentalism. *Human heredity*, 21, 517-522.

Gottesman, I. I. & Shields, J. (1982) *Schizophrenia: The epigenetic puzzle*. Cambridge: Cambridge University Press.

Grant, D. A. & Berg, E. A. (1948) A behavioral analysis of degree of reinforcement and ease of shifting to new responses in a weigh-type card-sorting problem. *Journal of Experimental Psychology*, 38, 404-411.

Grassian, G. (1983) Psychopathology of solitary confinement. *American Journal of Psychiatry*, 140, 1450-1454.

Grawe, K., Caspar, F. & Ambühl, H. (1990) Die Berner Therapievergleichsstudie: Wirkungsvergleich und differentielle Indikation. *Zeitschrift für klinische Psychologie*, 19, 338-361.

Grawe, K., Donati, R. & Bernauer, F. (1994) *Psychotherapie im Wandel. Von der Konfession zur Profession*. Göttingen: Hogrefe.

Green, M. F. (1993) Cognitive remediation in schizophrenia: Is it time yet? *American Journal of Psychiatry*, 150, 178-187.

Green, M. F., Hellman, S. & Kern, R. S. (1997) Feasibility studies of cognitive remediation in schizophrenia: Grasping the little picture. In H. D. Brenner, W. Böker & R. Genner (eds) *Towards a comprehensive therapy for schizophrenia*. Seattle: Hogrefe & Huber Publishers.

Green, M. F., Satz, P. & Vaclav, J. F. (1990) Teaching the Wisconsin Card Sorting Test to schizophrenic patients. *Archives of General Psychiatry*, 47, 91-92.

Green, M. F., Satz, P., Ganzell, S. & Vaclav, J. F. (1992) Wisconsin card sorting test performance in schizophrenia: Remediation of a stubborn deficit. *American Journal of Psychiatry*, 149, 62-67.

Green, M. F. & Nuechterlein, K. H. (1999) Should schizophrenia be treated as a neurocognitive disorder? *Schizophrenia Bulletin*, 25, 309-318.

Green, M. F. (1998) *Schizophrenia from a neurocognitive perspective. Probing the impenetrable darkness*. Boston: Allyn & Bacon.
Greenberg, L. S. & Safran, J. D. (1987) *Emotion in psychotherapy*. New York: Guilford.
Groves, T. (1990) After the asylums. The local picture. *British Medical Journal*, 300, 1128-1130.
Gruzelier, J. H. (1978) Bimodal states of arousal and lateralized dysfunction in schizophrenia: The effect of chlorpromazine upon psychophysiological, information processing, and endocrine measures. In L. Wynne, R. Cromwell & S. Matthysee (eds) *The nature of schizophrenia: New approaches to research and treatment*. New York: Wiley.
Guidano, V. F. & Liotti, G. (1983) *Cognitive processes and emotional disorders*. New York: Guilford Press.
Gunderson, J. (1978) Defining the therapeutic processes in psychiatric milieus. *Psychiatry*, 41, 327-335.
Gunderson, J. (1979) Individual psychotherapy. In L. Bellak (ed) *Disorders of the schizophrenic syndrome*. New York: Basic Books.
Gunderson, J. G., Frank, A. F., Katz, H. & Glass, L. (1993) Psychotherapy with Schizophrenic Patients: 1988. In G. Benedetti & P. M. Furlan (eds) *The psychotherapy of schizophrenia: Effective clinical approach - controversies, critiques and recommendations*. Seattle: Hogrefe.
Häfner, H. (1988) Rehabilitation Schizophrener. *Zeitschrift für Klinische Psychologie*, XVII, 187-209.
Hahlweg, K., Dürr, H. & Müller U (1995) *Familienbetreuung schizophrener Patienten*. Weinheim: Beltz, Psychologie-Verlags-Union.
Hain, C. H., Maier, W., Klingler, T. H. & Franke, P. (1993) Positive/Negative Symptomatology and Experimental Measures of Attention in Schizophrenic Patients. *Psychopathology*, 26, 62-68.
Hammond, K. R. & Summer, D. A. (1972) Cognitive control. *Psychological Review*, 79, 58-67.
Harrow, M. & Quinlan, D. M. (1985*) Disordered thinking and schizophrenic psychopathology*. New York: Gardner Press, INC.
Harrow, M., Lanin-Kettering, I. & Miller, J. G. (1989) Impaired perspective and thought pathology in schizophrenic and psychotic disorders. *Schizophrenia Bulletin*, 15, 605-623.
Hasher, L. & Zacks, R. T. (1979) Automatic and effortful processes in memory. *Journal of Experimental Psychology*, 108, 356-388.
Heaton, R. K. (1981) *Wisconsin Card Sorting Test Manual*. Odessa, FL: Psychological Assessment Resources.
Hecht, H., Faltermaier, A. & Wittchen, H. U. (1987*) Social Interview Schedule (SIS). Halbstrukturiertes Interview zur Erfassung der aktuellen sozialpsychologischen Situation*. Regensburg: Roderer Verlag.
Heider, F. (1958) *The psychology of interpersonal relations*. New York: Wiley.
Heimberg, C., Gur, R. & Erwin, R. J., et al (1992) Facial emotion discrimination: III. Behavioral findings in schizophrenia. *Psychiatry Research*, 42, 253-265.

Hell, D. (1991) "Verdrängungsmechanismen" in psychiatrischen Institutionen. *Praxis der Psychotherapie und Psychosomatik*, 36, 189-194.

Hellman, S., Green, M. F., Kern, R. S. & Christenson, C. D. (1992) The effects of instructions versus reinforcement of the Wisconsin Card Sorting Test. *Journal of Clinical and Experimental Neuropsychology*, 14, 63.

Hemsley, D. R. (1994) A cognitive model for schizophrenia and its possible neural basis. *Acta Psychiatrica Scandinavica*, 90, 80-86.

Hemsley, D. R. (1987) An experimental psychological model for schizophrenia. In H. Häfner, W. F. Gattaz & W. Janzarik (eds) *Search for the causes of schizophrenia*, Heidelberg: Springer Verlag.

Hermanutz, M. & Gestrich, J. (1991) Computer-assisted attention training in schizophrenia. *European Archives of Psychiatry and Clinical Neurology*, 240, 282-287.

Herzog, T. (1992) Nurses, patients and relatives: A study of family patterns on psychiatric wards. In C. L. Cazzullo & G. Invernizzi (eds) *Family intervention in schizophrenia- experiences and orientations in Europe*. Milan: ARS.

Hewstone, M. & Macrae, C. N. (1990) Social cognition. In M. W. Eysenck (ed) *The Blackwell dictionary of cognitive psychology*. Oxford: Blackwell Reference.

Higgins, E. T., Klein, R. & Straumann, T. (1985) Self-concept discrepancy theory: A psychological model for distinguishing among different aspects of depression and anxiety. *Social Cognition*, 3, 51-76.

Hirsch, S. R. & Jolley, A. G. (1989) The dysphoric syndrome in schizophrenia and its implications for relapse. *British Journal of Psychiatry*, 155 (suppl. 5), 46-50.

Hirschberg, W. (1988) Soziale Netzwerke bei schizophrenen Störungen – eine Übersicht. *Psychiatrische Praxis*, 15, 84-89.

Hodel, B. & Brenner, H. D. (1996) Ein trainigsprogramm zur Bewältigung von maladaptiven Emotionen bei schizophrenen Erkrankten. *Nervenarzt*, 67, 564-571.

Hodel, B. (1988) *Selbstbild Skala SIS. Das Selbstbild schizophren Erkrankter*. Unpublished manuscript. Bern: Psychiatric University Hospital.

Hodel, B. (1992) *Bilder mit Emotionen: Ein Test zur Erfassung von Emotionswahrnehmungen* Unpublished manuscript. Bern: Psychiatric University Hospital.

Hodel, B. (1993a) *Zur Frage der Pervasivität von Interventionseffekten bei Schizophrenieerkrankten*. Visp: Mengis.

Hodel, B. (1993b) Weiterentwicklung des IPT: Das Training "Umgang mit Emotionen" im Vergleich mit dem Training "Kognitive Differenzierung" (Abstract). *Schizophrenie* Sonderheft, 1,

Hodel, B., Brenner, H. D., Merlo M., Teuber J. (1998) Emotional management therapy in early psychosis. *British Journal of psychiatry*, 172(suppl.33), 128-133.

Hogarty, G. E. (1977) Treatment and the course of schizophrenia. *Schizophrenia Bulletin*, 3, 587-599.

Hogarty, G. E. (1988) Resistance of schizophrenic patients to social and vocational rehabilitation. In S. J. Denker & F. Kulhanek (eds) *Treatment resistance in schizophrenia*. Braunschweig/Wiesbaden: Vieweg.

Hogarty, G. E., Anderson, C. M. & Reiss, D. J. (1987) Family psychoeducation, social skills training, and medication in schizophrenia: The long and short of it. *Psychopharmacological Bulletin*, 23, 12-13.

Hogarty, G. E., Anderson, C. M., Reiss, D. J. et al (1991) Family psychoeducation, social skills training and maintenance therapy in the aftercare treatment of schizophrenia: II. Two-year effects of a controlled study on relapse and adjustment. *Archives of General Psychiatry*, 48, 340-347.

Hogarty, G. E., Kornblith, S. J., Greenwald, D. et al (1995) Personal therapy: A disorder-relevant psychotherapy of schizophrenia. *Schizophrenia Bulletin*, 21, 379-393.

Hogarty, G. E., Anderson, C. M., Reiss, D. J. et al (1986) Family psychoeducation, social skills training, and maintenance chemotherapy in the aftercare treatment of schizophrenia. I. One-year effects of a controlled study on relapse and expressed emotion. *Archives of General Psychiatry*, 43, 633-42.

Hollon, S. D. & Kriss, M. R. (1984) Cognitive factors in clinical research and practice. *Clinical Psychology Review*, 4, 35-76.

Holmes, J. (1993) Attachment theory: A biological basis of psychotherapy. *British Journal of Psychiatry*, 163, 430-438.

Holzman, P. S. & Bivens, L. W. (1988) Basic behavioral sciences. *Schizophrenia Bulletin*, 14, 423-456.

Honigfeld, G. & Klett, C. J. (1965) The nurses' observations scale for inpatient evaluation. *Journal of Clinical Psychology*, 21, 65-71.

Honigfeld, G. (1974) NOSIE-30: History and current status of its use in pharmacopsychiatric research. In P. Pichot (ed) *Modern Problems of Pharmacopsychiatry* (Vol. 7, Psychological measurements in psychopharmacology). Basel: S. Karger Verlag.

Honigfeld, G., Gilles, R. D. & Klett, C. J. (1966) NOSIE-30: A treatment-sensitive ward behavior scale. *Psychological Review*, 19, 180-182.

Horowitz, H. (1975) A cognitive model of hallucinations. *American Journal of Psychiatry*, 132, 789-795.

Hurlburt, R. T. (1990) *Sampling normal and schizophrenic inner experience*. New York: Plenum Press.

Hymowitz, P. & Spohn, H. (1980) The effects of antipsychotic medication on the linguistic ability of schizophrenics. *Journal of Nervous and Mental Disease*, 168, 287-296.

Jackson, A. J., Minas, I. H. & Burgess, P. M. (1989) Negative symptoms and social skills performance in schizophrenia. *Schizophrenia Research*, 2, 457-463.

Jacob, M., Frank, E., Kupfer, D.J., Cornes, C. & Carpenter, L.L. (1987) A Psychoeducational Workshop for Depressed Patients, Family and Friends: Description.and Evaluation. *Hospital und Commnunity Psychiatry*, 38, 968-972.

Janzarik, W. (1959) *Dynamische Grundkonstellationen in endogenen Psychosen. Ein Beitrag zur Differentialtypologie der Wahnphänomene*. Berlin: Springer.

Janzarik, W. (1988) *Strukturdynamische Grundlagen der Psychiatrie*. Stuttgart: Ferdinand Enke.

Jenkins, J. H. & Karno, M. (1992) The meaning of expressed emotion: theoretical issues raised by cross-cultural research. *American Journal of Psychiatry*, 149, 9-21.

Jensen, A. R. & Munro, E. (1979) Reaction time, movement time and intelligence. *Intelligence*, 3, 121-126.

Jones, E. E. & Davis, K. E. (1965) From acts to dispositions: The attribution process in person perception. In L. Berkowitz (ed) *Advances in experimental social psychology*. Vol. 2. New York: Academic Press.

Kaehler, W. M. (1990) SPSS-X PC. Braunschweig: Vieweg.

Kahneman, D. (1973) *Attention and effort*. Englewood Cliffs: Prentice-Hall.

Kane, J. M. & Marder, S. R. (1993) Psychopharmacologic treatment of schizophrenia. *Schizophrenia Bulletin*, 19, 287-302.

Kaney, S. & Bentall, R. P. (1989) Persecutory delusions and attributional style. *British Journal of Medical Psychology*, 62, 191-198.

Kanfer, F. (1994) Beiträge eines Selbstregulationsmodells zur psychotherapeutischen Praxis. In M. Zielke & J. Sturm (eds) *Handbuch Stationäre Verhaltenstherapie*. Weinheim: Beltz Psychologie Verlags Union.

Kanfer, F. H. (1989) Basiskonzepte in der Verhaltenstherapie: Veränderungen während der letzten 30 Jahre. In I. Hand & H.-U. Wittchen (eds). *Verhaltenstherapie in der Medizin*. Berlin:Springer.

Kaplan, H. I., Sadock, B. J. & Grebb, J. A. (1994) *Synopsis of psychiatry. Behavioral sciences clinical psychiatry*. (2nd ed). Baltimore: Williams & Wilkins.

Karasu, T. B. (1982) Psychotherapy and pharmacotherapy: Toward an integrative model. *American Journal of Psychiatry*, 139, 1102-1113.

Käsermann, M. L. (1986) *Dialoge zwischen Psychiatriepatient und Arzt: Missverständnisse verstehen lernen*? Uni Press (Universität Bern), 49, 12-15.

Kavanagh, D. J. (1992) Recent developments in expressed emotion and schizophrenia. *British Journal of Psychiatry*, 160, 601-620.

Kelley, H. H. (1973) The processes of causal attribution. *American Psychologist*, 28, 107-128.

Kern, R. S. & Green, M. F. (1994) Cognitive prerequisites of skill acquisition in schizophrenia: Bridging micro- and macro-levels of processing. In W. Spaulding (ed) *Cognitive technology in psychiatric rehabilitation*. Lincoln, NE: University of Nebraska Press (pp. 49-66).

Kern, R. S., Green, M. F. & Satz, P. (1992) Neuropsychological predictors of skills training for chronic psychiatric patients. *Psychiatry Research*, 4, 223-230.

Kern, R. S., Green, M. F. & Goldstein, M. J. (1995) Modification of performance on the span of apprehension, a putative marker of vulnerability to schizophrenia. *Journal of Abnormal Psychology*, 104, 385-9.

Keshavan, M. S. & Schooler, N. R. (1992) First-episode studies in schizophrenia: Criteria and characterization. *Schizophrenia Bulletin*, 18, 491-513.

Kierkegaard, S. (1989) *The sickness unto death*. New York: Viking Penguin.

Killian, G. A., Holzman, P. S., Davis, J. M. & Gibbons, R. (1984) Effects of psychotropic medication on selected cognitive and perceptual measures. *Journal of Abnormal Psychology*, 93, 58-70.

Kingdon, D. G. & Bakewell, E. (1988) Aggressive behavior: evaluation of a non-seclusion policy of a district psychiatric service. *British Journal of Psychiatry*, 153, 631-634.

Kingdon, D. G. & Turkington, D. (1991) Preliminary report. The use of cognitive behavior therapy and a normalizing rationale in schizophrenia. *Journal of Nervous & Mental Disease*, 179, 207-211.

Kingdon, D. G. & Turkington, D. (1994) *Cognitive-behavioral therapy of schizophrenia*. New York: Guilford.

Kingdon, D. G., Turkington, D. & Collis, J. et al (1989) Befriending: Cost-effective community care. *Psychiatric Bulletin*, 13, 350-351.

Kingdon, D. G., Turkington, D. & Malcolm, K. et al (1991) Replacing the mental hospital: Community provision for a district chronically psychiatrically disabled in domestic environments. *British Journal of Psychiatry*, 158, 113-116.

Kingdon, D., Turkington, D. & John, C. (1994) Cognitive behavior therapy of schizophrenia. *British Journal of Psychiatry*, 164, 581-587.

Kleinginna, P. R. & Kleinginna, A. M. (1981) A categorized list of emotion definitions, with suggestions for a consensual definition. *Motivation & Emotions*, 5, 345-379.

Kline, J. S., Smith, J. E. & Ellis, H. C. (1992) Paranoid and nonparanoid schizophrenic processing of facially displayed affect. *Journal of Psychiatric Research*, 26, 169-182.

Klosterkötter, J., Albers, M., Steinmeyer, E.M., Hensen, A. & Sass H (1994) Positive oder negative Symptome. Was ist brauchbarer für die Diagnose Schizophrenie? *Nervenarzt*, 65, 444-53.

Knight, R. G. & Russell, P. N. (1978) Global capacity reduction and schizophrenia. *British Journal of Social and Clinical Psychology*, 17, 275-280.

Knight, R. G. (1984) Converging models of cognitive deficit in schizophrenia. In W. Spaulding & J. Cole (eds) *Theories of schizophrenia and psychosis. Nebraska symposium on motivation,* (Vol. 31). Lincoln, NE: University of Nebraska Press.

Koh, S. D. (1978) Remembering in schizophrenia. In S. Schwartz (ed) *Language and cognition in schizophrenia*. Hillsdale, N. J.: Lawrence Erlbaum.

Koh, S. D., Grinker, R. R., Marusarz, T. W. & Forman, P. L. (1981) Affective memory and schizophrenic anhedonia. *Schizophrenia Bulletin*, 7, 292-303.

Koh, S. D., Kayton, L. & Peterson, R. A. (1976) Affective encoding and consequent remembering in schizophrenic young adults. *Journal of Abnormal Psychology*, 85, 156-166.

Koh, S. D., Peterson, R. A. & Spivak, D. A. (1980) *The Pollyanna tendency in schizophrenic and hypomanic individuals*. Unpublished manuscript.

Konen, A., Neis, L., Hodel, B. & Brenner, H. D. (1993) A propos des thérapies cognitive-comportementales de la schizophrénie: Le programme intégratif de thérapies psychologiques (IPT). *L'Encéphale*, 19, 47-55.

Koukkou, M. & Manske, W. (1986) Functional states of the brain and schizophrenic states of behavior. In C. Shagass, R. C. Josiassen & R. A. Roemer (eds) *Brain electrical potentials and psychopathology*. Amsterdam: Elsevier.

Koukkou, M., Tremel, E. & Manske, W. (1991) Psychobiological models of pathogenesis of schizophrenic symptoms. *International Journal of Psychophysiology*, 19, 203-212.

Kraemer, S. (1998) Psychosoziale Interventionen unter Einbeziehung der Bezugspersonen von Patienten mit psychiatrischen Störungen. In W. Binder & W. Bender (eds) *Angehörigenarbeit in der Psychiatrie*, Claus Richter Verlag.

Kraemer, S., Beloch, E. & Heidenreich, T. (1999a) Das Störungsspektrum schizophrener Patienten und Veränderungen durch computergestütztes Training. *Schizophrenie*, 14, 28-39.

Kraemer, S., Dinkoff-Awiszus, G. & Möller, H. J. (1994) Modification of Integrated Psychological Therapy for schizophrenic patients (IPT) In H. D. Brenner, V. Roder , B. Hodel et al (eds) *Integrated Psychological Therapy for schizophrenic patients (IPT)*. Seattle: Hogrefe & Huber.

Kraemer, S., Lihl, M., Mergenthaler, E. & Lukesch, P. (1999b) Die Erkennung von Schlüsselstunden oder guten Phasen im Verlauf kognitiver Verhaltenstherapie bei schizophrenen Patienten. *Fortschritte der Neurologie und Psychiatrie*, Sonderheft 9/1999, S11(abstract).

Kraemer, S., Sulz, K. H. D., Schmid, R. & Lassle, R. (1987) Kognitive Therapie bei standardversorgten schizophrenen Patienten. *Nervenarzt*, 58, 84-90.

Kraemer, S., von Stark, J., Dietzel, A. & Dragon, E. (1999c) Kognitive Verhaltenstherapie schizophrener Patienten unter Berücksichtigung der therapeutischen Beziehung. *Psychotherapie*, 4, 57-65.

Kraemer, S., Zinner, H. J. & Möller, H. J. (1991) Kognitive Therapie und Sozialtraining: Vergleich zweier verhaltenstherapeutischer Behandlungskonzepte für chronisch schizophrene Patienten. In R. Schüttler (ed) *Theorie und Praxis kognitiver Therapieverfahren bei schizophrenen Patienten*. München: Zuckschwerdt Verlag.

Kraepelin, E. (1902) Dementia praecox. In E. Kraepelin (ed) *Clinical psychiatry: A textbook for students and physicians*. (6th ed). Leipzig: Thieme.

Kraus, A. (1987) Rollendynamische Aspekte bei Manisch-Depressiven. In K. P. Kisker, H. Lauter , J.-E. Meyer et al (ed) *Psychatrie der Gegenwart: Affektive Psychosen*, (Bd. 5). Berlin: Springer.

Kuipers, E. (1998) Working with carers: interventions for relative and staff carers of those who have psychosis. In T. Wykes, N. Tarrier & S. Lewis (eds) *Outcome and innovation in psychological treatment of schizophrenia*. Chichester, UK: John Wiley & Sons.

Lamberti, G., Wienke, K. H. & Brauke, N. (1988) Der Computer als Hilfe beim Aufmerksamkeitstraining - eine klinisch-experimentelle Studie. *Rehabilitation*, 27, 190-198.

Lang, P. J. & Buss, A. H. (1965) Psychological deficits in schizophrenia: II. Inference and activation. *Journal of Abnormal Psychology*, 70, 77-106.

Larsen, S. & Fromholt, P. (1976) Mnemonic organization and free recall in schizophrenics. *Journal of Abnormal Psychology*, 85, 61-65.

Leff, J. P. & Vaughn, C. (1981) The role of maintenance therapy and relatives expressed emotions in relapse of schizophrenia: A two year follow-up. *British Journal of Psychiatry*, 141, 121-134.

Leff, J. P. & Vaughn, C. E. (1985) *Expressed emotion in families*. New York: Guilford.

Leff, J. P. (1968) Perceptual phenomena and personality in sensory deprivation. *British Journal of Psychiatry*, 114, 1499-1508.

Lehman, A. F., Carpenter, W. T. Jr., Goldman, H. H. & Steinwachs, D. M. (1995) Treatment outcomes in schizophrenia: implications for practice, policy, and research. *Schizophrenia Bulletin*, 21, 669-75.

Lempp, R. (1992) *Vom Verlust der Fähigkeit, sich selbst zu betrachten. Eine entwicklungspsychologische Erklärung der Schizophrenie und des Autismus.* Bern: Hans Huber.

Lewandowski, L., Buchkremer, G. & Hermann, T. (1992) Zur Wirksamkeit ambulanter arbeitstherapeutischer Massnahmen für schizophrene Patienten. *Psychiatrische Praxis*, 19, 122-8.

Liberman, R. P. & Corrigan, P. W. (1993) Designing new psychosocial treatments for schizophrenia. *Psychiatry*, 56, 238-249.

Liberman, R. P. & Green, M. F. (1992) Whither cognitive-behavior therapy for schizophrenia. *Schizophrenia Bulletin*, 18, 27-35.

Liberman, R. P. & Wallace, C. (1990) Neuere Entwicklungen des Trainings sozialer Fertigkeiten für chronisch psychisch Kranke. In R. Olbrich (ed) *Therapie der Schizophrenie.* Stuttgart: Kohlhammer.

Liberman, R. P. (1988) *Psychiatric rehabilitation of chronic mental patients.* Washington DC: American Psychiatric Press.

Liberman, R. P., Delisi, W. J. & McCann, M. (1975) *Personal effectiveness.* Champaign: Research Press.

Liberman, R. P., DeRissi, W. J. & Mueser, K. T. (1989) *Social skills training for psychiatric patients.* New York, Oxford, Frankfurt: Pergamon Press.

Liberman, R. P., Falloon, I. R. H. & Wallace, C. J. (1984) Drug psychosocial interventions in the treatment of schizophrenia. In M. Mirabi (ed) *The chronically mentally ill: Research and services.* New York: SP Medical & Scientific Books.

Liberman, R. P., Jacobs, H. E., Boone, S. E. et al (1986) Fertigkeitstraining zur Anpassung Schizophrener an die Gemeinschaft. In W. Böker & H. D. Brenner (eds) *Bewältigung der Schizophrenie.* Bern: Huber.

Liberman, R. P., Massell, H. K., Mosk, M. D. & Wong, S. E. (1985) Social skills training for chronic mental patients. *Hospital and Community Psychiatry*, 36, 396-403.

Liberman, R. P., Mueser, K. T. & Wallace, C. J. (1986) Training skills in the psychiatrically disabled: Learning coping and competence. *Schizophrenia Bulletin*, 12, 631-647.

Liberman, R. P., Wallace, C., Blackwell, G. et al (1993) Innovation in skills training for the seriously mentally ill: The UCLA social and independent living skills modules. *Innovations & Research*, 2, 43-60.

Liberman, R. P., Spaulding, W. D. & Corrigan, P. W. (1995) Cognitive-Behavioural Therapies in Psychiatric Rehabilitation. In S. R. Hirsch & D. R. Weinberger (eds) *Schizophrenia.* London: Blackwell Sciences.

Lidz, T. (1973) *The origin and treatment of schizophrenic disorders.* New York: Basic Books.

Lieberman, J. & Koreen, A. R. (1993) Neurochemistry and neuroendocrinology of schizophrenia. *Schizophrenia Bulletin*, 19, 371-429.

Linehan, M. M. (1993) *Cognitive Behavioral Treatment of Borderline Personality Disorder*. New York: Guilford Press.
Liotti, G. & Onofri, A. (1987) La relazione terapeutica col paziente schizofrenico alla luce della teoria dell' attaccamento. *Schizofrenia*, 1, 31-36.
Liotti, G. (1986) Structural cognitive therapy. In W. Dryden & W. Golden (eds) *Cognitive-behavioral approaches to psychotherapy*. London: Harper & Row.
Liotti, G. (1991) Insecure attachment and agoraphobia. In C. M. Parkes & J. Stevenson-Hinde (eds) *Attachment across the life cycle*. London: Routledge.
Ludwig, A. M. (1966) Altered states of conciousness. *Archives of General Psychiatry*, 15, 225-234.
Luhmann, N. (1984) *Soziale Systeme. Grundrisse einer allgemeinen Theorie*. Frankfurt: Suhrkamp.
Lukoff, D., Nuechterlein, K. H. & Ventura, J. (1986) Manual for expanded brief psychiatric rating scale (BPRS). *Schizophrenia Bulletin*, 12, 594-602.
Lukoff, D., Snyder, K., Ventura, J. & Nuechterlein, K. H. (1984) Life events, familial stress, and coping in the developmental course of schizophrenia. *Schizophrenia Bulletin*, 10, 259-292.
Lundh, L. G. (1983) *Mind and meaning*. Acta Universitatis Upsaliensis. Uppsala, Sweden, 10.
Lysaker, P. & Bell, M. (1995) Work and meaning: disturbance of volition and vocational dysfunction in schizophrenia. *Psychiatry*, 58, 392-400.
Lysaker, P. H., Bell, M. D. & Bioty, S. M. (1995) Cognitive deficits in schizophrenia. Prediction of symptom change for participators in work rehabilitation. *The Journal of Nervous and Mental Disease*, 183, 332-6.
Magaro, P. A. (1980) *Cognition in schizophrenia and paranoia: The integration of cognitive processes*. Hillsdale: Erlbaum.
Magaro, P. A. (1984) Psychosis and schizophrenia. In W. Spaulding & J. K. Cole (eds) *The Nebraska symposium on motivation*. Lincoln: University of Nebraska Press.
Main, M. & Weston, D. R. (1982) Avoidance of the attachment figure in infancy. In C. M. Parkes & J. Stevenson-Hinde (eds) *The place of attachment in human behavior* New York: Basic Books.
Mandal, M. K. & Gewali, H. (1989) Identifying the components of facial emotion and schizophrenia. *Psychopathology*, 22, 295-302.
Mandler, G. (1984) *Mind and body. Psychology of emotion and stress*. New York: Norton.
Marder, S. R., Wirshing, W. C., Mintz, J. et al (1996) Two-year outcome of social skills training and group psychotherapy for outpatients with schizophrenia. *American Journal of Psychiatry*, 153, 1585-92.
Marker, K. (1989) *Cognition - 1. Handbuch zum Programm Version 2.2 (C)*. Dossenheim: Marker Software.
Markus, H. (1977) Self-schemata and processing information about the self. *Personality and Social Psychology*, 35, 63-78.
Marsella, A. J. (1988) Cross-cultural aspects of severe psychiatric disorders. *Acta Psychiatrica Scandinavica*, 78 (suppl. 344), 7-22.

Martinez-Diaz, J. A., Massell, H. K., Wong, S. E. et al (1983) *Training and generalization of conversation skills in chronic schizophrenics*. Presented at the annual meeting of the Association for the Advancement of Behavior Therapy, Washington, DC.

Massell, H. K., Corrigan, P. W., Liberman, R. P. & Milan, M. (1991) Conversation skills training in thought-disordered schizophrenics through attention focusing. *Psychiatry Research*, 38, 51-61.

McDougall, W. (1908) *An introduction to social psychology*. London: Methuen.

McFall, R. M. (1982) A review and reformulation of the concept of social skills. *Behavioral Assessment*, 4, 1-33.

McGlashan, T. H. (1988) A selective review of recent North American long-term followup studies of schizophrenia. *Schizophrenia Bulletin*, 14, 515-542.

McGorry, P. D. & Jackson, H. J. (eds) (1999) *The recognition and management of early psychosis: a preventive approach*. Cambridge, UK: Cambridge University Press.

Mead, G. H. (1934) *Mind, self, and society*. Chicago: University of Chicago Press.

Mednick, B. R. (1973) Breakdown in high risk subjects: Familial and early enviromental factors. *Journal of Abnormal Psychology*, 82, 469-475.

Meehl, P. E. & Cronbach, L. J. (1955) Construct validity in psychological tests. *Psychological Bulletin*, 52, 3-31.

Mefferd, R. B., Wieland, B. A. & James, W. E. (1966) Repetitive psychometric measures: Digit span. *Psychological Reports*, 18, 3-10.

Meichenbaum, D. & Cameron, R. (1973) Training schizophrenics to talk to themselves: A means of developing attentional controls. *Behavioral Therapy*, 4, 515-534.

Meichenbaum, D. (1977a) Methoden der Selbstinstruktion. In F.H. Kanfer & A.P. Goldstein (eds) *Möglichkeiten der Verhaltensänderung*. München, Wien, Baltimore: Urban & Schwarzenberg.

Meichenbaum, D. (1977b) *Cognitive-behavior modification: An integrative approach*. New York: Plenum Press.

Meichenbaum, D. (1991) *Intervention bei Streß*. Bern: Huber Verlag.

Meiselman, K. C. (1973) Broadening dual modality cue utilization in chronic nonparanoid schizophrenia. *Journal of Consulting and Clinical Psychology*, 41, 447-453.

Meltzer, H. Y., Kupfer, D. J. & Wyatt, R. et al (1970) Sleep disturbance and serum CPK activity in acute psychosis. *Archives of General Psychiatry*, 22, 398-405.

Meltzer, H. Y. & McGurk, S. R. (1999) The effects of clozapine, risperidone, and olanzapine on cognitive function in schizophrenia. *Schizophrenia Bulletin*, 25, 233-255.

Menditto, A. A., Baldwin, L. J. & O'Neal, L. G. (1989) *The use of shaping chips in a comprehensive social-learning program for chronically mentally-ill forensic patients*. Paper presented at the 23rd annual convention of the Association for the Advancement of Behavior Therapy, Washington, DC.

Mergenthaler, E. (1998) Cycles of Emotion-Abstraction-Patterns: A Way of Practice Oriented Process Research? *The British Psychological Society, Psychotherapy Section Newsletter*, 24, 16-29.

Merlo, M. C. G. & Studer, A. (1993) Computerunterstützte Diagnostik kognitiver Störungen bei schizophrenen Patienten. In F. Tretter & F. Goldhorn (eds) *Computer in der Psychiatrie. Diagnostik-Therapie-Rehabilitation* Heidelberg: Roland Asanger Verlag.

Merlo, M. C. G. (1989) Systemtheoretische Ueberlegungen zur Behandlung des akuten und postakuten Stadiums schizophrener Psychosen. *Psychiatrische Praxis*, 16, 121-125.

Merlo, M. C. G., Schwallbach, H. & Kröger, F. (1991) Changes in social perception during family therapy of young schizophrenics. *Small Group Research*, 22, 124-135.

Milner, B. (1963) Effects of different brain lesions on card sorting. The role of the frontal lobes. *Archives of Neurology*, 9, 90-100.

Milton, F., Patwa, V. K. & Hafner, R. J. (1978) Confrontation vs. belief modification in persistently deluded patients. *British Journal of Medical Psychology*, 51, 127-130.

Modestin, J., Lerch, M. & Böker, W. (1994) *Burnout in der psychiatrischen Krankenpflege: Resultate einer empirischen Untersuchung.* Berlin: Springer.

Mojtabai, R., Nicholson, R. A. & Carpenter, B. N. (1998) Role of psychosocial treatment in management of schizophrenia: a meta-analytic review of controlled outcome studies. *Schizophrenia Bulletin*, 24, 569-587.

Möller, H.-J. & von Zerssen, D. (1986) *Der Verlauf schizophrener Psychosen unter den gegenwärtigen Behandlungsbedingungen.* Berlin, Heidelberg: Springer.

Möller, H.-J. (1993) Grundsätzliches zur Therapie. In H.-J. Möller (ed) *Therapie psychiatrischer Erkrankungen.* Stuttgart: Enke Verlag.

Morrison, R. L. & Bellack, A. S. (1984) Social skills training. In A.S. Bellack (ed) Schizophrenia: *Treatment, management, and rehabilitation.* New York: Grune & Stratton.

Moscovici, S. (1981) On social representation. In J. P. Forgas (ed) *Social cognition.* London: Academic Press.

Mueser, K. T., Blanchard, J. J. & Bellack, A. S. (1995) Memory and social skill in schizophrenia: the role of gender. *Psychiatry Research*, 57, 141-53.

Mueser, K. T., Gingerich, S. L. & Rosenthal, C. K. (1994) Educational Family Therapy for schizophrenia: a new treatment model for clinical service and research. *Schizophrenia Research*, 13, 99-107.

Müller, P., Gaebel, W., Bandelow, B. et al (1998) Zur sozialen Situation schizophrener Patienten. *Nervenarzt*: 69:204-209.

Mundt, C., Fiedler, P., Pracht, B. & Retting, R. (1985) InSka (Intentionalitätsskala). Ein neues psychopathometrisches Instrument zur quantitativen Erfassung der schizophrenen Residualsymptomatik. *Nervenarzt*, 56, 146-149.

Murray, R. M., Kerwin, R. W. & Nimgaonker, V. (1988) What have we learned about the biology of schizophrenia? In K. Granville-Grossman (ed) *Recent advances in clinical psychiatry.* Churchill Livingstone: Edinburgh.

Mussgay, L. & Olbrich, R. (1988) Trainingsprogramme in der Behandlung kognitiver Defizite Schizophrener. Eine kritische Würdigung. *Zeitschrift für Klinische Psychiatrie*, 17, 341-353.

Mussgay, L. (1993) Der Computer als Hilfsmittel bei der Reduktion kognitiver Defizite Schizophrener: Voraussetzungen und Grenzen In F. Tretter & F. Goldhorn (eds) *Computer in der Psychiatrie*. Heidelberg: Roland Asanger Verlag.

Muzekari, L. H. & Bates, M. E. (1977) Judgement of emotion among chronic schizophrenics. *Journal of Clinical Psychology*, 33, 662-666.

National Institute of Mental Health (1970) 12-CGI: Clinical Global Impressions. In W. Guy & R.R. Bonato (eds) *Manual for the ECDEU Assessment Battery*. 2nd Rev. Maryland: Ed. Chevy Chase.

Neimeyer, R. A. & Mahoney, M. J. (eds) (1996) *Constructivism in psychotherapy*. Washington, DC: American Psychological Association.

Neisser, U. (1976) *Cognition and reality. Principles and implications of cognitive psychology*. San Francisco: Freeman.

Norman, R. M. G. & Malla, A. K. (1993) Stressful life events and schizophrenia. I: A review of the research. *British Journal of Psychiatry*, 162, 161-174.

Novic, J., Luchins, D. J. & Perline, R. (1984) Facial affect recognition in schizophrenia: Is there a differential deficit? *British Journal of Psychiatry*, 144, 533-537.

Nuechterlein, K. H. & Asarnow, R. F. (1989) Cognition and perception. In H. I. Kaplan & B. J. Sadock (eds) *Comprehensive Textbook of Psychiatry*. Baltimore: Williams & Wilkins.

Nuechterlein, K. H. & Dawson, M. E. (1984a) A heuristic vulnerability/stress model of schizophrenic episodes. *Schizophrenia Bulletin*, 10, 300-312.

Nuechterlein, K. H. & Dawson, M. E. (1984b) Information processing and attentional functioning in the developmental course of schizophrenic disorders. *Schizophrenia Bulletin*, 10, 160-203.

Nuechterlein, K. H. (1977) Reaction time and attention in schizophrenia: A critical evaluation of the data and theories. *Schizophrenia Bulletin*, 3, 373-382.

Nuechterlein, K. H. (1990) Testing vulnerability models: Stability of potential vulnerability indicators across clinical state. In H. Häfner & W.F. Gattaz (eds) *Search for the causes of schizophrenia*. (Vol. 2), Heidelberg: Springer-Verlag.

Nuechterlein, K. H. (1991) Vigilance in schizophrenia and related disorders. In H.A. Nasrallah (ed) *Handbook of schizophrenia (Vol.5), Neuropsychology, psychophysiology and information processing*. Amsterdam: Elsevier.

Nuechterlein, K. H. (1994) Information processing abnormalities as neuropsychological vulnerability factors for schizophrenia. *Acta Psychiatrica Scandinavica*, 89 (suppl. 382), 71-9.

Nuechterlein, K. H., Snyders, S. & Mintz, J. (1992) Paths to relapse: Possible transactional processes connecting patient illness onset, expressed emotion, and psychotic relapse. *British Journal of Psychiatry*, 161 (suppl. 18), 88-96.

Nugter, M.A., Dingemans, P.M., Linszen, D.H., Van der Does, A.J. & Gersons, B.P. (1997) The relationships between expressed emotion, affective style and communication deviance in recent-onset schizophrenia. *Acta Psychiatrica Scandinavica*, 96, 445-51.

Öhman, A. & Magnusson, D. (1987) An interactional paradigm for research on psychopathology. In D. Magnusson & A. Öhman (eds) *Psychopathology. An interactional perspective*. New York: Academic Press.

Olbrich, R. & Mussgay, L. (1990) Reduction of schizophrenic deficits by cognitive training: an evaluative study. *European Archives of Psychiatry and Clinical Neurological Sciences*. 239, 366-369.

Olbrich, R. (1993) *Computer-based training programs for cognitive deficits in schizophrenia*. Dublin: Abstract's book of the WAPR congress.

Oltmanns, T. F. & Neale, J. M. (1975) Schizophrenic performance when distractors are present: Attentional deficit of differential task difficulty? *Journal of Abnormal Psychology*, 84, 205-209.

Orzack, M. H., Kornetsky, C. & Freeman, H. (1967) The effects of daily administration of carphenazine on attention in the schizophrenic patient. *Psychopharmacologia*, 11, 31-38.

Oswald, I. (1974) *Sleep*, (3rd ed) Harmondsworth: Penguin.

Oswald, W.D. & Roth, E. (1978) *Der Zahlen-Verbindungs-Test (ZVT)*. Göttingen. Testzentrale Göttingen.

Overall, J. E. & Gorham, D. R. (1962) The Brief Psychiatric Rating Scale. *Psychological Reports*, 10, 799-812.

Paul, G. L. & Lentz, R. J. (1977) *Psychosocial treatment of chronic mental patients: Milieu vs. social learning programs*. Cambridge: Harvard University Press.

Penn, D., van der Does, J., Spaulding, W., Garbin, C., Linzen, D. & Dingamans, P. (1993) Information processing and social-cognitive problem solving in schizophrenia: Assessment of interrelationshiips and changes over time. *Journal of Mental Disease*, 181, 13-20.

Penn, D.L. & Mueser, K.T. (1996) Research update on the psychosocial treatment of schizophrenia. *American Journal of Psychiatry*, 153, 607-17.

Perris, C. (1986) Intensive cognitive-behavioral in-patient treatment of young severely ill patients. In C. Perris & M. Eisemann (eds). *Cognitive Psychotherapy. An Update*. Umea: Dopuu Press.

Perris, C. (1987) Development of psychiatry in Sweden with particular reference to one of the northern countries. *International Journal of Mental Health*, 16, 198-224.

Perris, C. (1988a) *Kognitiv psykoterapi vid schizofrena störningar*. Stockholm: Pilgrim Press.

Perris, C. (1988b) Intensive cognitive-behavioral psychotherapy with patients suffering from schizophrenic psychotic or post-psychotic syndromes: Theoretical and pratical aspects. In C. Perris, I.M. Blackburn & H. Perris (eds) *Cognitive psychotherapy. Theory and practice*. Heidelberg: Springer.

Perris, C. (1988c) Cognitive psychotherapy and milieutherapeutic processes in psychiatric inpatient units. *Journal of Cognitive Psychotherapy*, 2, 35-50.

Perris, C. (1989) *Cognitive therapy with schizophrenic patients*. New York: Guilford Press.

Perris, C. (1991) An interactionistic integrating view of depressive disorders and their treatment. *Acta Psychiatrica Scandinavica*, 84, 41113-423.

Perris, C. (1993) *Psicoterapia del paziente difficile*. Lanciano (Italy), Metis.

Perris, C. (1997) Schema-focused integrative treatment of patients with schizophrenic disorder. In H.D. Brenner, W. Böker & R. Genner (eds) *Towards a comprehensive therapy for schizophrenia*. Seattle: Hogrefe & Huber Publishers.

Perris, C., Blackburn, I. M. & Perris, H. (1988) *Cognitive psychotherapy: Theory and practice*. Berlin: Springer Verlag.

Perris, C. & Skagerlind, L. (1994) Cognitive therapy with schizophrenic patients. *Acta Psychiatrica Scandinavica*, 89 (suppl. 382), 65-70.

Perry, W. & Braff, D. L. (1994) Information-processing deficits and thought disorder in schizophrenia. *American Journal of Psychiatry*, 151,363-7.

Piaget, J. (1954) *Les relations entre l'affectivité et l'intelligence dans le dévelopment mental de l'enfant*. Paris: C.D.U.

Piaget, J. (1976) *Die Aequilibration der kognitiven Strukturen*. Stuttgart: Klett Verlag.

Pitman, R. K., Kolb, B., Orr, S. P. et al (1987) Ethological study of facial behavior in nonparanoid and paranoid schizophrenic patients. *American Journal of Psychiatry*, 144, 99-102.

Pitschel-Walz, G., Bäuml, J. & Kissling, W. (1999) Die Beeinflussung des Krankheitsverlaufs schizophrener Patienten durch psychoedukative Gruppen. Unveröffentlichtes Manuskript München.

Plutchik, R. (1962) *The emotions. Facts, therories, and a new model*. New York: Random House.

Podvoll, E. M. (1990) *The seduction of madness*. New York: Harper Collins Publisher.

Pribram, K. H. (1981) Emotions. In S.B. Filskov & T.J. Boll (eds) *Handbook of clinical neuropsychology*. New York: Wiley.

Prochaska, J. O., Di Clemente, C. C. & Norcross, J.C. (1992) In search of how people change: Applications to addictive behaviors. *American psychologist* 1102-1114.

Pym, B. (1989) *Run it your own way*. Community Care, 6th April. Unpublished paper.

Racamier, P.-C. (1982) *Die Schizophrenien. Eine psychoanalytische Interpretation*. Berlin: Springer Verlag.

Reker, T. & Eikelmann, B. (1993) Die gegenwärtige Praxis der psychiatrischen Arbeitsrehabilitation. *Psychiatrische Praxis*, 20, 95-101.

Reker, T. & Eikelmann, B. (1994) Ambulante Arbeitstherapie. Ergebnisse einer multizentrischen prospektiven Evaluationsstudie. *Nervenarzt*, 65, 329-37.

Retzer, A. (1994) *Familie und Psychose*. Stuttgart: Gustav Fischer.

Rey, E.-R. & Bailer, J. (eds) (1996) *Prognose und Verlauf ersthospitalisierter Schizophrener*. Frankfurt am Main: Lang.

Rittmannsberger, H., Grausgruber, A., Morth, I., Atzlinger, G. & Heilbrunner, C. (1996) Berufliche Wiedereingliederung psychisch Kranker. *Psychiatrische Praxis*, 23, 79-83.

Roder, V. & Brenner, H. D. (1990) Spezifische Therapieinterventionen im kognitiven und sozialen Bereich mit schizophrenen Patienten. In R. Olbrich (ed) *Therapie der Schizophrenie*. Stuttgart: Kohlhammer.

Roder, V. (1989) *Behavior and problem analysis in the therapeutical process with psychiatric patients.* Paper presented at the VIIIth World Congress of Psychiatry, October 12-19. Athens, Greece:

Roder, V. (1993) *Verhaltenstherapeutische Rehabilitation schizophrener Menschen in Wohn-, Arbeits- und Freizeitbereich: Entwicklung entsprechender Therapiemanuale.* Unpubished paper. Psychiatrische Universitätsklinik Bern.

Roder, V., Brenner, H. D., Kienzle, N. & Hodel, B. (1988) *Integriertes Psychologisches Therapieprogramm für schizophrene Patienten (IPT).* München: Psychologie Verlags Union.

Roder, V., Brenner, H. D., Kienzle, N. & Hodel, B. (1992) *Integriertes Psychologisches Therapieprogramm für schizophrene Patienten*, (2nd ed) Weinheim: Psychologie Verlags Union.

Roder, V., Eckman, T. A., Brenner, H. D., Kienzle, N. & Liberman, R. P. (1990) Behavior therapy. In M.I. Herz, S. J. Keith & J.P. Docherty (eds) *Handbook of schizophrenia.* Vol. 4. Amsterdam: Elsevier.

Roder, V., Jenull, B. & Brenner, H. D. (1998) Teaching schizophrenic patients recreational, residential and vocational skills. *International Review of Psychiatry,* 10, 35-41.

Roder, V., Zorn, P. & Brenner, H.D. (1997) Verhaltenstherapeutische Ansätze zu sozialen Fertigkeiten und Problemlösefertigkeiten schizophrener Patienten: Ein Überblick. In W. Böker & H.D. Brenner (eds) *Behandlung schizophrener Psychosen.* Stuttgart: Enke.

Romme, M. A. J. & Escher, D. M. A. (1989) Hearing voices. *Schizophrenia Bulletin,* 15, 209-216.

Rosen, H. (1985) *Piagetian dimensions of clinical relevance.* New York: Columbia University Press.

Rosenbaum, G., Mackavey, W. R. & Grisell, J. L. (1957) Effects of biological and social motivation on schizophrenic reaction times. *Journal of Abnormal and Social Psychology,* 54, 364-368.

Rosvold, H. E., Mirsky, A., Sarason, I., Bransome, E. D. Jr. & Beck, L. H. (1956) A continuous performance test of brain damage. *Journal of Consulting Psychology,* 20, 343.

Rudas, S. (1990) Evaluation sich verändernder psychiatrischer Versorgungssysteme-Beiträge zur Versorgungsforschung am Beispiel Wiens. *Psychiatrische Praxis,* 17, 206-15.

Russel, J. A. & Fehr, B. (1987) Relativity in the perception of emotion in facial expressions. *Journal of Experimental Psychology,* 116, 223-237.

Rutter, D. R. (1985) Language in schizophrenia. *British Journal of Psychiatry,* 146, 399-404.

Saccuzzo, D. P. & Miller, S. (1977) The critical interstimulus interval in delusional schizophrenics and normals. *Journal of Abnormal Psychology,* 86, 261.

Saccuzzo, D. P. (1986) An information processing interpretation of theory and research in schizophrenia. In R. E. Ingram (ed) *Information approaches to clinical psychology.* New York: Academic Press.

Safran, J. (1990) Toward a refinement of cognitive therapy in light of interpersonal theory: 1.Theory. *Clinical Psychology Review,* 10, 87-105.

Safran, J. D. & Segal, Z. V. (1990) *Interpersonal processes in cognitive therapy.* New York: Basic Books.

Sandner, M., Hodel, B. & Brenner, H. D. (September 14-16, 1991) *Treatment of emotional and cognitive vulnerability of schizophrenic patients.* Geneva: Abstract of the International Congress on Schizophrenia and Affective Psychoses.

Schachter, S. & Singer, J. E. (1962) Cognitive, social, and physiological determinants of emotional state. *Psychological Review*, 69, 379-399.

Scharfetter, C. (1980) *General psychopathology.* Cambridge: Cambridge University Press.

Scharfetter, C. (1990) *Schizophrene Menschen.* München: Urban & Schwarzenberg.

Scheflen, A. (1981) *Levels of schizophrenia.* New York: Brunner/Mazel.

Schindler, L. (1989) Das Codiersystem zur Interaktion in der Psychotherapie (CIP): Ein Instrument zur systematischen Beobachtung des Verhaltens von Therapeut und Klient im Therapieverlauf. *Zeitschrift für Klinische Psychologie*, 18, 68-79.

Schneider, F., Heimann, H. & Himer, W. et al (1990) Computer-based analysis of facial action in schizophrenic and depressed patinents. *European Archives of Psychiatry & Clinical Neuroscience*, 240, 67-76.

Schulz, H., Nuebling, R. & Rueddel, H. (1995) Entwicklung einer Kurzform eines Fragebogens zur Psychotherapiemotivation. Verhaltenstherapie, 5, 89-95.

Searles, H. F. (1955) Dependency processes in the psychotherapy of schizophrenia. *Journal of the American Psychoanalytic Association*, 3, 19-36.

Seltzer, M. A., Sullivan, T. B., Carsky, M. & Terkelsen, K. G. (1989) *Working with the person with schizophrenia. The treatment alliance.* New York: New York University.

Selvini-Palazzoli, M., Boscolo, L., Cecchin, G. & Prata, G. (1980) Hypothesizing-Circularity-Neutrality: Three guidelines for the conductor of the session. *Family Process*, 19, 3-12.

Silverman, J. (1964) The problem of attention in research and theory in schizophrenia. *Psychological Review*, 71, 352-379.

Skantze, K., Malm, U., Dencker, S. J., May, P. R. & Corrigan, P. (1992) Comparison of quality of life with standard of living in schizophrenic out-patients. *British Journal of Psychiatry*, 161, 797-801.

Smith, M., Glass, G. V. & Miller, T. I. (1980) *The benefits of psychotherapy.* Baltimore: John Hopkins University Press.

Snyder, K. S., Wallace, C. J., Moe, K. & Liberman, R. P. (1994) Expressed emotion by residential care operators and residents' symptoms and quality of life. *Hospital and Community Psychiatry*, 45, 1141-3.

Soni, S. D., Gaskell, K. & Reed, P. (1994) Factors affecting rehospitalisation rates of chronic schizophrenic patients living in the community. *Schizophrenia Research*, 12, 169-77.

Spaulding, W. D. & Sullivan, M. (1991) From the laboratory to the clinic: Psychological methods and principles in psychiatric rehabilitation. In R.P. Liberman (ed) *Handbook of psychiatric rehabilitation.* Elmsford: Pergamon Press.

Spaulding, W. D., Storms, L., Goodrich, V. & Sullivan, M. (1986) Applications of experimental psychopathology in psychiatric rehabilitation. *Schizophrenia Bulletin*, 12, 560-577.

Spaulding, W., Garbin, C. & Dras, S. (1989b) Cognitive functioning in chronic psychiatric patients and schizotypal college students. *Journal of Nervous and Mental Disease*, 177, 717-728.

Spaulding, W., Garbin, C. P. & Crinean, W. J. (1989a) The logical and psychometric prerequisites for cognitive therapy for schizophrenia. *British Journal of Psychiatry*, 155 (suppl. 5), 69-73.

Spaulding, W., Hargrove, D., Crinean, J. & Martin, T. (1981) A microprocessor-based laboratory for psychopathology research in rural settings. *Behavior Research Methods and Instrumentation*, 616-623.

Spaulding, W., Reed, D., Elting, D., Sullivan, M. & Penn, D. (1997) Cognitive changes in the course of rehabilitation. In H. D. Brenner, W. Böker & R. Genner (eds) *Towards a comprehensive therapy for schizophrenia*. Seattle: Hogrefe & Huber Publishers.

Spohn, H. E. & Strauss, M. (1989) Relation of neuroleptic and anticholinergic medication to cognitive functions in schizophrenia. *Journal of Abnormal Psychology*, 98, 367-380.

Spohn, H. E., Lacoursiere, R. B., Thompson, R. & Coyne, L. (1977) Phenothiazine effects on psychological and psychophysiological dysfunction in chronic schizophrenics. *Archives of General Psychiatry*, 34, 633-644.

Spring, B. J. & Ravadin, L. (1992) Cognitive remediation in schizophrenia: Should we attempt it? *Schizophrenia Bulletin*, 18, 15-20.

Spring, B., Lemon, M. & Fergeson, P. (1990) Vulnerabilities to schizophrenia: Information processing Markers. In E.R. Straube & K. Hahlweg (eds) *Schizophrenia. Concepts, Vulnerability, and Intervention*. Berlin: Springer.

Stark, F. M., Lewandowski, L., Buchkremer, G. (1992) Therapist-patient relationship as a predictor of the course of schizophrenic illness. *European Psychiatry*, 7, 161-169.

Stierlin, H. (1978) *Delegation und Familie*. Frankfurt am Main: Suhrkamp.

Stokes, T. F. & Osnes, P. G. (1989) An operant pursuit of generalization. *Behavior Therapy*, 20, 337-356.

Storms, L. & Broen, W. (1969) A theory of schizophrenic behavioral disorganization. *Archives of General Psychiatry*, 20, 129-144.

Straube, E. R. & Oades, R. D. (1992) *Schizophrenia. Empirical research and findings*. San Diego: Academic Press.

Strauss, J. S. (1969) Hallucinations and delusions as point on continua function. *Archives of General Psychiatry*, 21, 581-586.

Strauss, J. S. & Carpenter, W. T. Jr. (1991) *Schizophrenia*. New York, NY: Plenum Publishing Cooperation.

Strauss, J. S., Hafez, H., Lieberman, P. & Harding, C. M. (1985) The course of psychiatric disorder: III. Longitudinal principles. *American Journal of Psychiatry*, 142, 289-296.

Strauss, M., Foureman, W. & Parwatikur, S. (1974) Schizophrenics' size estimation of thematic stimuli. *Journal of Abnormal Psychology*, 83, 117-123.

Strongman, K. T. (1987) *The psychology of emotion* (3rd ed). Chichester, New York: John Wiley & Sons.

Süllwold, L. & Herrlich, J. (1987) *Befindlichkeits-Skala (FBS) für schizophren Erkrankte.* Heidelberg: Springer.

Süllwold, L. & Herrlich, J. (1990) *Psychologische Behandlung schizophren Erkrankter.* Stuttgart, Berlin, Köln: Kohlhammer.

Süllwold, L. & Huber, G. (1986) *Schizophrene Basisstörungen.* Berlin: Springer.

Süllwold, L. (1986a) *Der Frankfurter Beschwerdefragebogen.* Berlin, Heidelberg, New York: Springer.

Süllwold, L. (1986b) *Schizophrenie* (2nd ed). Stuttgart: Kohlhammer.

Summerfelt, A. T., Alphs, L. D., Funderburk, F. R., Strauss, M. W. & Wagmann, A. M. I. (1991) Impaired Wisconsin Card sorting performance in schizophrenia may reflect motivational deficits. *American Journal of Psychiatry*, 149, 62-67.

Theilemann, S. & Peter, K. (1994) Zur Evaluation kognitiver Therapie bei schizophren Erkrankten. *Zeitschrift für Klinische Psychologie*, 23, 20-33.

Tomm, K. (1985) Circular interviewing: A multifaceted clinical tool. In D. Champbell & R. Draper (eds) *Applications of systemic family therapy. The Milan approach.* London: Grune & Statton.

Tulving, E. (1972) Episodic and semantic memory. In E. Tulving & W. Donaldson (eds) *Organization of memory.* New York: Academic Press.

Tune, L. E., Strauss, M. E., Lew, M. F., Breitlinger, E. & Coyle, J. T. (1982) Serum levels of anticholinergic drugs and impaired recent memory in chronic schizophrenic patients. *American Journal of Psychiatry*, 139, 1460-1462.

Turkington, D., Larkin, E. & Kingdon, D. G. (1990) Patient and relative attitudes to mental hospital closure and transfer to a hospital hostel. *Psychiatric Bulletin*, 14, 717-718.

Turpin, G. & Clements, K. (1992) Psychophysiological contributions to clinical assessment and treatment. In: D.J. Kavanagh (ed) *Schizophrenia. An overview and practical handbook.* London: Chapman & Hall.

Ullrich, R. & Ullrich de Muynck, R. (1976) *Die Unsicherheitsfragebogen-Testmappe und Anleitungen für den Therapeuten.* München: Pfeiffer.

United Nations (1990) *Human development report 1990: Development programme.* Oxford: Oxford University Press.

Vaccaro, J. V., Liberman, R. P., Blackwell, G. & Wallace, C. J. (1992) Combining social skills training and assertive case managment. In R.P. Liberman (ed) *New directions for mental health services: Effective psychiatric rehabilitation.* San Francisco: Jossey-Bass.

Vaitl, P., Bender, W., Hubmann, W., Krug, M. & Oberecker L (1987) Rehabilitation chronisch schizophrener Patienten in Dauerwohngemeinschaften. *Nervenarzt*, 58, 116-20.

Van der Does, A. J. W. & Van den Bosch, R. J. (1992) What determines Wisconsin Card Sorting Performance in schizophrenia? *Clinical Psychology Review*, 12, 567-584.

Vaughn, C. E. & Leff, J. (1976) The influence of family and social factors on the course of psychiatric illness. *British Journal of Psychiatry*, 129, 125-137.

Vauth, R. & Stieglitz, R. D. (1994) Verhaltenstherapeutische Interventionen bei persistierender halluzinatorischer und wahnhafter Symptomatik schizophrener Patienten. *Verhaltenstherapie*, 4, 177-185.

Venables, P. H. (1964) Input dysfunction in schizophrenia. In B.A. Maher (ed) *Progress in experimental personality research*, (Vol. 1). New York: Academic Press.

Venables, P. H. (1991) Overview of psychophysiology in relation to psychopathology with special reference to schizophrenia. In H.A. Nasrallah (ed) *Handbook of schizophrenia. Neuropsychology, psychophysiology, and information processing*, (Vol. 5). Amsterdam: Elsevier.

Verres, R. (1990) Wirkfaktoren in der Verhaltenstherapie. In H. Lang (ed) *Wirkfaktoren der Psychotherapie*. Berlin: Springer.

von Cramon, D. & Zihl, J. (1988) *Neuropsychologische Rehabilitation*. Berlin, Heidelberg, New York: Springer.

von Zerssen, D. (1976) *Die Beschwerden-Liste. Manual*. Weinheim: Beltz.

von Zerssen, D. (1981) Klinische Selbstbeurteilungsskalen. In Collegium Internationale Psychiatriae Scalarum (CIPS) *Internationale Skalen für Psychiatrie*. Weinheim: Beltz.

Wagman, A. & Wagman, W. (1992) On the Wisconsin. In E. Walker, R. Dworking & B. Cornblatt (eds) *Progress in experimental personality* research, (Vol. 15). New York: Springer.

Wagner, B. R. (1968) The training of attending and abstracting responses in chronic schizophrenia. *Journal of Experimental Research in Personality*, 3, 77-88.

Walker, E., McGuire, M. & Bettes, B. (1984) Recognition and identification of facial stimuli by schizophrenics and patients with affective disorders. *British Journal of Clinical Psychology*, 23, 37-44.

Wallace, C. J. & Liberman, R. P. (1985) Social skills training for patients with schizophrenia: A controlled clinical trial. *Psychiatry Research*, 15, 239-247.

Wallace, C. J. (1982). In J.P. Curran & P.M. Monti (eds) *Social skills training: A practical handbook for assessment and treatment*. New York: Guilford Press.

Wallace, C. J. (1986) Functional assessment in rehabilitation. *Schizophrenia Bulletin*, 24, 112-117.

Wallace, C. J., Liberman, R. P., MacKain, S. J. et al (1992) Effectiveness and replicability of modules for teaching social and instrumental skills to the severely mentally ill. *American Journal of Psychiatry*, 149, 654-658.

Wallace, C. J., Nelson, C., Liberman, R. P. et al (1980) A review and critique of social skills training for schizophrenics. *Schizophrenia Bulletin*, 6, 42-60.

Watt, N. F., Anthony, E. J., Wynne, L. C. & Rolf, J. E. (1984) *Children at risk for schizophrenia. A longitudinal perspective*. Chambridge: Chambridge University Press.

Watts, F. & Bennett, D. (1983) Management of the staff team. In F.N. Watts & D.H. Bennett (eds) *Theory and practice of psychiatric rehabilitation*. Chichester: John Wiley & Sons.

Waxler, N. E. (1974) Parent and child effects on cognitive performance: An experimental approach to the etiological and responsive therories of schizophrenia. *Family Process*, 13, 1-22.

Weinberger, D. R., Berman, K. F. & Illowsky, B. P. (1988) Physiologic dysfunction of dorsolateral prefrontal cortex in schizophrenia. III. A new cohort and evidence for a monoaminergic mechanism. *Archives of General Psychiatry*, 45, 609-615.

Weinberger, D. R., Berman, K. F. & Zec, R. F. (1986) Physiologic dysfunction of dorsolateral prefrontal cortex in schizophrenia: I. Regional cerebral blood flow evidence. *Archives of General Psychiatry*, 43, 114-124.

Weingaertner, A. H. (1971) Self-administered aversive stimulation with hallucinating hospitalized schizophrenics. *Journal of Consulting and Clinical Psychology*, 36, 422-429.

Wessler, R. L. & Hankin-Wessler, S. W. R. (1986) Cognitive appraisal therapy. In W. Dryden & W. Golden (eds) *Cognitive-behavioral approaches to psychotherapy*. London: Harper & Row.

Wiedl, K.H. (1997) Coping-orientated therapy with schizophrenic patients: General guidelines, starting points and issues of evaluation. In H. D. Brenner, W. Böker & R. Genner (eds) *Towards a comprehensive therapy for schizophrenia*. Seattle: Hogrefe & Huber Publishers.

Willke, H. (1991) *Systemtheorie*, (3rd ed). Stuttgart: Gustav Fischer Verlag.

Wing, J. K. & Brown, G. W. (1970) *Institutionalism and schizophrenia*. London: Cambridge University Press.

Wing, J. K. (1974) Principles of evaluation. In J.K. Wing & A.M. Hailey (eds) *Evaluating a community psychiatric service*. London: Oxford University Press.

Wing, J. K., Cooper, J. E. & Sartorius, N. (1974) *Measurement and classification of psychiatric symptoms: An instruction manual for the P.S.E. and Catego program*. Cambridge: Cambridge University Press.

Wishner, J. & Wahl, O. (1974) Dichotic listening in schizophrenia. *Journal of Consulting and Clinical Psychology*, 42, 538-546.

Wong, S. E. & Woolsey, J. E. (1989) Re-establishing conversational skills in overtly psychotic, chronic schizophrenic patients: Discrete trials training on the psychiatric ward. *Behavior Modification*, 13, 415-430.

World Health Organization (WHO) (1980) *International classification of impairments, disabilities, and handicaps*. Geneva: World Health Organization.

World Health Organization (WHO) (1988) *WHO psychiatric disability assessment schedule (WHO/DAS)*. Geneva: World Health Organization.

World Health Organization (WHO) (1993) *The ICD-10 Classification of Mental and Behavioural disorders: Diagnostic criteria for research*. Geneva: World Health Organization.

Wundt, W. (1910) *Grundriss der physiologischen Psychologie*, (vol. 2, 6th ed). Leipzig: Engelmann.

Yates, A. J. (1966) Psychological deficit. *Annual Review of Psychology*, 17, 111-114.

Zahn, T. P. (1975) Psychophysiological concomittants of task performance in schizophrenia. In M.L. Kietzman, S. Sutton & J. Zubin (eds) *Experimental approches to psychopathology*. New York: Academic Press.

Zec, R. F. & Weinberger, D. R. (1986) Relationship between CT scan findings and neuropsychological performance in chronic schizophrenia. *Psychiatric Clinics of North-America*, 9, 49-61.

Zigler, E. & Levine, J. (1983) Hallucination vs. delusions: A developmental approach. *Journal of Nervous and Mental Disease*, 171, 141-146.

Zinner, H. J., Kraemer, S. & Möller, H. J. (1990) Empirische Untersuchungen zur Konkordanz verschiedener Minussymptomatik-Skalen sowie zur Korrelation mit testpsychologischen Befunden. In H. J. Möller & E. Pelzer (eds) *Neuere Ansätze zur Diagnostik und Therapie schizophrener Minussymptomatik*. Berlin: Springer Verlag.

Zubin, J. & Spring, B. (1977) Vulnerability - A new view of schizophrenia. *Journal of Abnormal Psychology*, 86, 103-126.

Author Index

Abels, D., 104
Adams, H., 21, 54
AMDP, 142, 143, 148, 156, 158, 159, 161, 162, 175
Andreasen, N.C., 104, 142, 156, 176
Andres, K., 129
Angermeyer, M.C., 54
Angst, J., 97
Anonymous, 4
APA, 103, 104
Arieti, S., 85, 90
Asarnow, R.F., 47, 48, 108, 179
Bailer, J., 98
Baker, L.A., 47
Bakewell, E., 67
Bales, R.F., 71
Balint, E., 72
Balint, M., 72
Ball, A., 15, 71
Bandura, A., 50, 139
Bates, M.E., 126
Bäuml, J., 139, 162
Beatty, J., 52
Bebbington, P., 6, 14, 15, 71, 170, 171
Beck, A.T., 21, 34, 42, 59, 60, 67, 167, 168, 169
Bell, M.D., 98
Bellack, A.S., 20, 21, 25, 26, 53, 55, 96, 98, 125, 127
Bellissimo, A., 108
Benedict, R.H., 20
Benjamin, L.S., 164
Bennett, D., 68, 69, 70, 98
Bentall, R.P., 61
Berenbaum, H., 125, 126, 127

Berg, E.A., 168, 180
Binder, L.M., 168
Birchwood, M., 10, 12, 96
Birley, J.L.T., 171
Bivens, L.W., 135
Blanco, S., 87, 88
Blankenburg, W., 7, 13
Bleuler, E., 47, 134
Bleuler, M., 3, 32
Bliss, E., 86
Böker, W., 10, 18, 124
Bowen, L., 26, 117
Bowers, K.S., 34
Bowlby, J., 10, 42, 85, 86, 91, 173
Braff, D.L., 119, 125, 168, 178
Breier, A., 64
Brenner, H.D., 5, 7, 14, 18ff., 19, 22, 23, 26, 32, 55, 56, 60, 69, 70, 95, 96, 99, 100, 108, 124, 125ff., 126, 127, 128, 134, 135, 137, 140, 153, 162, 167, 169, 170
Bretherton, I., 85
Brickenkamp, R., 104, 142, 156, 179
Broen, W.E., 47, 48, 49, 51
Brown, G.W., 12, 73, 74, 169, 171
Buchkremer, G., 98
Buss, A.H., 125
Butzlaff, R.L., 6, 14, 170
Cairns, V.E., 104, 176
Calev, A., 52
Callaway, E., 48
Cameron, R., 20, 127, 134
Carmin, C. N., 37
Carpenter, W.T. Jr., 11, 74
Carr, V., 64
Chadwick, P., 10, 96

Childers, S.E., 54
Ciompi, L., 3, 6, 32, 33, 35, 97
CIPS, 23, 104
Clare, A.W., 104, 176
Clarkin, J., 162
Clements, K., 172
Cohen, C.I., 98
Cohen, S., 70
Cohen, S.P., 71
Colon, F., 20
Cornblatt, B.A., 125
Corrigan, P.W., 4, 26, 27, 47ff., 58, 125, 134
Cortese, L., 11
Cramer, P., 62
Cromwell, R.L., 58
Cronbach, L.J., 48
Csernansky, J.G., 47
Cutting, J.C., 126, 167
Dahl, D., 103
David, A.S., 139, 167
Davis, J.M., 3,
Davis, K.E., 167
Dawson, M.E., 25, 32, 48, 49, 95, 125, 168
De Luca, G., 75ff.
Décarie, T.G., 35
Deister, A., 98
Delahunty, A., 20, 96
Diaz, A., 20
Dixon, L.B., 96
Dougherty, F.E., 126
Dowd, E.T., 37
Duffy, M., 55
Dworkin, R.H., 125
D'Zurilla, T.J.,
Eckman, T.A., 21
Eikelmann, B., 97
Ellis, A., 61, 169
Ellis, E.S., 54
Engel, G., 3
Erickson, R.C., 168
Erlenmeyer-Kimling, L., 33
Escher, D.M.A., 64
Estes, W.K., 179
Eysenck, H.J., 60
Fahrenberg, J., 23, 129, 142, 156

Falloon, I.R.H., 33, 55, 64, 84, 85, 91, 127, 134
Fecteau, G.W., 55
Fehr, B., 126
Feinberg, T.E., 126
Ferguson, B., 67
Fitts, P.M., 50
Folkman, S., 174
Forsyth, D.R., 167
Foss, L., 3
Frank, A.F., 10
Friedrich, W., 23
Frith, C.D., 5, 6, 7
Fröhlich, W.D., 138
Fromholt, P., 20, 52
Gansert, U., 20, 140
Garbin, C., 107ff.
Gekle, W., 3ff., 46, 69, 71, 73
Gessler, S., 126
Gestrich, J., 20, 162
Gewali, H., 126
Gislon, M.C., 75ff.
Gjerde, P.F., 49, 125
Glick, I.D., 74
Gmür, M., 95, 96
Gold, J.M., 140, 178
Goldberg, T.E., 20, 53, 54, 140, 167, 178
Goldfried, M.R., 169
Goldman-Rakic, P.S., 4
Goldstein, M.J., 16, 58
Gorham, D.R., 104, 142, 156, 175
Gottesman, I.I., 32, 33, 60
Grant, D.A., 168, 180
Grassian, G., 59
Grawe, K., 131, 173
Green, M.F., 20, 21, 25, 26, 54, 117, 168, 178
Greenberg, L.S., 34
Groves, T., 66
Gruzelier, J.H., 49
Guidano, V.F., 89, 90
Gunderson, J.G., 9, 10, 39, 43
Häfner, H., 95, 98, 136
Hahlweg, K., 96, 98
Hain, C.H., 140
Hammond, K.R., 20

Author Index

Hankin-Wessler, S.W.R., 36
Harding, C.M., 54
Harris, A., 20
Harrow, M., 6
Hasher, L., 48, 49
Heaton, R.K., 20, 53, 180
Hecht, H., 104, 156, 177
Heider, F., 167
Heimberg, C., 125, 126
Hell, D., 72
Hellmann, S.,
Hemsley, D.R., 19, 125, 140, 153
Henning, W., 23
Hermanutz, M., 20, 162
Herrlich, J., 12, 129, 176
Hersen, M., 21
Herzog, T., 71
Hewstone, M., 5
Higgins, E.T., 173
Hirsch, S.R., 64
Hirschberg, W., 97
Hodel, B., 7, 14, 18ff., 22, 23, 26, 125ff., 128, 129, 135
Hofer, H., 16, 68ff., 167ff.
Hogarty, G.E., 14, 33, 55, 96, 98
Hollon, S.D., 34
Holmes, J., 173
Holzman, P.S., 135
Honigfeld, G., 110, 130, 176
Hooley, J.M., 6, 14, 170
Horowitz, H., 86
Huber, G., 23, 176
Hurlburt, R.T., 5
Hymowitz, P., 41
Iqbal, Z., 12
Jackson, A.J., 125
Jackson, H.J., 10, 68
Jacob, M., 163
Janzarik, W., 6
Jenkins, J.H., 98
Jensen, A.R., 179
Jolley, A.G., 64
Jones, E.E., 167
Kaehler, W.M., 135
Kahneman, D., 48, 49
Kane, J.M., 96
Kaney, S., 61

Kanfer, F.H., 138, 139
Kaplan, H.I., 174
Karasu, T.B., 33
Karno, M., 98
Käsermann, M.L., 126
Kavanagh, D.J., 6, 14, 170
Kelley, H.H., 167
Kern, R.S., 25, 26, 117, 134
Keshavan, M.S., 172
Khan, A.,
Kierkegaard, S., 14
Killian, G.A., 47
Kingdon, D.G., 10, 12, 59ff., 66, 67, 74
Kleinginna, A.M., 169
Kleinginna, P.R., 169
Klett, C.J., 176
Kline, J.S., 126
Klosterkötter, J., 98
Knight, R.G., 48, 112
Koh, S.D., 47, 52
Konen, A., 128
Koreen, A.R., 7
Koukkou, M., 4, 18
Kraemer, S., 55, 127, 134, 136ff., 139, 140, 161, 163
Kraepelin, E., 7, 32, 47
Kraus, A., 7, 13
Kriss, M.R., 34
Kuipers, E., 8, 15, 16
Kuipers, L., 6, 14, 15, 71, 170, 171
Lamberti, G., 20
Lang, P.J., 125
Larsen, S., 20, 52
Leff, J.P., 33, 60, 98, 169, 170
Lehman, A.F., 96
Lempp, R., 3
Lentz, R.J., 108
Levine, J., 86
Lewandowski, L., 98
Liberman, R.P., 21, 25, 27, 33, 55, 56, 95, 96, 100, 108, 127, 134, 138, 156, 162
Lidz, T., 85
Lieberman, J., 7
Linehan, M.M., 136
Liotti, G., 14, 34, 84ff., 85, 89, 90

Ludwig, A.M., 60
Luhmann, N., 69
Lukoff, D., 60, 175
Lundh, L.G., 35
Lysaker, P.H., 98
MacCrimmon, D.J., 47, 108
Macrae, C.N., 5
Magaro, P.A., 49, 50
Magnusson, D., 32
Mahoney, M.J., 16, 169
Main, M., 85
Malla, A.K., 171
Mandal, M.K., 126
Mandler, G., 35
Manske, W., 4
Marder, S.R., 96, 100
Marker, K., 143
Markus, H., 35
Marneros, A., 98
Marsella, A.J., 32
Martinez-Diaz, J.A., 55
Massell, H.K., 21, 55, 56
McDougall, W., 169
McFall, R.M., 21
McGlashan, T.H., 97
McGorry, P.D., 10, 68
McGurk, S.R., 106
Mead, G.H., 7, 10, 13, 14, 15, 173
Mednick, B.R., 85
Meehl, P.E., 48
Mefferd, R.B., 180
Meichenbaum, D., 20, 127, 134, 139, 156, 169
Meiselman, K.C., 20, 51
Meltzer, H.Y., 63, 106
Menditto, A.A., 57
Mergenthaler, E., 163
Merlo, M.C.G., 3ff., 16, 46, 68ff., 69, 71, 73, 167
Miller, S., 108
Milner, B., 168, 180
Milton, F., 63
Modestin, J., 72
Mojtabai, R., 3, 9
Möller, H.J., 95, 96
Morrison, R.L., 21, 55, 125
Moscovici, S., 174

Mueser, K.T., 25, 96, 100
Müller, C., 97
Müller, P., 136
Mundt, C., 104, 156
Munro, E., 179
Murray, R.M., 60
Mussgay, L., 96, 99, 140, 153
Muzekari, L.H., 126
Naghdi, S., 48
Neale, J.M., 47
Neimeyer, R.A., 16, 169
Neisser, U., 172
NIMH, 175
Norman, R.M.G., 171
Novic, J., 126
Nuechterlein, K.H., 19, 25, 32, 47, 48, 49, 95, 125, 134, 168, 175, 178, 179
Nugter, M.A., 6
Oades, R.D., 167
Öhman, A., 32
Olbrich, R., 20, 96, 99, 140, 153
Oltmanns, T.F., 47, 125, 127
Onofri, A., 85
Orzack, M.H., 47
Osnes, P.G., 58
Oswald, I., 59, 104
Overall, J.E., 104, 142, 156, 175
Paul, G.L., 108
Penn, D.L., 96, 107ff., 116
Perris, C., 3, 10, 11, 21, 31ff., 33, 37, 38, 40, 43, 45, 84, 91, 173
Perry, W., 168
Peter, K., 99
Piaget, J., 35, 78, 173
Pitman, R.K., 127
Pitschel-Walz, G., 163
Plutchik, R., 169
Podvoll, E.M., 7, 71, 73
Posner, M.L., 50
Pribram, K.H., 125
Prochaska, J.O., 138, 162
Pym, B., 66
Quinlan, D.M., 6
Racamier, P.-C., 14
Ravadin, L., 20
Reda, M.A., 14, 84ff.

Reker, T., 97
Retzer, A., 16
Rey, E.-R., 98
Rittmannsberger, H., 97
Roder, V., 22, 26, 40, 45, 55, 95ff.,
    96, 99, 100, 101, 129, 139, 140,
    156, 170
Romme, M.A.J., 64
Rosen, H., 85
Rosenbaum, G., 20, 51
Rosvold, H.E., 178
Roth, E., 104
Rothenberg, K., 3
Rudas, S., 98
Russel, J.A., 48, 126
Rutter, D.R., 62
Saccuzzo, D.P., 47, 108, 119
Safran, J.D., 34, 35, 85
Sandner, M., 128
Schachter, S., 169
Scharfetter, C., 13, 62
Scheflen, A., 85
Schindler, L., 163
Schneider, F., 127
Schooler, N.R., 172
Schulz, H., 104
Searles, H.F., 84, 90
Segal, Z.V., 35
Seltzer, M.A., 3, 10, 12, 16, 69, 71,
    72, 73
Selvini-Palazzoli, M., 16
Shields, J., 32, 33, 60
Silverman, J., 51
Singer, J.E., 169
Skagerlind, L., 45
Skantze, K., 172
Smith, M., 131
Snyder, K.S., 15
Soni, S.D., 96
Spaulding, W.D., 25, 26, 48, 56, 58,
    107ff., 108, 109, 153, 169, 180
Spohn, H.E., 41, 47
Spring, B.J., 20, 32, 58, 95, 162, 174
Stark, F.M., 163
Steffy, R.A., 108
Stieglitz, R.D., 96
Stierlin, H., 7

Stokes, T.F., 58
Storms, L., 48
Straube, E.R., 167
Strauss, J.S., 11, 59, 64
Strauss, M., 47, 108
Strongman, K.T., 169
Studer, A., 167
Süllwold, L., 12, 23, 37, 129, 156,
    176
Summer, D.A., 20
Summerfelt, A.T., 20
Taylor, H.A., 179
Theilemann, S., 99
Tomm, K., 16
Tulving, E., 86
Tune, L. E., 47
Turkington, D., 10, 12, 59ff., 66, 74
Turpin, G., 172
Ullrich de Muynck, R., 156
Ullrich, R., 156
United Nations, 172
Vaccaro, J.V., 21
Vaitl, P., 97
van der Bosch, R.J., 53
van der Does, A.J.W., 53
Vaughn, C.E., 33, 98, 169, 170
Vauth, R., 96
Venables, P.H., 49, 51, 172
Ventura, J., 175
Verres, R., 135
von Cramon, D., 143
von Zerssen, D., 96, 104, 142, 156,
    175, 176
Wagman, A., 108
Wagman, W., 108
Wagner, B.R., 20, 50
Wahl, O., 20
Walker, E., 126
Wallace, C.J., 6, 21, 55, 96
Watt, N.F., 178
Watts, F., 69, 70, 98
Waxler, N.E., 70
Weinberger, D.R., 7, 47
Weingaertner, A.H., 54
Wessler, R.L., 36
Weston, D.R., 85
WHO, 103, 104, 170

Wiedl, K.H., 25
Willke, H., 69, 70, 72
Wing, J.K., 12, 39, 40, 60, 73, 74
Wishner, J., 20
Wong, S.E., 21, 56
Woolsey, J.E., 21, 56
Wundt, W., 169
Yates, A.J., 48
Zacks, R.T., 48, 49

Zahn, T.P., 49
Zapparoli, G.C., 14, 75ff.
Zec, R.F., 47
Zigler, E., 86
Zihl, J., 143
Zinner, H.J., 140
Zorn, P., 95ff.
Zubin, J., 32, 58, 95, 174

Subject Index

Association for Methodology and Documentation in Psychiatry, (AMDP) 142, 143, 148, 156, 158, 159, 161, 162, 175
Attribution, 61, 74, 75, 80, 83, 86, 89, 90, 91, 167, 168, 171
Automatic thoughts, 34, 36, 37, 38, 61, 81, 86, 167
Backward masking test, 50, 108, 114, 119, 168, 178, 180
Basic cognitive (dys)functions (disturbances, impairments), 4, 5, 9, 15, 140, 153, 154, 156, 157, 158, 161, 163, 168, 170, 171
Brief Psychiatric Rating Scale (BPRS), 23, 24, 104, 105, 142, 143, 147, 148, 149, 150, 156, 158, 159, 160, 161, 175
Clinical Global Impression (CGI), 158, 159, 175
COGLAB, 25, 108, 109, 110, 111, 112, 113, 114, 115, 116, 117, 118, 119, 120, 122, 179, 180
Cognition, 6, 16, 21, 34, 35, 42, 43, 45, 48, 52, 54, 61, 64, 107, 108, 117, 128, 153, 168, 169, 173, 174
Cognitive remediation, 9, 19, 20, 25, 26, 27, 48, 49, 53, 54, 57, 58, 127, 134, 156, 168, 169
Cognitive therapy, 9, 16, 17, 21, 25, 26, 27, 31, 32, 34, 35, 37, 38, 40, 41, 42, 43, 44, 45, 49, 59, 60, 66, 67, 78, 79, 70, 96, 99, 100, 101, 102, 136, 137, 138, 139, 140, 154, 155, 156, 158, 159, 160, 161, 163, 167, 169
Continuous Performance Test (CPT), 26, 140, 156, 157, 158, 161, 168, 178, 179

d2 test, 104, 140, 142, 144, 156, 157, 158, 179
Disability, 38, 39, 43, 67, 74, 97, 104, 167, 170, 172
Disturbance-List (D-L), 156, 175
Emotion expressed (EE), 6, 14, 15, 71, 98, 134, 169, 170
Emotions, 4, 5, 6, 7, 8, 9, 10, 13, 14, 16, 17, 21, 26, 34, 35, 36, 37, 39, 42, 43, 69, 71, 72, 73, 74, 75, 77, 79, 81, 85, 86, 87, 88, 89, 90, 91, 98, 101, 125, 126, 127, 129, 130, 131, 132, 133, 134, 135, 136, 137, 163, 167, 169, 170, 171, 173
Frankfurt Complaint Questionnaire, (FCQ), 23, 24, 129, 130, 131, 132, 133, 156, 159, 161, 176
Frankfurt Subjective Condition Scale (FCS), 129, 130, 131, 132, 133, 176
Handicap, 40, 74, 80, 170
Impairment, 4, 5, 18, 19, 20, 21, 22, 23, 24, 25, 26, 27, 39, 40, 47, 48, 50, 55, 65, 57, 58, 84, 85, 91, 99, 104, 109, 110, 112, 114, 116, 117, 120, 121, 122, 123, 124, 125, 127, 161, 168, 169, 170, 176, 178, 179
Integrated Psychological Therapy Program (IPT) 22, 23, 24, 26, 55, 56, 99, 100, 101, 103, 104, 105, 108, 125, 127, 128, 129, 134, 140, 169, 170, 171
Nurses' Observation Scale for Inpatient Evaluation (NOSIE), 23, 24, 109, 110, 111, 112, 113, 114, 115, 116, 117, 118, 119, 120, 121, 122, 123, 130, 131, 132, 133, 176
Paranoid-Depressivity Scale (PD-S), 142, 143, 148, 156, 158, 159, 176

Psychophysiology, 52, 53, 58, 84, 87, 90, 154, 167, 172
Quality of life, 8, 15, 58, 69, 124, 136, 137, 162, 172
Reaction Time Test, 20, 50, 51, 108, 114, 116, 119, 140, 141, 145, 146, 156, 157, 158, 161, 162, 168, 179, 180
Repeated Psychological Measurement (RPM) 23, 129, 142, 145, 156, 157, 158, 179
Scale for Assessment of Negative Symptoms (SANS), 104, 105, 142, 143, 147, 149, 151, 156, 159, 161, 176
Schema, 4, 5, 6, 7, 9, 35, 36, 37, 38, 41, 43, 45, 61, 79, 81, 84, 85, 86, 89, 90, 91, 126, 168, 169, 172, 173
Secure base, 10, 17, 42, 89, 173
Social cognition, 21, 57, 91, 173
Social Maladjustment Schedule (SMS), 156, 176
Span of Apprehension Test (SAT) 25, 50, 108, 114, 119, 120, 140, 141, 142, 143, 144, 145, 146, 156, 157, 158, 161, 162, 168, 179, 180
Vulnerability-stress-model, 12, 16, 18, 37, 58, 60, 95, 100, 154, 156, 171, 172, 174
Wisconsin Card Sorting Test (WCST), 20, 25, 53, 54, 104, 108, 168, 180